DATE DUE

ELECTR——————————————————G DATA

This book he———————————————ıealth record
(EHR) syster———————————————n. It analyzes
both the shoı———————————————'s response to
the creation ———————————————mework, and
developing ———————————————echnological
improvemen———————————————ddresses not
only privacy———————————————ıges, such as
those related———————————————ır formulates
a large body———————————————security, and
efficacy for ———————————————al data.

Sharona Ho———————————————tern Reserve
University. S———————————————EHR systems
and medical———————————————uter Science
Andy Podgu———————————————lence at the
Centers for———————————————Surveillance,
Epidemiolog———————————————hor of *Aging*
with a Plan———————————————*ır Tomorrow*
(2015).

CAMBRIDGE BIOETHICS AND LAW

This series of books was founded by Cambridge University Press with Alexander McCall Smith as its first editor in 2003. It focuses on the law's complex and troubled relationship with medicine across both the developed and the developing world. Since the early 1990s, we have seen in many countries increasing resort to the courts by dissatisfied patients and a growing use of the courts to attempt to resolve intractable ethical dilemmas. At the same time, legislatures across the world have struggled to address the questions posed by both the successes and the failures of modern medicine, while international organizations such as the WHO and UNESCO now regularly address issues of medical law.

It follows that we would expect ethical and policy questions to be integral to the analysis of the legal issues discussed in this series. The series responds to the high profile of medical law in universities, in legal and medical practice, and in public and political affairs. We seek to reflect the evidence that many major health-related policy debates in the United Kingdom, Europe, and the international community involve a strong medical law dimension. With this in mind, we seek to address how legal analysis might have a transjurisdictional and international relevance. Organ retention, embryonic stem cell research, physician-assisted suicide, and the allocation of resources to fund healthcare are but a few examples among many. The emphasis of this series is thus on matters of public concern and/or practical significance. We look for books that could make a difference to the development of medical law and enhance the role of medicolegal debate in policy circles. That is not to say that we lack interest in the important theoretical dimensions of the subject, but we aim to ensure that theoretical debate is grounded in the realities of how the law does and should interact with medicine and healthcare.

Series Editors

Margaret Brazier, *University of Manchester*
Graeme Laurie, *University of Edinburgh*
Richard Ashcroft, *Queen Mary, University of London*
Eric M. Meslin, *Indiana University*

Books in the Series

Marcus Radetzki, Marian Radetzki, & Niklas Juth, *Genes and Insurance: Ethical, Legal and Economic Issues*

Ruth Macklin, *Double Standards in Medical Research in Developing Countries*

Donna Dickenson, *Property in the Body: Feminist Perspectives*

Matti Häyry, Ruth Chadwick, Vilhjálmur Árnason, & Gardar Árnason, *The Ethics and Governance of Human Genetic Databases: European Perspectives*

Electronic Health Records and Medical Big Data

LAW AND POLICY

SHARONA HOFFMAN

Case Western Reserve University School of Law

CAMBRIDGE
UNIVERSITY PRESS

CAMBRIDGE
UNIVERSITY PRESS

One Liberty Plaza, 20th Floor, New York, NY 10006, USA

Cambridge University Press is part of the University of Cambridge.

It furthers the University's mission by disseminating knowledge in the pursuit of education, learning, and research at the highest international levels of excellence.

www.cambridge.org
Information on this title: www.cambridge.org/9781107166547

First published 2016

Printed in the United States of America by Sheridan Books, Inc.

A catalog record for this publication is available from the British Library.

Library of Congress Cataloging-in-Publication Data
Hoffman, Sharona, author.
Electronic health records and medical big data : law and policy / Sharona Hoffman.
New York : Cambridge University Press, 2016. | Series: Cambridge bioethics and law ; 32
LCCN 2016048561 | ISBN 9781107166547 (hardback)
LCSH: Medical records – Law and legislation – United States. | Medical records – Data processing – United States. | Medical records – Access control – United States. | Data protection – Law and legislation – United States.
LCC KF3827.R4 H64 2016 | DDC 651.5/042610285–dc23
LC record available at https://lccn.loc.gov/2016048561

ISBN 978-1-107-16654-7 Hardback
ISBN 978-1-316-61768-7 Paperback

To my husband, Andy Podgurski

Contents

Acknowledgments

I came to the topic of health information technology and the law through marriage. My husband, Andy Podgurski, is a Professor of Computer Science and Electrical Engineering at Case Western Reserve University, where I am a professor of law and bioethics and specialize in health law. Soon after we were married in 2005, we began to realize that our areas of academic interest overlapped and that what brought them together was health information technology. During many dinners and long walks, we discussed (sometimes argued about) the emerging issues raised by the advent of electronic health record (EHR) systems. We eventually wrote a large number of law review articles together, some of which form a partial basis for chapters in this book. I am deeply grateful to Andy for all he has taught me, for being a wonderful co-author, and for enriching my life in so many other ways.

Case Western Reserve University (CWRU) has been my intellectual home for most of the last two decades and has given me the opportunity to have an incredibly fulfilling career. I am grateful for being included among its faculty and also for financial support in the form of numerous summer grants for my scholarship. I also thank the many academic colleagues at CWRU and elsewhere who invited me to give talks about my work and read and commented on drafts of my health information technology articles over the years. Your input has always made my scholarship better.

A special thank you goes to my faculty colleague, Max Mehlman, for so carefully reading a full draft of this manuscript and providing detailed suggestions for improvement. Tracy (Yeheng) Li, a CWRU Cowen Research Fellow, provided extensive research assistance that was vital to this book. Santiago Reich and Brandon Wojtasik also provided valuable research help.

During my sabbatical semester in 2014, the Centers for Disease Control and Prevention (CDC) in Atlanta welcomed me as a Distinguished Scholar in

Residence at its Center for Surveillance, Epidemiology and Laboratory Services. I thank the many CDC officials who met with me and discussed their work relating to electronic health records, data-sharing policies, open data, cloud computing, and many other areas. I learned a great deal from them.

Finally, I am grateful to my editing team at Cambridge University Press for their assistance, support, and extremely capable editing work. They are Matt Gallaway, Kristina Deusch, Emma Collison, and Jeevitha Baskaran.

Introduction

Electronic health record (EHR) systems are not a new idea. A short YouTube video entitled "1961 Electronic Medical Records"[1] discusses a project that Akron General Hospital in Ohio undertook in the early 1960s. The grainy black-and-white film shows the hospital's newly installed, very large computers being used by satisfied clinicians. The narrator enthusiastically asserts that thanks to the new technology, "It is going to be possible to relieve the nurses and doctors of some of their paperwork. It is going to be possible to have correlation of diseases which we have not had before. And it is going to be possible to eliminate errors in medications and tests of this kind which would have been harmful to the patients."

In truth, however, EHRs did not begin to take off until forty years later, in the early twenty-first century. On April 26, 2004, President George W. Bush announced a plan to ensure that all Americans' health records would be computerized within ten years.[2] The following day, the president issued an executive order establishing the position of National Health Information Technology Coordinator to promote implementation of a "nationwide inter-operable health information technology infrastructure."[3] At the same time, many other developed countries in Europe and elsewhere undertook major initiatives to transition to use of EHR systems.[4]

---

[1] "1961 Electronic Medical Records"; available at: www.youtube.com/watch?v=t-aiKlIc6uk (accessed February 9, 2016).

[2] The White House, "Transforming Health Care: The President's Health Information Technology Plan," in *Promoting Innovation and Competitiveness: President Bush's Technology Agenda*, April 26, 2004; available at: http://georgewbush-whitehouse.archives.gov/infocus/technology/economic_policy200404/chap3.html (accessed September 8, 2015).

[3] Exec. Order No. 13,335, *Fed. Reg.* 69: 24,059 (April 27, 2004).

[4] eHealth Stakeholder Group, "Patient Access to Electronic Health Records: eHealth Stakeholder Group," led by Illaria Passarani, European Commission, June 2013; available at: http://ec.europa.eu/digital-agenda/en/news/commission-publishes-four-reports-ehealth-stakeholder-group (accessed January 7, 2016).

Arguably, it was high time that medical professionals digitize their practices. Almost all other industries had long ago embraced computerization. Nevertheless, the rate of adoption of EHR systems was quite low at first. By 2008, only 17 percent of doctors' offices and 10 percent of hospitals had basic EHR systems in the United States.[5] In Europe, by 2007, only seven countries routinely used EHRs.[6] The transition from paper medical records to EHR systems was proving to be far more complicated, cumbersome, and hazardous than many anticipated.

In 2009, as part of President Obama's economic stimulus plan, Congress enacted the Health Information Technology for Economic and Clinical Health (HITECH) Act.[7] This law dedicated approximately $27 billion to promoting health information technology, including incentive payments for healthcare providers who adopted and appropriately used certified EHR systems.[8] As a result, by 2013, 70 percent of US physicians had implemented at least a basic EHR system, and 76 percent of US hospitals had done so by 2014.[9] By 2015, 95 percent of hospitals and 84 percent of primary care physicians in the United States were estimated to use EHR systems, as did the vast majority of primary care physicians in other developed countries.[10]

There is no going back – we now live in a world in which computers populate the clinical setting as much as doctors, nurses, and patients do. Computers are

---

[5] Robert Wachter, *The Digital Doctor: Hope, Hype, and Harm at the Dawn of Medicine's Computer Age* (New York: McGraw Hill Education, 2015), 12.

[6] World Health Organization, "Legal Frameworks for eHealth," *Global Observatory for eHealth Series* 5 (2012): 45; available at: http://apps.who.int/iris/bitstream/10665/44807/1/9789241503143 _eng.pdf (accessed January 7, 2016).

[7] Health Information Technology for Economic and Clinical Health (HITECH) Act, Pub. L. No. 111–15, 123 Stat. 226 (2009) (codified as amended in scattered sections of 42 USC).

[8] David Blumenthal and Marilyn Tavenner, "The 'Meaningful Use' Regulation for Electronic Health Records," *New England Journal of Medicine* 363 (2010): 501; Sharona Hoffman and Andy Podgurski, "Meaningful Use and Certification of Health Information Technology: What about Safety?," *Journal of Law, Medicine & Ethics* 39 (Suppl. 1) (2011): 77. Providers can receive up to $44,000 through Medicare or $63,750 through Medicaid. See Chapter 2.

[9] Dustin Charles, Meghan Gabriel, and Talisha Searcy, "Adoption of Electronic Health Record Systems among US Non-Federal Acute Care Hospitals: 2008–2014," *ONC Data Brief* 23 (2015); available at: http://healthit.gov/sites/default/files/data-brief/2014HospitalAdoptionDataBrief .pdf (accessed September 8, 2015); Dawn Heisey-Grove and Vaishali Patel, "Physician Motivations for Adoption of Electronic Health Records," *ONC Data Brief* 21 (2015); available at: www.healthit.gov/sites/default/files/oncdatabrief-physician-ehr-adoption-motivators-2014 .pdf (accessed September 8, 2015); Julia Adler-Milstein et al., "Electronic Health Record Adoption in US Hospitals: Progress Continues, But Challenges Persist," *Health Affairs* 34, no. 12 (2015): 2174.

[10] Robin Osborn et al., "Primary Care Physicians in Ten Countries Report Challenges Caring for Patients with Complex Health Needs," *Health Affairs* 34, no. 12 (2015): 2104–12; available at: http://content.healthaffairs.org/content/34/12/2104.full?keytype=ref&siteid=healthaff&ijkey= Wvt51Tp9QSL/g#T4; HealthIT.gov, "Health IT Quick Stats"; available at: http://dashboard .healthit.gov/quickstats/quickstats.php (accessed December 28, 2015).

a standard feature in the examination room and at the bedside. But this change does not please everyone. I am sure I'm not alone in having witnessed a clinician curse the computer during an office visit or in feeling at times as though doctors are paying more attention to their data-input duties than they are to me during our encounters.

EHR systems are central not only to clinical care but also to medical research, public health initiatives, quality-improvement efforts, and other health-related endeavors. EHRs enable the creation of "medical big data," that is, very large electronic data resources that can be put to secondary, nonclinical uses. Medical big data can have tremendous benefits as a tool for scientific discoveries and other advances, but the creation and use of vast EHR databases raises acute concerns about privacy breaches and consequent harm to data subjects.

Just as the transition to EHR systems has had a profound impact on the delivery of medical care, research, and health data analysis, so too it has changed the laws and regulations of the healthcare industry. Countless legal questions are raised by the new technology. For example, how can privacy best be protected when medical records are stored electronically? Does use of EHR systems increase or decrease clinicians' vulnerability to medical malpractice claims? How can complex and ever-changing EHRs be transformed into discoverable documents that are accessible to plaintiffs? Should medical research regulations respond in any way to the increasing prevalence of EHR-based research? Are American anti-discrimination laws strong enough to protect individuals when employers and others may discover private health information on the Internet?

This book's purpose is to analyze the intersection of law and health information technology. It will evaluate what EHR systems and big data have to offer and what their shortcomings are. It will also explore how the law has responded to the advent of EHR systems so far, highlight gaps in the current legal framework, and develop detailed recommendations for future regulatory, policy, and technological improvements. A central premise of the book is that the law is a vital tool for safeguarding and enhancing the quality and security of EHR systems. Although the US Department of Health and Human Services has engaged with the need to oversee the new technology and has implemented a series of regulations, they are far from comprehensive. While this book largely focuses on regulations and policies in the United States, much of the analysis is applicable to other regions of the world, and the text is often enriched with references to international studies and doctrine.

A Note about Terminology. For the sake of consistency, I use the term "electronic health record" (EHR) rather than "electronic medical record"

(EMR) in this book. I do not believe that there is a substantive difference between the two, and I mean EHR to encompass any digital version of a patient's medical chart. The term "electronic health record (EHR) system," as I use it here, means a system that adds to EHRs information management tools such as clinical alerts and reminders, decision aids, tools for data analysis, and more.[11]

Discussions of the law in this book focus on legal concerns arising from the use of EHR systems. Thus I do not assess many other legal-medical challenges that are important to contemporary patients. For example, I do not devote space to general health privacy interests or to provisions of the Health Insurance Portability and Accountability Act (HIPAA) Privacy Rule that do not relate specifically to electronically stored information. Likewise, discussion of medical big data in this book focuses on government or private-entity databases that draw data from EHRs or healthcare providers. Therefore I generally do not address big data that is obtained from nontraditional sources such as social media, consumer purchasing records, or website searches.

This book proceeds in two primary parts. The first part focuses on EHR systems as they are used in clinical settings to treat patients. The second part is devoted to medical big data that is derived from EHRs and used for research and other nonclinical, secondary purposes.

More specifically, this book covers a wide array of EHR system and medical big data topics. Part I begins with a chapter that details the capacities of EHR systems and analyzes their benefits and shortcomings. It proceeds to a discussion of the federal "meaningful use" and certification regulations that govern EHR systems and assesses their efficacy. Chapter 3 is devoted to EHR data security and the HIPAA Security Rule. Chapter 4 focuses on the liability risks that EHR systems generate and the effects that record digitization will have on discovery in medical malpractice cases. Part II of this book begins with a discussion of what medical big data is and what benefits it offers. Chapter 6 probes the privacy and autonomy concerns that medical big data research raises. It is followed by a discussion of the data-quality problems and analytical challenges that analysts working with medical big data may face. Finally, Chapter 8 explores the emerging phenomenon of open medical data, that is, health information that is publicly available to anyone with Internet access and that may or may not be thoroughly deidentified. Many of these chapters conclude with a set of proposals to address the challenges that they highlight.

[11] Edward H. Shortliffe and James J. Cimino, eds., *Biomedical Informatics: Computer Applications in Health Care and Biomedicine* (New York: Springer, 2006), 937.

My hope is that readers gain an in-depth understanding of EHR systems and medical big data. This book serves not only as a general primer but also analyzes the many legal, ethical, and policy implications of EHRs and big data and the relationship between law and medical technology. It also formulates a large body of recommendations to improve the technology's safety, security, and efficacy for both clinical and secondary uses. The field of medicine is now firmly rooted in the digital age. This book, which is up-to-date as of July 2016, is devoted to illuminating both its promise and its perils.

PART I

EHR Systems

Attributes, Benefits, and Shortcomings

Electronic health record (EHR) systems are now a fixture in medical examination rooms and hospital corridors. EHR systems have a wealth of potential capabilities, but they also constitute very complex technology. The federal government has embraced and promoted the transition to these systems with great fanfare and for good reasons. This enthusiasm, however, is not universally shared, and many clinicians complain bitterly about the technology's shortcomings. Before analyzing the legal, ethical, and policy implications of EHR system use, it is important to understand fully what the technology is, what it does, and what it doesn't do. This chapter describes the many features of EHR systems. It also details their benefits and explores their pitfalls and shortcomings.

1.1 WHAT ARE EHR SYSTEMS?

1.1.1 EHR System Attributes

In the past, doctors' medical records were just that – repositories of medical information about each patient. Contemporary EHR systems, however, do much more than serve a record-keeping function. They also help clinicians to manage many aspects of patient care through a variety of technological capabilities. The Institute of Medicine (IOM), the Robert Wood Johnson

This chapter is based in part on the following articles: Sharona Hoffman and Andy Podgurski, "Finding a Cure: The Case for Regulation and Oversight of Electronic Health Record Systems," *Harvard Journal of Law & Technology* 22, no. 1 (2008): 103; Sharona Hoffman and Andy Podgurski, "E-Health Hazards: Provider Liability and Electronic Health Record Systems," *Berkeley Technology Law Journal* 24, no. 4 (2009): 1523; Sharona Hoffman, "Medical Big Data and Big Data Quality Problems," *Connecticut Insurance Law Journal* 21, no. 1 (2015): 289.

Foundation, and other experts[1] have identified the following eight elements as
"core EHR functionalities":

- **Clinical documentation and health information display.** EHR systems
  record and display laboratory test results, allergies, patient medication
  lists, medical diagnoses, patient demographics, clinicians' notes,
  advance directives, and other information.
- **Results management.** EHRs create searchable electronic clinical data
  repositories, including previous and current laboratory test results, radiology procedure results, and other diagnostic or treatment results. These
  enhance provider access to needed information.
- **Computerized provider order entry and management (CPOE).** EHR
  systems enable providers to order prescriptions, diagnostic tests, treatments, and referrals electronically. Providers can also store, retrieve, and
  modify their orders.
- **Clinical decision support (CDS).** This potentially lifesaving feature
  generates alerts and reminders for clinicians. Examples are warnings
  about drug interactions, drug allergies, and appropriate medication
  doses and prompts relating to preventive and wellness care. CDS
  thus offers monitoring for potential medication errors or other adverse
  events. It can also suggest possible diagnoses and treatments and
  educate doctors about clinical practice guidelines[2] and standard
  protocols.
- **Electronic communication and connectivity.** EHR systems can facilitate online communication among medical team members, with other
  providers such as laboratories or pharmacies, and between patients and
  clinicians. Available tools include e-mail, secure web messaging, telemedicine,[3] and home telemonitoring.[4] Ideally, communication should
  be possible among providers in different geographic locations and

---

[1] Institute of Medicine, *Key Capabilities of an Electronic Health Record System* (Washington,
    DC: National Academies Press, 2003), 7–11; Timothy G. Ferris et al., "A Framework for
    Measuring the Effects of Health Information Technology on Health Care Quality," in
    Health Information Technology in the United States: Where We Stand, ed. by David
    Blumenthal et al. (Princeton, NJ: Robert Wood Johnson Foundation, 2008), 178–9.

[2] *Clinical practice guidelines* can be defined as "[s]ystematically developed statements to assist
    practitioner and patient decisions about appropriate health care for specific clinical circum-
    stances." Edward H. Shortliffe and James J. Cimino, eds., *Biomedical Informatics: Computer
    Applications in Health Care and Biomedicine* (New York: Springer, 2006): 924.

[3] *Telemedicine* is "the delivery of health care at a distance, increasingly but not exclusively by
    means of the Internet." Shortliffe and Cimino, *Biomedical Informatics*, 991.

[4] *Telemonitoring* is "[t]he use of telecommunications media to monitor the health status and/or
    vital signs of patients at distance." US Department of Health and Human Services Indian
    Health Service, *Telehealth Care in Indian Health: Directory and New Directions 2005*, ed. by

medical organizations, even if they use EHR systems that are produced by different vendors.

- **Patient support.** EHR systems can promote patient education and assist patients in accessing and obtaining copies of their health records. Some systems offer patients a personal health record (PHR). A PHR can be defined as "an electronic application through which individuals can access, manage, and share their health information ... in a private, secure, and confidential environment."[5] The systems also generate reminders to patients for purposes of preventive and follow-up care.
- **Administrative processes.** Electronic scheduling systems, insurance eligibility verification, billing, and claims processing are additional components of EHR systems. Computerized tools can also be used to identify individuals who are potentially eligible for clinical trials, those who should be informed about drug recalls, or candidates for chronic disease management programs. Search capabilities can also be used for quality assessment, quality improvement, and initiatives to reduce disparities among people of different ethnicities or socioeconomic status.
- **Reporting and population health management.** EHR systems enable the collection of clinical data to meet public, private, and institutional reporting requirements. They should also support medical research and public health activities. Federal regulations, for example, require clinicians to use EHR systems to report clinical quality measures, immunization data, cancer cases, and other illnesses to appropriate federal and state governmental entities.[6]

A 2008 report produced by the George Washington University, Massachusetts General Hospital, and the Robert Wood Johnson Foundation provides a more detailed listing of EHR functions. For those who might benefit from a comprehensive checklist, it is as follows:

Mark Carroll, Mark Horton, and Mark Thomas, 56; available at: ftp://ftp.ihs.gov/pubs/Teleh ealth/Telehealth%20Directory%20030405.pdf (accessed August 14, 2015).

[5] Paul C. Tang et al., "Personal Health Records: Definitions, Benefits, and Strategies for Overcoming Barriers to Adoption," *Journal of the American Medical Informatics Association* 13, no. 2 (2006): 122.

[6] Institute of Medicine, *Key Capabilities of an Electronic Health Record System*, 7–11; Ferris et al., "A Framework for Measuring the Effects of Health Information Technology on Health Care Quality," 178–9; Institute of Medicine, *Health IT and Patient Safety: Building Safer Systems for Better Care* (Washington, DC: National Academies Press, 2012), 38–44; Centers for Medicare and Medicaid Services, "Stage 1 vs. Stage 2 Comparison Table for Eligible Professionals"; last modified August 2012; available at: www.cms.gov/Regulations-and-Guidan ce/Legislation/EHRIncentivePrograms/Downloads/Stage1vsStage2CompTablesforEP.pdf (accessed August 14, 2015).

1. Electronic notes and health information management
   a. Enable full electronic management of medical records
   b. Manage patient advance directives
   c. Manage patient past medical history, family history, and social history
   d. Manage problem list
   e. Manage structured medication list
   f. Manage allergy list (without active drug-allergy checks)
   g. Voice recognition capabilities for documentation
   h. Manage flow sheets
   i. Manage progress notes
   j. Generate and record patient-specific instructions
   k. Capture patient preferences
2. Results management
   a. View laboratory results
   b. Provide alerts for critical laboratory values
   c. Manage (prioritize and sort) laboratory results
   d. Notification of results availability
   e. Document point-of-care laboratory results
3. Provider order entry with decision support for nonmedication orders
   a. Prescribe medications
   b. Provide alerts for redundant laboratory orders
   c. Send an order for a test (if on site)
   d. Provide alerts for laboratory charges
   e. Provide decision support for immunization orders (including flu shot and pneumovax reminders)
   f. Enter electronic referrals
4. Medication prescribing support
   a. Provide alerts regarding generic substitution
   b. Provide alerts for expensive medications
   c. Provide alerts regarding formulary compliance
   d. Provide default drug dosages
   e. Check for drug–drug interactions
   f. Provide renal dosing guidance
   g. Perform drug-allergy checks
   h. Perform drug laboratory checks
   i. Provide dosage checking
   j. Prompt corollary laboratory ordering

k. Perform drug–condition checks
l. Perform drug–diet checks

5. Clinical reminders during patient encounter
   a. Present alerts for preventive services and wellness (e.g., Pap smears and mammograms)

6. Clinical guidelines, protocols, or reference tools
   a. Provide reminders for adherence to guidelines for chronic disease management
   b. Provide alerts for adherence to standard care plans, guidelines, and protocols
   c. Display patient-specific data for chronic disease management
   d. Capture deviations from standard care plans, guidelines, and protocols
   e. Enable links to external knowledge sources

7. Population health management tools
   a. Enable report generation for public reporting
   b. Enable physicians to manage panels of patients
   c. Provide surveillance for adverse events, including adverse drug events
   d. Support quality-improvement measurement
   e. Immunization tracking
   f. Support performance measurement

8. Electronic communication
   a. Enable interprovider communication

9. Administrative, billing, and coding
   a. Manage patient consents and authorizations
   b. Manage patient demographics and administrative information
   c. Maintain an electronic record of all patient encounters
   d. Provide rules-driven financial and administrative coding assistance
   e. Support supply management, including documentation of medication and immunization administration in the office
   f. Document and schedule follow-up appointments
   g. Support the creation of legal documentation[7]

---

[7] Rainu Kaushal and Douglas E. Levy, "Economic Analyses of Health Information Technology," in *Health Information Technology in the United States*, ed. by Blumenthal et al. (Princeton, NJ: Robert Wood Johnson Foundation, 2008), 163–4. Copyright 2008, Robert Wood Johnson Foundation. Used with permission from the Robert Wood Johnson Foundation.

1.1.2 *Cloud-Based EHR Systems*

Some EHR systems use providers' in-house servers, but others are cloud based. Cloud computing uses a network of remote servers hosted on the Internet to store, manage, and process data. The National Institute of Standards and Technology (NIST) defines *cloud computing* as "a model for enabling ubiquitous, convenient, on-demand network access to a shared pool of configurable computing resources (e.g., networks, servers, storage, applications, and services) that can be rapidly provisioned and released with minimal management effort or service provider interaction."[8]

Cloud computing can relieve organizations of the need to build and maintain their own computer infrastructure – all they need is an Internet connection. Multiple customers can share cloud infrastructure, services, and applications, a phenomenon known as *multitenancy*. According to one study, over 80 percent of small practices in urban settings have adopted cloud-based EHRs.[9] Cloud computing also makes it easy for healthcare providers to access EHRs from outside the office. Another of its advantages is scalability; that is, consumers can use as much or as little computing capability as they need at a given time.[10]

1.1.3 *The EHR Vendor Marketplace*

Hundreds of vendors are producing EHR systems, but many experts predict that in the coming years the EHR vendor market will shrink considerably through departures and consolidation.[11] According to the Office of the National Coordinator for Health Information Technology, as of March 2015, 179 health information technology (IT) vendors supplied certified EHR products to hospitals, and 779 vendors supplied certified products to healthcare professionals. However, a few vendors, such as Cerner, MEDITECH, and

---

[8] National Institute of Standards and Technology, *The NIST Definition of Cloud Computing: Recommendations of the National Institute of Standards and Technology*, by Peter Mell and Timothy Grance (NIST Special Publication 800-145) (Gaithersburg, MD: National Institute of Standards and Technology, 2011), 2; available at: http://csrc.nist.gov/publications/nistpubs/800–145/SP800-145.pdf (accessed December 10, 2015).

[9] "Cloud-Based Electronic Health Record Firms Sweep Top Physician Satisfaction Rankings for Small and Solo Practices, Reveals 2015 Black Book Survey," *PRWEB*, May 27, 2015; available at: www.prweb.com/releases/2015/05/prweb12744687.htm (accessed December 10, 2015).

[10] National Institute of Standards and Technology, *The NIST Definition of Cloud Computing*, 2.

[11] "6 EHR Trends to Watch in 2015," Health Care Data Solutions; available at: www.healthcaredatasolutions.com/wp-content/uploads/2015/03/HDS-Whitepaper-6-EHR-Trends-to-Watch-in-2015.pdf (accessed December 10, 2015).

Epic Systems, dominated the market. The top ten EHR vendors provided the primary certified EHR systems for nine of ten hospitals and two of three professionals.[12] A different report indicated that fifteen vendors sold 75 percent of EHR systems to healthcare providers, and among hospitals,[13] just six vendors accounted for 75 percent of purchases.[14]

Commentators agree that given these trends, market consolidation is inevitable. Several large companies have already merged,[15] and at least one, GE Healthcare, has left the hospital EHR business, though it continues to sell EHR products for other medical practices.[16] Mergers and departures can be highly problematic for customers because they may force users to switch to a different EHR system after having invested considerable time, money, and effort in adopting their original product.[17]

1.2 EHR SYSTEM BENEFITS

It is no wonder that many healthcare providers and policymakers have eagerly advocated for and welcomed the implementation of EHR systems. The

[12] Office of the National Coordinator for Health Information Technology, "Electronic Health Record Vendors Reported by Hospitals Participating in the CMS EHR Incentive Programs," *Health IT Quick-Stat* 29 (2015); available at: http://dashboard.healthit.gov/quickstats/pages/FIG-Vendors-of-EHRs-to-Participating-Hospitals.php (accessed January 7, 2016); Office of the National Coordinator for Health Information Technology, "Electronic Health Record Vendors Reported by Health Care Professionals Participating in the CMS EHR Incentive Programs and ONC Regional Extension Centers Program," *Health IT Quick-Stat* 30 (2015); available at: http://dashboard.healthit.gov/quickstats/pages/FIG-Vendors-of-EHRs-to-Participating-Professionals.php (accessed January 7, 2016).

[13] The healthcare providers and hospitals studied all participated in the federal "meaningful use" incentive program that requires participants to purchase certified EHR systems in compliance with federal regulations. See discussion in Chapter 4.

[14] J. Wanderer, P. Mishra, and J. Ehrenfeld, "Innovation and Market Consolidation among Electronic Health Record Vendors: An Acute Need for Regulation," *Journal of Medical Systems* 38, no. 1 (2014): 8.

[15] Examples are Greenway-Vitera and Cerner-Siemens.

[16] Tony Schueth, "What's Next for EHR Market Consolidation?," *HealthTech Zone*, October 16, 2014; available at: www.healthtechzone.com/topics/healthcare/articles/2014/10/16/391527-whats-next-ehr-market-consolidation.htm (accessed January 7, 2016); Neil Versel, "GE Healthcare: We're Leaving the Hospital EMR Business," *MedCity News*, April 14, 2015; available at: http://medcitynews.com/2015/04/ge-healthcare-leaving-hospital-emr-business/ (accessed January 7, 2016).

[17] Westat, "EHR Contracts: Key Contract Terms for Users to Understand," Office of the National Coordinator for Health Information Technology, June 25, 2013; available at: www.healthit.gov/sites/default/files/ehr_contracting_terms_final_508_compliant.pdf (accessed January 7, 2016); Marisa Torrieri, "When Your EHR Vendor Goes Out of Business," *Physicians Practice*, March 5, 2013; available at: www.physicianspractice.com/ehr/when-your-ehr-vendor-goes-out-business (accessed January 7, 2016).

potential benefits of the new technology are considerable. EHR systems can reduce errors, improve patient safety, enhance communication, potentially reduce costs, and promote research, quality improvement, and public health initiatives. This section provides a detailed discussion of EHR system benefits.

1.2.1 *Improving Quality of Care through Decision Support and Search Capabilities*

EHR systems can reduce errors and improve patient safety, particularly through decision support mechanisms. EHR systems can incorporate reminders, prompts, and links to medical literature to promote accurate, timely, and responsible care.[18] Well-timed, clear alerts about patients' allergies, drug–drug interactions, incorrect dosages, and other potential hazards can reduce medical errors and prescribing mistakes. Some studies have shown that EHR systems improve preventive care, clinician adherence to practice guidelines, and documentation thoroughness. For example, one study found that computerized reminders "increased the use of pneumococcal and influenza vaccinations from practically zero to approximately 35 and 50 percent, respectively, for hospitalized patients."[19]

Respondents to a survey of trauma centers indicated that they used EHR systems to enhance care through "custom patient tracking lists, real-time feeds of clinical data, and automated blood alcohol content screening." Furthermore, EHR systems can prevent doctors from ordering unneeded diagnostic tests because they make prior laboratory results visible and easily accessible.[20]

Currently, the lag between the discovery of new treatments and their consistent use in medical practice can be up to twenty years.[21] EHR systems, however, could significantly expedite the broad dissemination of knowledge about effective new treatments through decision support mechanisms.[22] Electronic messages could alert physicians to new studies or guidelines that suggest that they should change particular practices or switch to different therapies.

---

[18] Anne Bobb et al., "The Epidemiology of Prescribing Errors: The Potential Impact of Computerized Prescriber Order Entry," *Archives of Internal Medicine* 164, no. 7 (2004): 788–9.

[19] Paul R. Dexter et al., "A Computerized Reminder System to Increase the Use of Preventive Care for Hospitalized Patients," *New England Journal of Medicine* 345 (2001): 968.

[20] Jennifer King et al., "Clinical Benefits of Electronic Health Record Use: National Findings," *Health Services Research* 49, no. 1 (2014): 397; Erik G. Van Eaton et al., "A Nationwide Survey of Trauma Center Information Technology Leverage Capacity for Mental Health Comorbidity Screening," *Journal of American College of Surgeons* 219, no. 3 (2014): 508.

[21] Institute of Medicine, *Crossing the Quality Chasm: A New Health System for the 21st Century* (Washington, DC: National Academies Press, 2001), 145.

[22] Louise Liang, "The Gap between Evidence and Practice," *Health Affairs* 26, no. 2 (2007): w120.

EHR systems also have a potential role to play in reducing health disparities. Health inequities between whites and blacks have been the subject of much commentary and debate in recent years and have fueled governmental interest in formulating effective responses.[23] Technology that provides resource-poor practices with automatic decision support, reminders, and alerts based on the most advanced medical knowledge could enhance the care available to patients in remote rural areas and to those who are economically disadvantaged. Clinicians in such areas, who are pressed for time and resources, would have information at their fingertips that might otherwise be inaccessible.

Public health emergency response efforts could likewise benefit from EHR systems. With appropriate support from EHR vendors and public health officials, decision support in EHR systems could be rapidly adapted to alter the behavior of clinicians responding to public health threats or other important changes in recommended modes of care.[24] For example, EHR systems nationwide might be quickly reconfigured to advise caregivers to treat patients with particular symptoms as possible carriers of an emerging infectious disease.

Advanced search capabilities could also contribute significantly to patient safety. Using electronic searches, physicians could reduce the time they spend reviewing patient records for particular details and diminish the risk of missing key information. Physicians could type in search terms, just as they do in Google, and the data they need could appear instantly. In addition, electronic searches can enable clinicians to identify patients who should be informed about matters such as drug recalls.[25]

1.2.2 *Facilitating Communication among Treating Clinicians and between Patients and Doctors: Interoperability, Electronic Messaging, and More*

EHR systems can enhance communication among medical team members and between patients and physicians, and better communication can lead to better medical outcomes. First, EHR systems make records available to

---

[23] See, e.g., Ruqaiijah Yearby, "When Is a Change Going to Come?: Separate and Unequal Health Care Fifty Years after Title VI of the Civil Rights Act of 1964," *SMU Law Review* 67 (2014): 287–338.

[24] These adaptations could be similar to automatic antivirus downloads, which are now commonly available.

[25] Richard J. Baron et al., "Electronic Health Records: Just around the Corner? Or over the Cliff?," *Annals of Internal Medicine* 143, no. 3 (2005): 225–6; Office of the National Coordinator for Health Information Technology (ONC), "Report to Congress: Update on the Adoption of Health Information Technology and Related Efforts to Facilitate the Electronic Use and Exchange of Health Information (October 2014)," 11; available at: www.healthit.gov/sites/defa ult/files/rtc_adoption_and_exchange9302014.pdf (accessed August 14, 2015).

clinicians anytime and anywhere, and they are always legible.[26] Physicians can access patients' records remotely, so they can look at them even if they are speaking to patients by phone from home. In addition, patients who have PHRs can look at them from home as well. Second, EHR systems potentially enable healthcare providers to obtain critical medical information about their patients from any other clinician or medical facilities as soon as the need arises.

To realize these benefits fully, however, we must have EHR systems that are interoperable. Interoperable systems can communicate with each other, exchange data, and operate seamlessly and in a coordinated fashion across organizations.[27] Interoperable EHR systems could allow doctors with proper authorization access to the medical histories, drug lists, allergies, and other relevant information of all their patients, no matter where they had been treated previously. This capability could be essential in treating patients who arrive in an emergency room unconscious, confused, or with dementia. It could also significantly facilitate and enhance the treatment of economically disadvantaged patients who may not have access to medical facilities and family doctors who carefully manage their care.[28] Such patients may have particularly fragmented and incomplete records in the absence of interoperability.

Furthermore, many patients have medical records that are fragmented among different physicians. According to one source, elderly patients see an average of four specialists in a year.[29] If these doctors do not communicate and carefully coordinate the patient's care, any one of them might miss vital information that is critical to the individual's welfare.

Third, EHR systems can enhance communication not only among medical professionals but also among patients and their doctors. Many doctors do not provide their patients with e-mail addresses because of privacy and security concerns. E-mails can be copied to multiple people, can be easily sent to the wrong addressee, can be inadvertently deleted, or can go to junk mail folders. Secure messaging capabilities built into EHR systems solve many of these problems. As of 2014, only about 25 percent of medical practices used secure

---

[26] Thomson Kuhn et al., "Clinical Documentation in the 21st Century: Executive Summary of a Policy Position Paper from the American College of Physicians," *Annals of Internal Medicine* 162, no. 4 (2015): appendix.

[27] Shortliffe and Cimino, *Biomedical Informatics*, 952.

[28] Lawrence O. Gostin, "'Police' Powers and Public Health Paternalism: HIV and Diabetes Surveillance," *Hastings Center Report* 37, no. 2 (2007): 10.

[29] Barbara Starfield et al., "Ambulatory Specialist Use by Nonhospitalized Patients in US Health Plans: Correlates and Consequences," *Journal of Ambulatory Care Management* 32, no. 3 (2009): 218, 222.

messaging capabilities,[30] but patients are eager to communicate electronically with their doctors, and secure messaging is likely to become more commonplace in the future.[31]

During patient visits, clinicians can use Internet resources to educate patients and answer their questions. Pharmacists may use photos of different pills, surgeons can discuss anatomic drawings, and physicians can show videos that explain proposed treatments and procedures.[32]

Finally, PHRs allow patients to view portions of their EHRs and to obtain test results, clinical summaries, appointment schedules, and more. PHRs are thus another way in which physicians can communicate information to patients quickly and accurately.

1.2.3 *Achieving Cost Savings*

Many commentators associate significant cost savings with EHR systems despite the expenses of purchasing, implementing, and operating them. Optimists' estimates of financial benefits range from between $8,400 and $140,100 over five years per physician,[33] to $37 million to $59 million over five years for large hospitals,[34] to overall national savings of $77.8 billion a year if a standardized, interoperable national health information network is established.[35]

[30] Helen Gregg, "6 Statistics on Physician Use of Telemedicine, Secure Messaging, Remote Monitoring," *Health IT & CIO Review*, June 4, 2014; available at: www.beckershospitalreview .com/healthcare-information-technology/6-statistics-on-physician-use-of-telemedicine-secure-messaging-remote-monitoring.html (accessed December 28, 2015).

[31] Melissa Jayne Kinsey, "Please Hold for the Doctor: Why You Still Can't Email Your Physicians with a Simple Question (Hint: It's Not Their Fault.)," *Slate*, June 26, 2014; available at: www .slate.com/articles/technology/future_tense/2014/06/telemedicine_e_visits_doctors_should _start_using_email.html (accessed August 17, 2015).

[32] Zuzanna Czernik and C. T. Lin, "Time at the Bedside (Computing)," *JAMA* 315, no. 22 (2016): 2399.

[33] William W. Stead, "Rethinking Electronic Health Records to Better Achieve Quality and Safety Goals," *Annual Review of Medicine* 58 (2006): 37; Robert H. Miller et al., "The Value of Electronic Health Records in Solo or Small Group Practices," *Health Affairs* 24, no. 3 (2005): 1127, 1131 (finding that "[f]inancial benefits averaged approximately $33,000 per … [full time] provider per year").

[34] Beverly Bell and Kelly Thornton, "From Promise to Reality: Achieving the Value of an EHR," *Healthcare Financial Management* 65, no. 2 (2011): 51–6; Michael D. Ries, "Electronic Medical Records: Friends or Foes?," *Clinical Orthopaedics and Related Research* 472, no. 1 (2014): 17.

[35] Jan Walker et al., "The Value of Health Care Information Exchange and Interoperability," *Health Affairs* (2005): w5–16; US Congress, Congressional Budget Office, *Evidence on the Costs and Benefits of Health Information Technology*, 2008, 4; available at: www.cbo.gov/sites/ default/files/05-20-healthit.pdf (accessed August 17, 2015) (stating that researchers have estimated the cost savings would total approximately $80 billion per year).

Cost savings may be generated by a variety of factors. These include (1) fewer duplicated tests, (2) reductions in administrative expenditures, and (3) a decrease in medical errors and adverse drug events.[36] For example, doctors should be able to retrieve the EHRs of patients who present at emergency rooms no matter where those records are housed and thus would not need to conduct diagnostic tests that the patient has already recently undergone. Furthermore, access to a patient's complete EHR, including medical history, allergies, and current medication list, could prevent medical errors that might lead to lengthy hospitalization, surgery, and other expensive care.

At the same time, EHR systems may help physicians to generate more income. The technology can improve clinicians' ability to record details of medical treatments and examinations and thus to bill more accurately (or, in the view of skeptics, more extensively) for their services. In professional lingo, this is known as improved *charge capture*.[37]

1.2.4 *Enabling Secondary Uses: Research, Quality Assessment and Improvement, and Public Health Initiatives*

The use of health information for nontreatment purposes is often called *secondary use*.[38] EHR data may be put to secondary use by medical providers, governmental entities, and other interested parties.

First and foremost, EHRs could promote medical research and the development of much-needed evidence concerning the efficacy of various treatment alternatives. EHRs can facilitate the identification of patients for clinical studies by allowing investigators to search their own patients' records electronically for individuals who have specific conditions and meet the criteria for inclusion in particular clinical trials. Second, many studies can be based directly on analysis of the extensive and comprehensive data contained in electronic records.[39]

---

[36] Rainu Kaushal et al., "Return on Investment for a Computerized Physician Order Entry System," *Journal of the American Medical Informatics Association* 13, no. 3 (2006): 265; Walker et al., "The Value of Health Care Information Exchange and Interoperability," w5–16.

[37] Taleah H. Collum, Nir Menachemi, and Bisakha Sen, "Does Electronic Health Record Use Improve Hospital Financial Performance? Evidence from Panel Data," *Health Care Management Review* 41, no. 3 (2016): 267.

[38] Taxiarchis Botsis et al., "Secondary Use of EHR: Data Quality Issues and Informatics Opportunities," *Summit on Translational Bioinformatics* 2010 (2010): 1–5; Jessica S. Ancker et al., "Root Causes Underlying Challenges to Secondary Use of Data," *AMIA Annual Symposium Proceedings* 2011 (2011): 57.

[39] John Powell and Iain Buchan, "Electronic Health Records Should Support Clinical Research," *Journal of Medical Internet Research* 7, no. 1 (2005): e4.

Randomized, controlled clinical trials are considered to be the gold standard of medical studies.[40] However, research can also be accomplished through observational studies.[41] Thus, rather than conducting a controlled experiment, investigators might review the charts or electronic files of patients receiving different medications or different types of surgery to treat a particular condition in order to determine the efficacy of each approach.[42]

EHR databases could allow researchers to access a vast quantity of information about millions of patients who are treated in varied clinical settings, have diverse attributes, and live in different regions of the country.[43] Available information could include patients' medical histories over their entire lifetimes. The data reviewed in database studies, consequently, may be far more abundant and comprehensive than the data generated by clinical trials, which are rigorously controlled and often involve fewer than 3,000 patients.[44]

The federal government and many medical experts have embraced the objective of conducting extensive comparative effectiveness research (CER).[45] The Patient Protection and Affordable Care Act of 2010 defines CER as "research evaluating and comparing health outcomes and the clinical

---

[40] Friedrich K. Port, "Role of Observational Studies versus Clinical Trials in ESRD Research," *Kidney International* 57 (2000): S3. *Clinical studies* have been defined as "involving the collection of data on a process when there is some manipulation of variables that are assumed to affect the outcome of a process, keeping other variables constant as far as possible." Bryan F. J. Manly, *The Design and Analysis of Research Studies* (Cambridge University Press, 1992), 1.

[41] Manly, *The Design and Analysis of Research Studies*, 1 (explaining that observational studies involve the collection of data "by observing some process which may not be well understood"); Charles P. Friedman and Jeremy C. Wyatt, *Evaluation Methods in Biomedical Informatics*, 2nd edn. (New York: Springer, 2006), 369 (defining observational studies as involving an "[a]pproach to study design that entails no experimental manipulation" in which "[i]nvestigators typically draw conclusions by carefully observing ... [subjects] with or without an information resource").

[42] Kjell Benson and Arthur J. Hartz, "A Comparison of Observational Studies and Randomized Controlled Trials," *New England Journal of Medicine* 342 (2000): 1879–83.

[43] *Ibid.*; Liang, "The Gap between Evidence and Practice," w120 (asserting that EHRs "have the potential to take over where clinical trials and evidence-based research leave off, by providing real-world evidence of drugs' and treatments' effectiveness across subpopulations and over longer periods of time"); Lynn M. Etheredge, "A Rapid-Learning Health System," *Health Affairs* 26 (2007): w111; James H. Ware and Mary Beth Hamel, "Pragmatic Trials – Guides to Better Patient Care?," *New England Journal of Medicine* 364 (2011): 1685 (discussing the shortcomings of clinical trials).

[44] Sheila Weiss Smith, "Sidelining Safety – The FDA's Inadequate Response to the IOM," *New England Journal of Medicine* 357 (2007): 961.

[45] Patient Protection and Affordable Care Act of 2010, 42 USC § 1320e (2010); Institute of Medicine, *Initial National Priorities for Comparative Effectiveness Research* (Washington, DC: National Academies Press, 2009); available at: www.iom.edu/Reports/2009/Comparative EffectivenessResearchPriorities.aspx (accessed August 17, 2015) (emphasizing the need for CER and proposing initial CER priorities).

effectiveness, risks, and benefits of 2 or more medical treatments, services, and items."[46] CER can be conducted in part through observational studies, which can be particularly illuminating because they reflect actual usage of treatments.[47] The outcomes of CER and other observational studies may ultimately enable the healthcare community to alleviate human suffering more effectively, reduce medical costs, and save patients' lives.[48]

EHR systems also can help healthcare providers to collect quality measures concerning the services they provide for quality assessment and improvement purposes.[49] Medical facilities and government authorities conduct a variety of oversight activities. Healthcare providers may seek data for internal quality assessment purposes in order to evaluate their own performance.[50] Likewise, insurers may require facilities to submit process and outcome information in order to assess their performance.[51] In addition, the Centers for Medicare and Medicaid Services (CMS) and many state governments require quality measurements and public reporting.[52] A prime example is CMS's Hospital Compare, which features publicly available data about the quality of care at over 4,000 hospitals.[53]

[46]   42 USC § 1320e(a)(2)(A) (2010).

[47]   42 USC § 1320e(d)(2)(A) (2010). See John Concato et al., "Observational Methods in Comparative Effectiveness Research," *American Journal of Medicine* 123, no. 12 (2010): e16; S. Schneeweiss et al., "Assessing the Comparative Effectiveness of Newly Marketed Medications: Methodological Challenges and Implications for Drug Development," *Clinical Pharmacology & Therapeutics* 90, no. 6 (2011): 777.

[48]   42 USC § 1320e(d)(2)(A) (2010); L. Manchikanti et al., "Facts, Fallacies, and Politics of Comparative Effectiveness Research, Part 1: Basic Consideration," *Pain Physician* 13, no. 1 (2010): e39; Adam G. Elshaug and Alan M. Garber, "How CER Could Pay for Itself – Insights from Vertebral Fracture Treatments," *New England Journal of Medicine* 364 (2011): 1392–3.

[49]   Kitty S. Chan et al., "Electronic Health Records and the Reliability and Validity of Quality Measures: A Review of the Literature," *Medical Care Research and Review* 67, no. 5 (2010): 504.

[50]   Monica M. Horvath et al., "The DEDUCE Guided Query Tool: Providing Simplified Access to Clinical Data for Research and Quality Improvement," *Journal of Biomedical Informatics* 44, no. 2 (2011): 273.

[51]   Paul C. Tang et al., "Comparison of Methodologies for Calculating Quality Measures Based on Administrative Data versus Clinical Data from an Electronic Health Record System: Implications for Performance," *Journal of the American Medical Informatics Association* 14, no. 1 (2007): 10.

[52]   Joseph S. Ross, Sameer Sheth, and Harlan M. Krumholz, "State-Sponsored Public Reporting of Hospital Quality: Results Are Hard to Find and Lack Uniformity," *Health Affairs* 29, no. 12 (2010): 2318–19; Hanys Quality Institute, *Understanding Publicly Reported Hospital Quality Measures: Initial Steps toward Alignment, Standardization, and Value* (Rensselaer: Healthcare Association of New York State, 2007), 1–3; available at: www.hanys.org/publications/upload/hanys_quality_report_card.pdf (accessed August 17, 2015).

[53]   US Department of Health and Human Services, "What Is Hospital Compare?"; available at: www.hospitalcompare.hhs.gov/About/WhatIs/What-Is-HOS.aspx (accessed August 17, 2015); Ross, Sheth, and Krumholz, "State-Sponsored Public Reporting of Hospital Quality," 2318.

Third, federal and state government agencies may rely on EHR data to support public health initiatives. Federal "meaningful use" regulations require clinicians to use their EHR systems to send various types of data to public health authorities. These include laboratory results, immunization information, cancer cases, and more.[54] Public health authorities, in turn, deposit the submitted information in databases and use it to conduct disease surveillance and to respond to public health threats.[55]

1.3 EHR SYSTEM SHORTCOMINGS

Despite the many potential benefits of EHR systems, they are not an unalloyed good. Their design implementation, use, and maintenance raise important concerns that must not be overlooked.

1.3.1 Data Veracity

EHRs are created by very busy clinicians who face increasing demands to see more patients and do more documentation. On average, doctors spend only thirteen to eighteen minutes with each patient.[56] Whether they attempt to enter data during the patient encounter or attend to documentation afterwards, they are likely to work quickly and to make mistakes. Surely, paper medical records often contained illegible handwriting, misspellings, and other errors. One of the promises of EHR technology was that it would cure the data-accuracy problem. Unfortunately, thus far this promise has not been fulfilled, and computerization may in fact create many new error vulnerabilities.

---

[54] 45 CFR § 170.205 (2015). See Chapter 2 for further discussion.

[55] Chapter 5 extensively addresses the use of EHR data for research and other secondary purposes. Chapter 7 analyzes the limitations of contemporary EHR databases.

[56] Andrew Gottschalk and Susan A. Flocke, "Time Spent in Face-to-Face Patient Care and Work Outside the Examination Room," *Annals of Family Medicine* 3, no. 6 (2005): 491 (finding that the average time per patient was 13.3 minutes); Kimberly S. H. Yarnall et al., "Family Physicians as Team Leaders: 'Time' to Share the Care," *Preventing Chronic Disease* 6, no. 2 (2009); available at: www.cdc.gov/pcd/issues/2009/apr/08_0023.htm (accessed August 17, 2015) (finding that the mean length for an acute care visit is 17.3 minutes, the mean for a chronic disease care visit is 19.3 minutes, and the average for a preventive care visit is 21.4 minutes and that of total clinical time spent by physicians, these comprise 45.8, 37.4, and 16.8 percent, respectively); Kevin Fiscella and Ronald M. Epstein, "So Much to Do, So Little Time: Care for the Socially Disadvantaged and the 15-Minute Visit," *Archives of Internal Medicine* 168, no. 17 (2008): 1843 ("The average office visit in the United States lasts for about 16 minutes").

1.3.1.1 Input Errors

Busy clinicians who face enormous time pressures can easily mistype words and numbers when entering data into EHRs. Moreover, documentation in EHRs is often performed using drop-down lists, checkboxes, macros, and templates,[57] which create several other opportunities for errors. Studies have shown that users select wrong menu items from drop-down menus, choose erroneous diagnosis codes, check boxes incorrectly, or uncheck boxes inappropriately if the default setting has all boxes checked.[58]

The existence of both structured data fields and free-text sections in EHRs adds opportunities for misleading errors. If dosages or treatment instructions are entered in the structured areas and also typed in free-text format, they are sometimes different or contradictory, thereby confusing other clinicians.[59]

Presumably, the vast majority of errors are made innocently; however, there are also some perverse incentives at play. If a clinician checks a few too many boxes, for example, she can make it look like she did more during the clinical encounter than she actually did, and consequently, she can bill a higher amount. Similarly, selecting a code for a slightly more serious condition than the patient has may justify increased charges. Such billing manipulations are known as *up-coding*. According to one study, up-coding services provided to Medicare patients is so common that it may account for as much as 15 percent of Medicare's expenditures for general office visits, or $2.13 billion annually (in 2007 dollars).[60]

1.3.1.2 Data Entered into Wrong Patient Charts

Data can be entered into the wrong patient chart if multiple patient charts are open at the same time or if a prior user did not log off properly after viewing another patient's EHR.[61] Such errors are particularly likely in hospitals.

---

[57] Kuhn et al., "Clinical Documentation in the 21st Century," appendix.

[58] Farah Magrabi et al., "An Analysis of Computer-Related Patient Safety Incidents to Inform the Development of a Classification," *Journal of the American Medical Informatics Association* 17, no. 6 (2010): 665, 669; Hoffman and Podgurski, "E-Health Hazards," 1544–5 (discussing input errors).

[59] Sue Bowman, "Impact of Electronic Health Record Systems on Information Integrity: Quality and Safety Implications," *Perspectives in Health Information Management* 10 (2013): 1, 2; available at: www.ncbi.nlm.nih.gov/pmc/articles/PMC3797550/pdf/phim0010-0001c.pdf (accessed August 17, 2015).

[60] Christopher S. Brunt, "CPT Fee Differentials and Visit Upcoding under Medicare Part B," *Health Economics* 20 (2011): 840.

[61] Elizabeth Borycki, "Trends in Health Information Technology Safety: From Technology-Induced Errors to Current Approaches for Ensuring Technology Safety," *Healthcare Informatics Research* 19, no. 2 (2013): 70.

During a typical hospitalization, approximately 150 individuals view each patient's chart, and multiple records may be handled at once in nursing stations.[62]

1.3.1.3 Copy and Paste Problems

The EHR copy and paste feature is particularly notorious as a source of errors.[63] It is designed to save time by allowing physicians to copy a narrative from a prior visit and paste it into new visit notes. However, if the copied information is not carefully edited and updated, the physician will inadvertently introduce errors into the record.[64] For example, in one reported case, the record of a patient hospitalized for many weeks because of complications from surgery indicated each day that this was "post-op day no. 2" because the note was never edited. In another case, the statement "Patient needs drainage, may need OR [operating room]" appeared in notes for several consecutive days, even after the patient successfully underwent a procedure to drain his abscess.[65] In yet another instance, a patient's EHR indicated erroneously that he had a below-the-knee amputation (BKA) because a voice-recognition dictation system entered "BKA" into the record instead of the real problem – diabetic ketoacidosis, whose acronym is DKA.[66]

Copying and pasting information from prior visits or other areas of the EHR can cause all of the following problems:

- Incorrect or outdated information,
- Repetitive information,
- Inability to determine the true author and purpose of documentation,

[62] Judy Foreman, "At Risk of Exposure: In the Push for Electronic Medical Records, Concern Is Growing about How Well Privacy Can Be Safeguarded," *Los Angeles Times*, June, 26, 2006; available at: http://articles.latimes.com/2006/jun/26/health/he-privacy26 (accessed August 17, 2015).

[63] Eugenia L. Siegler and Ronald Adelman, "Copy and Paste: A Remediable Hazard of Electronic Health Records," *American Journal of Medicine* 122, no. 6 (2009): 495–6; Justin M. Weis and Paul C. Levy, "Copy, Paste, and Cloned Notes in Electronic Health Records: Prevalence, Benefits, Risks, and Best Practice Recommendations," *Chest* 145, no. 3 (2014): 632, 637.

[64] Lena Mamykina et al., "Clinical Documentation: Composition or Synthesis?," *Journal of American Medical Informatics Association* 19, no. 6 (2012): 1027.

[65] Kevin B. O'Reilly, "EHRs: 'Sloppy and Paste' Endures Despite Patient Safety Risk," *American Medical News*, February 4, 2013; available at: www.amednews.com/article/20130204/profession/130209993/2/ (accessed August 17, 2015).

[66] Paul Hsieh, "Can You Trust What's in Your Electronic Medical Record?," *Forbes*, February 24, 2014; available at: www.forbes.com/sites/paulhsieh/2014/02/24/electronic-medical-record/ (accessed August 17, 2015).

- Inability to determine when the entry was created,
- Propagation of false information,
- Clinical notes that are inconsistent and confusing, and
- Clinical notes that are unnecessarily lengthy.[67]

Copy and paste is very commonly used. In a study of 100 randomly selected hospital admissions, copied text was found in 78 percent of medical residents' electronic sign-out notes (written when their shift ended) and 54 percent of patient progress notes.[68] A review of 2,068 notes from intensive care unit (ICU) patients showed that 82 percent of residents' notes and 74 percent of attending physicians' notes consisted of at least 20 percent copied information in the assessment and plan sections alone.[69]

The data-quality problems that copying and pasting generates have been widely recognized. In 2014, the American Health Information Management Association issued a statement calling for copy/paste functionality to be "permitted only in the presence of strong technical and administrative controls which include organizational policies and procedures, requirements for participation in user training and education, and ongoing monitoring."[70] In the absence of such measures, the errors caused by copying and pasting EHR text can confuse treating clinicians and claims administrators, harm patients, and taint records that will later be employed for secondary use by researchers and other analysts.

1.3.1.4 Estimating Error Rates

A number of studies have focused on error rates in EHR systems. A study of e-prescribing errors in community hospitals collected data during forty-five hours of observation in five pharmacies and follow-up interviews with twenty participants. Pharmacy personnel identified seventy-five e-prescribing errors and estimated that five in 100 e-prescriptions contained errors, the most common being incorrect drug quantity, dosing directions, therapy duration, and dosage formulation.[71]

---

[67] Bowman, "Impact of Electronic Health Record Systems on Information Integrity."

[68] Jesse O. Wrenn et al., "Quantifying Clinical Narrative Redundancy in an Electronic Health Record," *Journal of the American Medical Informatics Association* 17, no. 1 (2010): 49, 52.

[69] J. Daryl Thornton et al., "The Prevalence of Copied Information by Attendings and Residents in Critical Care Progress Notes," *Critical Care Medicine* 41, no. 2 (2013): 382.

[70] American Health Information Management Association, *Appropriate Use of the Copy and Paste Functionality in Electronic Health Records*, March 17, 2014, 1; available at: http://library.ahima .org/xpedio/groups/public/documents/ahima/bok1_050621.pdf (accessed August 17, 2015).

[71] Olufunmilola K. Odukoya, Jamie A. Stone, and Michelle A. Chui, "E-Prescribing Errors in Community Pharmacies: Exploring Consequences and Contributing Factors," *International Journal of Medical Informatics* 83, no. 6 (2014): 434–5.

Other studies have found considerable missing data. For example, in the outpatient setting, medication lists were incomplete for 27 percent of oncology patients and 53 percent of primary care patients. In addition, between 7 and 29 percent of patients with heart failure and diabetes did not have these chronic conditions documented in their EHR problem lists.[72] Consequently, one must assume that many EHRs have significant imperfections.

1.3.2 *Software and Programming Defects*

Software defects arising from errors in a computer program source code or design can adversely affect both EHR data quality and data analysis. To ensure software integrity, highly skilled software professionals must carefully design and then thoroughly test their products.[73]

Software bugs can cause computer programs to produce incorrect or unexpected results or to behave in unintended ways. To illustrate, when calculating the appropriate drug dosage for a patient, the weight-based dosing algorithm may fail to convert a weight measure that was entered in pounds to a weight measure in kilograms, the unit on which the calculation is based. In such a case, the patient would receive approximately double the correct dose.[74]

Software can also be programmed incorrectly. Numerous instances of dangerous programming problems have been reported. In one case, a woman's cervical cancer was not detected for four years because an EHR system's default setting displayed a prior normal Pap smear result to her physician rather than her more recent abnormal test results. Because detection of her disease was delayed, the patient, a young woman who had not yet had children, ended up needing a full hysterectomy.[75] In another case, a doctor ordered "daily" blood draws for a hospitalized patient, which conventionally means that they are performed at 6:00 a.m. Instead, however, the EHR system had been programmed to interpret the term "daily" to mean 4:00 p.m., so blood was taken

[72] Kitty S. Chan et al., "Electronic Health Records and the Reliability and Validity of Quality Measures: A Review of the Literature," *Medical Care Research and Review* 67, no. 5 (2010): 503, 514–15.

[73] Rebecca Sanders and Diane Kelly, "Dealing with Risk in Scientific Software Development," *IEEE Software* 25, no. 4 (2008): 25, 27; Diane F. Kelly, "A Software Chasm: Software Engineering and Scientific Computing," *IEEE Software* 24, no. 6 (2007): 118; Les Hatton, "The Chimera of Software Quality," *Computer* 40 (2007): 104.

[74] Dean F. Sittig and Hardeep Singh, "Defining Health Information Technology–Related Errors: New Developments since to Err Is Human," *Archives of Internal Medicine* 171, no. 14 (2011): 1283.

[75] Stacy Singer, "Electronic Medical Records May Cause Patient Care Errors, Florida Medical Board Says," *Palm Beach Post*, June 6, 2010; available at: www.palmbeachpost.com/news/news/electronic-medical-records-may-cause-patient-care-/nL7Yc/ (accessed August 18, 2015).

in the afternoon. When the patient was seen the next morning, the doctor did not know that the test results were from the previous day. Consequently, the patient was given an excessive amount of the anticoagulant warfarin, which caused a serious bleeding risk, though the error did not ultimately lead to harm.[76]

EHRs' limited ability to display graphical information may cause additional problems. Dean Sittig and colleagues evaluated the graphical displays of laboratory test results in eight EHR systems. They found most to be sorely inadequate, displaying data in nonstandardized fashion and suffering from other shortcomings in graphical capabilities. The authors caution that "many current EHR-generated graphs do not meet evidence-based criteria aimed at improving laboratory data comprehension."[77]

1.3.3 *The Challenges of Decision Support*

At times it is medically appropriate for doctors to discount decision support messages. In many instances, decision support prompts and alerts can be excessive and disruptive and, therefore, are justifiably overridden.[78] For example, drug-allergy alerts may indicate that some patients suffer mild reactions, and the alerts may appear even for patients who have tolerated the medication perfectly well for years. One study found that it took over 2,700 warnings to prevent one serious drug error and that only about 10 percent of alerts actually prevented adverse events and generated cost savings.[79] Furthermore, drug-related alerts often do not distinguish, by formatting or color, between warnings of high clinical significance and the much more routine notices of benign drug sensitivities so that physicians cannot immediately tell which warnings require their full attention.[80] For example, a

---

[76] Center for Surveillance, Epidemiology and Laboratory Services, Centers for Disease Control and Prevention, *The Essential Role of Laboratory Professionals: Ensuring the Safety and Effectiveness of Laboratory Data in Electronic Health Record Systems*, by M. Sawchuk et al. (Atlanta, May 2014); available at: www.cdc.gov/labhit/paper/Laboratory_Data_in_EHRs_2014 .pdf (accessed August 18, 2015).

[77] Dean Sittig et al., "Graphical Display of Diagnostic Test Results in Electronic Health Records: A Comparison of 8 Systems," *Journal of the American Medical Informatics Association* 22, no. 4 (2015): 900–4.

[78] Saeid Eslami et al., "Evaluation of Outpatient Computerized Physician Medication Order Entry Systems: A Systematic Review," *Journal of the American Medical Informatics Association* 14, no. 4 (2007): 404; Gilad J. Kuperman et al., "Medication-Related Clinical Decision Support in Computerized Provider Order Entry Systems: A Review," *Journal of the American Medical Informatics Association* 14, no. 1 (2007): 30.

[79] S. Weingart et al., "An Empirical Model to Estimate the Potential Impact of Modification Safety Alerts on Patient Safety, Health Care Utilization, and Cost in Ambulatory Care," *Archives of Internal Medicine* 169 (2009): 1465–70.

[80] Kuperman et al., "Medication-Related Clinical Decision Support in Computerized Provider Order Entry Systems," 404.

warning that a clinician is about to administer forty times the appropriate amount of a drug, a mistake that could kill the patient, might look no different from a warning that some patients develop a temporary rash from taking the drug.

Researchers have found that doctors override up to 95 percent of alerts.[81] Although many overrides are harmless, doctors who override decision support as a matter of course may inadvertently ignore lifesaving alerts.

Among 2,590 primary care physicians who responded to a survey, 86.9 percent indicated that they received an excessive quantity of alerts, and 69.6 percent reported that the number of alerts was so high that doctors could not manage them effectively. The median number of alerts received each day was sixty-three. Of even greater concern was the response of over half (55.6 percent) of physicians, who felt that contemporary decision support made it possible for clinicians to miss test results. In fact, almost a third (29.8 percent) reported that they had personally missed results and that the affected patients' care had consequently been delayed.[82]

Another study concluded that primary care physicians received a mean of 56.4 alerts per day that contained new information. Furthermore, it estimated that they spent an average of forty-nine minutes per day processing these alerts.[83]

1.3.4 *Inflexibility and Lack of Customization*

EHR systems may not always meet the needs of clinicians because they limit the choices doctors have in entering and displaying medical data. Sean Smith and Ross Koppel discuss three examples of such limitations[84]:

1. **Too coarse.** EHR systems may not allow doctors to choose descriptions that are detailed or refined enough. For example, it may be clinically important to note how old an infant is in terms of hours or minutes, but

[81] Jeremy S. Stultz and Milap C. Nahata, "Computerized Clinical Decision Support for Medication Prescribing and Utilization in Pediatrics," *Journal of the American Medical Informatics Association* 19, no. 6 (2012): 942–53; Allison B. McCoy et al., "Clinical Decision Support Alert Appropriateness: A Review and Proposal for Improvement," *Ochsner Journal* 14, no. 2 (2014): 195–202.

[82] Hardeep Singh et al., "Information Overload and Missed Test Results in Electronic Health Record–Based Settings," *JAMA Internal Medicine* 173, no. 8 (2013): 702–4.

[83] Daniel R. Murphy et al., "Notifications Received by Primary Care Practitioners in Electronic Health Records: A Taxonomy and Time Analysis," *American Journal of Medicine* 125, no. 2 (2012): e5.

[84] Sean W. Smith and Ross Koppel, "Healthcare Information Technology's Relativity Problems: A Typology of How Patients' Physical Reality, Clinicians' Mental Models, and Healthcare Information Technology Differ," *Journal of the American Medical Informatics* 21, no. 1 (2014): 117–31.

the EHR may only allow doctors to note age in terms of number of days. As a second example, the EHR may not allow doctors to indicate whether the patient's weight is recorded in pounds or kilograms. Because medication dosage calculations are done in the metric system, incorrect assumptions about which weight measurement unit has been used can lead to fatal dosage errors, especially for pediatric patients.

2. **Too fine.** By contrast, EHR systems may require doctors to make decisions that do not reflect their thinking or judgment at a particular time. For example, at an early stage of diagnosis, the doctor may suspect that a patient has stomach cancer but not know any details about the cancer. Yet the EHR may require him to name the specific cancer from a drop-down menu of thirty-eight different types of stomach cancer. A clinician who reads this entry in the future may be misled regarding the patient's diagnosis and level of certainty about it.

3. **Missing reality.** In this case, the system does not enable a clinician to enter details that she considers significant. For example, a system may not allow a physician to record the smell of a patient's breath, even though the smell may be an important symptom of some diseases (e.g., diabetes). Likewise, the system may not allow doctors who treat fetuses *in utero* to record the patient's age in terms of time before birth.

Other experts confirm that EHR systems can be too inflexible. A qualitative study focusing on primary care practices found that EHR implementation "has generally been done in the absence of an in-depth understanding of the workflow, cognitive, and interactional activities in primary care."[85] Likewise, a report generated by the American College of Physicians asserts that "not all clinical data lend themselves to structured documentation" and that the "mental activity involved in converting a patient narrative into coded values on a highly structured screen can lead to errors."[86]

1.3.5 *Effects on Clinician Workload and the Physician–Patient Relationship*

Clinicians have complained that EHRs are time-consuming and cumbersome to use both because they demand too much documentation and because they are difficult to navigate and read.[87] Researchers have found that physicians

---

[85] Nancy Pandhi et al., "Approaches and Challenges to Optimizing Primary Care Teams' Electronic Health Record Usage," *Informatics in Primary Care* 21, no. 3 (2014): 142, 148.

[86] Kuhn et al., "Clinical Documentation in the 21st Century," appendix.

[87] *Ibid.*; Oladimeji Farri et al., "A Qualitative Analysis of EHR Clinical Document Synthesis by Clinicians," *AMIA Annual Symposium Proceedings* 2012 (2012): 1211–20.

spend more time reading their computer screens than they did reviewing paper medical records. Many believe that clinicians also spend more time on documentation tasks than they did in the paper era.[88] According to one study, contemporary internal medicine interns spend 40 percent of their time handling computer tasks and only 12 percent of their time at the bedside, though there is some evidence that doctors did not interact with patients for much longer periods of time in the pre-EHR era.[89]

Data review can be just as challenging and time-consuming as data input. Whereas having to write notes by hand encouraged brevity, physicians entering notes electronically may copy large segments of information from elsewhere in the record for the sake of completeness and may not have time to edit copied notes carefully to make them concise and readable. Copy and paste may make records so lengthy that it is far more difficult for providers to obtain an overview of the patient's current condition or to locate needed details quickly.[90] In addition, EHR screens often are cluttered with information that is not relevant to patient care but is required for other purposes by government regulators, insurers, public health authorities, and others. Repetition of data (such as medication lists) in multiple areas of the EHR exacerbates clutter and makes EHRs all the more voluminous.[91]

The challenges of reviewing a patient's EHR may be compounded by data-display problems. Doctors may need to scroll through numerous screens to find the detail they seek. Information may be organized awkwardly or fragmented throughout the EHR. Scanned documents, such as prior surgery reports, may be buried in separate sections of the EHR, and doctors may be unaware of them if there is no prominent notation regarding their existence.

---

[88] Onur Asan, Paul D. Smith, and Enid Montague, "More Screen Time, Less Face Time: Implications for EHR Design," *Journal of Evaluation in Clinical Practice* 20 (2014): 896, 899; David S. Sanders et al., "Impact of an Electronic Health Record Operating Room Management System in Ophthalmology on Documentation Time, Surgical Volume, and Staffing," *JAMA Ophthalmology* 132, no. 5 (2014): 586, 588–9.

[89] Kathlyn E. Fletcher et al., "The Composition of Intern Work while on Call," *Journal of General Internal Medicine* 27, no. 11 (2012): 1432; Zuzanna Czernik and C. T. Lin, "Time at the Bedside (Computing)," 2399–400 (discussing a 1959 study that found that residents spent only 13 to 16 percent "of their time in the hospital in direct patient contact" and a 1988 study that concluded that residents "spent 42 to 45 percent of their time in the hospital charting and only 20 percent of their time with patients").

[90] Anne Armstrong-Coben, "The Computer Will See You Now," *New York Times*, March 5, 2009, A27 ("In the past, I could pick up a chart and flip through it easily . . . Now . . . important points often get lost").

[91] Kuhn et al., "Clinical Documentation in the 21st Century," appendix; Richelle J. Koopman et al., "Physician Information Needs and Electronic Health Records (EHRs): Time to Reengineer the Clinic Note," *Journal of the American Board of Family Medicine* 28, no. 3 (2015): 316, 321.

Thus physicians may not know that they should look at the scanned documents part of the EHR for relevant information concerning the patient's history or condition. Finally, all data might look the same, and distinct types of data may not be differentiated by color, font, or format, which can make it difficult for physicians to skim the EHR for the information needed at a particular moment.[92]

Many clinicians feel frustrated, overworked, and worried about the impact of EHR systems on their relationships with patients. Some report working many more hours than they did in the paper era. Others try to accomplish as much data input as possible while they are seeing their patients in order to avoid spending many extra hours in the office. They may also be distracted by excessive alerts during the patient visit or compulsively and unnecessarily look up details of the patient's history or other information on the computer. As a result, they have less time to examine and watch the patient; listen to the patient describe her symptoms, complaints, and history; and think deeply about possible diagnoses and treatments.

EHR systems thus can diminish clinicians' work satisfaction. Indeed, a 2015 survey found that in the United States, only 52 percent of primary care physicians reported that they are very satisfied or satisfied with their EHR systems, though the percentage was generally higher in other developed countries.[93] A different study by researchers at the Mayo Clinic involved 6,560 physicians in a large number of specialties and found even lower rates of satisfaction.[94] Dissatisfaction was particularly pronounced among physicians who were sixty years old or older, only 33.9 percent of whom were happy with their EHR systems, whereas 45.9 percent of respondents younger than forty indicated that they were content.[95] Furthermore, "by a greater than 2 to 1 margin, physicians disagreed with the notion that their EHRs or patient portal had improved their efficiency."[96]

---

[92] Ross Koppel, "Role of Computerized Physician Order Entry Systems in Facilitating Medication Errors," *Journal of the American Medical Association* 293, no. 10 (2005): 1199–201; Heather L. Farley et al., "Quality and Safety Implications of Emergency Department Information Systems," *Annals of Emergency Medicine* 62, no. 4 (2013): 399.

[93] Robin Osborn et al., "Primary Care Physicians in Ten Countries Report Challenges Caring for Patients with Complex Health Needs," *Health Affairs* 34, no. 12 (2015): 2104–12. In other countries, the percentages of very satisfied or satisfied primary care physicians were as follows: Australia – 80 percent, Canada – 68 percent, Germany – 77 percent, Netherlands – 76 percent, New Zealand – 69 percent, Norway – 64 percent, Sweden – 37 percent, Switzerland – 70 percent, and United Kingdom – 86 percent.

[94] Tait D. Shanafelt et al., "Relationship between Clerical Burden and Characteristics of the Electronic Environment with Physician Burnout and Professional Satisfaction," *Mayo Clinic Proceedings* 91, no. 7 (2016): 836, 840.

[95] *Ibid.*

[96] *Ibid.*, 844.

Dr. Paul Hyman expressed his distress as follows: "The pull of the computer leads me to miss so many subtle (and not-so-subtle) cues that patients are giving me. And it leaves me feeling empty – wanting more fulfilling interactions."[97] Similarly, Dr. Jayshil Patel observes: "The sick individual is at risk of being objectified, diluted to numbers and images, an 'i-patient.'"[98]

Dr. Robert Wachter, author of *The Digital Doctor: Hope, Hype, and Harm at the Dawn of Medicine's Computer Age*, captures these concerns in a compelling anecdote. He interviewed John Birkmeyer, a renowned surgeon and researcher at Dartmouth University. Birkmeyer related that in pre-EHR days, he was accustomed to reviewing his notes the night before operations so that he could remember personal details about each patient and procedure. For example, his notes might indicate that a patient's hernia was particularly painful when he played tennis, a fact that would distinguish this patient from others on the hernia surgery schedule. In the EHR system era, however, the practice environment is quite different:

> I do the same procedures over and over again, and so it's click right [for the side of the hernia] or left; autopopulate this; click him or her . . . and suddenly every one of my notes looks the same. Now when I show up for surgery, it's useless to have read my notes beforehand because every patient also looks exactly the same. It's like I never saw them before. I can't even picture their faces.[99]

Physicians' preoccupation with their computers has not escaped patients. One study videotaped patients' visits with their doctors and then asked patients to complete satisfaction surveys. Researchers found that the more time physicians spent gazing at their computers and not speaking with patients, the lower their scores were for communication skills and patient centeredness.[100] Powerful evidence of this comes in the form of a drawing by a seven-year-old patient. In her depiction of her doctor's appointment, she sits on the examination table, interacting with her family. The doctor, however, sits apart, facing the other direction, completely absorbed in his computer work.[101]

---

[97] Paul Hyman, "The Day the EHR Died," *Annals of Internal Medicine* 160, no. 8 (2014): 576.

[98] Jayshil J. Patel, "Writing the Wrong," *Journal of the American Medical Association*, 314, no. 7 (2015): 671–2.

[99] Robert Wachter, *The Digital Doctor: Hope, Hype, and Harm at the Dawn of Medicine's Computer Age* (New York: McGraw-Hill Education, 2015), 79.

[100] Richard L. Street Jr. et al., "Provider Interaction with the Electronic Health Record: The Effects on Patient-Centered Communication in Medical Encounters," *Patient Education Counseling* 96, no. 3 (2014): 315.

[101] Copyright 2011 Thomas G. Murphy, M.D., reproduced with permission.

The Cost of Technology

© 2011 Thomas G. Murphy, MD.

1.3.6 *Privacy and Security Concerns*

Digitized medical records are vulnerable to improper disclosure through a variety of mishaps or wrongdoings. Computers can be hacked. Laptops and other portable electronic devices with unencrypted personal health information have been stolen or misplaced. E-mails are sent to incorrect addresses. At times, healthcare professionals themselves knowingly reveal patient data on social media by posting videos or narratives in which patients are recognizable.[102] A growing problem is the phenomenon of ransomware attacks in which hackers seize control of an institution's computer system, lock it by encrypting files, and demand ransom for a decryption key.[103]

Cloud computing raises additional concerns. Privacy breaches can occur during the process of transferring information to the cloud. Moreover, healthcare providers must trust third-party cloud operators to maintain security at the

---

[102] Sharona Hoffman and Andy Podgurski, "In Sickness, Health, and Cyberspace: Protecting the Security of Electronic Private Health Information," *Boston College Law Review* 48 (2007): 332–4; Donna Vanderpool, "HIPAA – Should I Be Worried?," *Innovations in Clinical Neuroscience* 9, no. 11–12 (2012): 51–5.

[103] Alisa Chestler and Samuel Felker, "Ransomware Attack on Hospital Highlights the Importance of Being Prepared," *BNA's Health Law Reporter* 25, no. 13 (2016): 421–2.

highest level, and because of multitenancy, a single breach may affect numerous healthcare providers. Finally, the information's availability through the Internet might make it all the more vulnerable to privacy threats.[104]

Sadly, privacy breaches are reported all too frequently. In 2014 alone, the Department of Health and Human Services (HHS) received 17,779 health information privacy complaints.[105] Furthermore, as of December 28, 2015, the HHS website listed 1,423 large breaches that affected 500 or more individuals and occurred after September 2009.[106] In what is likely the largest medical data theft case to date, hackers breached the security of Anthem Blue Cross and Blue Shield in early 2015. They accessed records of up to 80 million Anthem customers and employees, including names, Social Security numbers, birthdays, mailing addresses, e-mail addresses, and employment information.[107]

1.4 NET EFFECT OF EHR USE TO DATE

Early assessments of the overall effect of EHR use are mixed. Many researchers have found that EHRs generate meaningful benefits for their users. In a study involving 5,047,089 patients treated at 550 hospitals, hospitals using advanced EHRs reported lower costs per patient admission than those without such systems.[108] Likewise, a second study found that healthcare providers who

[104] Joel J. P. C. Rodrigues et al., "Analysis of the Security and Privacy Requirements of Cloud-Based Electronic Health Records Systems," *Journal of Medical Internet Research* 15, no. 8 (2013): e186; Assad Abbas and Samee U. Khan, "A Review on the State-of-the-Art Privacy-Preserving Approaches in the e-Health Clouds," *Biomedical and Health Informatics* 18, no. 4 (2014): 1431–41.

[105] US Department of Health and Human Services, "Health Information Privacy Complaints Received by Calendar Year"; available at: www.hhs.gov/ocr/privacy/hipaa/enforcement/data/complaintsyear.html (accessed August 16, 2016). HHS fully investigated 1,954 complaints in 2014 and found no violation in 34 percent of the cases. It asserts that it obtained "corrective action" in the remaining 66 percent of cases. US Department of Health and Human Services, "Enforcement Results by Year"; available at: www.hhs.gov/ocr/privacy/hipaa/enforcement/data/historicalnumbers.html#eleventh (accessed August 16, 2016).

[106] US Department of Health and Human Services, "Breaches Affecting 500 or More Individuals"; available at: https://ocrportal.hhs.gov/ocr/breach/breach_report.jsf (accessed August 18, 2015). Large breach notification requirements took effect in September of 2009, and HHS did not specifically track such breaches before that date.

[107] Tara Siegel Bernard, "What Anthem Customers Should Do Next after Data Breach," *New York Times*, February 6, 2015; available at: www.nytimes.com/2015/02/07/your-money/what-anthem-customers-should-do-next-after-data-breach.html (accessed August 18, 2015). The storage, use, and disclosure of health information are governed by the HIPAA Privacy and Security Rules, discussed in Chapter 3.

[108] Abby Swanson Kazley et al., "Association of Electronic Health Records with Cost Savings in a National Sample," *American Journal of Managed Care* 20, no. 6 (2014): e183–90.

implemented EHR systems expertly, including establishing typing shortcuts and good templates, experienced cost savings. It predicted that hospitals would save between $37 million and $59 million in five years.[109]

Other work, however, is less sanguine about the advantages of EHR use. A study that focused on the treatment of stroke patients concluded that EHR use did not generate improved quality of care or better outcomes for those who suffered strokes.[110] A study using survey data from forty-nine community practices in the Massachusetts e-Health Collaborative estimated that "the average physician would lose $43,743 over five years [and] just 27 percent of practices would have achieved a positive return on investment" during the five-year timeframe.[111] A third study found that EHRs were not associated with reductions in the cost of hospital inpatient pediatric care but rather with a 7 percent cost increase per case.[112]

Furthermore, contemporary EHR systems are not widely interoperable. Dr. Karen DeSalvo, National Coordinator for Health Information Technology, acknowledged that the healthcare community has "not reached . . . [its] shared vision of having . . . [a nationally] interoperable system where data can be exchanged and meaningfully used to improve care."[113] A report to Congress on

[109] Michael D. Ries, "Electronic Medical Records: Friends or Foes?," 17. See also Yosefa Bar-Dayan et al., "Using Electronic Health Records to Save Money," *Journal of the American Medical Informatics Association* 20, no. e1 (2013): e17.

[110] K. E. Joynt et al., "Lack of Impact of Electronic Health Records on Quality of Care and Outcomes for Ischemic Stroke," *Journal of the American College of Cardiology* 65, no. 18 (2015): 1964–72.

[111] Julia Adler-Milstein et al., "A Survey Analysis Suggests that Electronic Health Records Will Yield Revenue Gains for Some Practices and Losses for Many," *Health Affairs* 32, no. 3 (2013): 565.

[112] Ronald J. Teufel II et al., "Hospital Electronic Medical Record Use and Cost of Inpatient Pediatric Care," *Academic Pediatrics* 12, no. 5 (2013): 431–3. See also Rishi P. Singh et al., "The Practice Impact of Electronic Health Record System Implementation within a Large Multispecialty Ophthalmic Practice," *JAMA Ophthalmology* 133, no. 6 (2015): 668 (finding no "significant differences in revenue or productivity following EHR conversion" at the Cleveland Clinic's Cole Eye Institute); Michele C. Lim et al., "The Long-Term Financial and Clinical Impact of an Electronic Health Record on an Academic Ophthalmology Practice," *Journal of Ophthalmology* 2015 (2015); Leila Agha, "The Effects of Health Information Technology on the Costs and Quality of Medical Care," *Journal of Health Economics* 34, no. 1 (2014): 29 (concluding that EHR adoption results in a 1.3 percent increase in billed charges but no cost savings or improved quality of care).

[113] Daniel R. Verdon, "ONC's DeSalvo Issues Next Health IT Challenge: Build Interoperable EHR Systems," *Medical Economics*, March 4, 2014; available at: http://medicaleconomics .modernmedicine.com/medical-economics/content/tags/health-it/oncs-desalvo-issues-next-he alth-it-challenge-build-interope?page=full (accessed August 14, 2015). The Office of the National Coordinator for Health Information Technology is part of the US Department of Health and Human Services and is charged with promoting and facilitating the country's transition to widespread use of health information technology.

information blocking likewise noted a "recurring allegation . . . that certain EHR developers refuse to establish interfaces or connections with certain technologies or entities."[114] In December 2015, the Bipartisan Policy Center issued a report finding that only 37 percent of physicians and 27 percent of hospitals electronically shared information with other providers, and most of the data sharing occurred among affiliated entities.[115] In other countries, the percentage of primary care physicians who could exchange patient clinical summaries with doctors outside their practices ranged from a low of 19 percent in Canada to a high of 82 percent in Norway in 2015.[116]

A 2013 analysis published in *Health Affairs* concluded that health information technology has failed to deliver quickly on its promise of dramatically improved healthcare safety, efficiency, and costs. However, it noted that the failure "is not due to . . . lack of potential but to shortcomings in the design and implementation of health IT systems." More specifically, the article pointed in part to "the reluctance of many clinicians to invest the considerable time and effort required to master difficult-to-use technology, and the failure of many healthcare systems to implement the process changes required to fully realize health IT's potential."[117] Thus, as EHR systems become essentially universal and clinicians grow to be expert and sophisticated users of these tools, the new technology may indeed fulfill its promise.

---

[114] Office of the National Coordinator for Health Information Technology (ONC), "Report to Congress: Report on Health Information Blocking (April 2015)," 16; available at: www.healthit .gov/sites/default/files/reports/info_blocking_040915.pdf (accessed August 14, 2015).

[115] Bipartisan Policy Center, *Improving Health through Interoperability and Information Sharing Advancing Medical Innovation for a Healthier America* (Washington, DC, 2015), 6–7; available at: www.bipartisanpolicy.org/wp-content/uploads/2015/11/BPC-Improving-Health-Interoperabi lity.pdf (accessed December 18, 2015).

[116] Robin Osborn et al., "Primary Care Physicians in Ten Countries Report Challenges Caring for Patients with Complex Health Needs," *Health Affairs* 34, no. 12 (2015): 2104–12.

[117] Arthur Kellerman and Spencer S. Jones, "What It Will Take to Achieve the As-Yet-Unfulfilled Promises of Health Information Technology," *Health Affairs* 32, no. 1 (2013): 64.

EHR System Regulation

Meaningful Use and Certification Standards

The degree to which the government should regulate industry is often a matter of debate. On the one hand, excessive regulation can discourage innovators from entering the market and suppress competition. On the other hand, anemic regulation can endanger public welfare. Countries that have implemented electronic health record (EHR) systems have struggled with how and to what extent to regulate them. The European Union is only now developing a legal framework for EU-wide EHR system testing and certification.[1] The United States has already taken several steps to establish quality control for EHR systems.

In 2009, the US Congress enacted the Health Information Technology for Economic and Clinical Health (HITECH) Act.[2] This law established an incentive program by which qualified providers could receive incentive payments if they became meaningful users of certified EHR systems.[3] In order to implement the HITECH Act, the Centers for Medicare and Medicaid Services (CMS) issued a series of regulations that establish the standards for meaningful use and EHR system certification. This chapter describes these regulations and critiques them. It argues that while they

This chapter is based partly on Sharona Hoffman and Andy Podgurski, "Meaningful Use and Certification of Health Information Technology: What about Safety?," *Journal of Law, Medicine, and Ethics* 39, Suppl. 1 (2011): 77.

1 "Action 77: Foster EU-wide standards, interoperability testing and certification of eHealth," in European Commission, *Digital Agenda in the Europe 2020 Strategy*; available at: http://ec.eu ropa.eu/digital-agenda/en/pillar-vii-ict-enabled-benefits-eu-society/action-77-foster-eu-wide-sta ndards-interoperability (accessed January 7, 2016).

2 Health Information Technology for Economic and Clinical Health (HITECH) Act, Pub. L. No. 111-5, 123 Stat. 226 (2009) (codified as amended in scattered sections of 42 USC).

3 David Blumentahl and Marilyn Tavenner, "The 'Meaningful Use' Regulation for Electronic Health Records," *New England Journal of Medicine* 363, no. 6 (2010): 501; Hoffman and Podgurski, "Meaningful Use and Certification of Health Information Technology," 77. Providers could receive up to $44,000 through Medicare or $63,750 through Medicaid depending on eligibility.

constitute a good first step toward regulating the quality of EHR systems, they do not adequately address concerns about the technology's safety and usability.

2.1 THE MEDICARE AND MEDICAID INCENTIVE PROGRAMS

The Medicare and Medicaid incentive programs began in 2011. Medicare payments will continue through 2016, and Medicaid payments will continue until 2021. Different rules apply to eligible professionals and eligible hospitals or critical access hospitals (CAHs).

2.1.1 Eligible Professionals

Eligible professionals must choose to participate in either the Medicare or Medicaid program. Under the Medicare program, eligible professionals[4] who demonstrate meaningful use of certified EHR technology can receive up to $43,720 over five consecutive years if they began participating by 2012. The regulations specify how participants can demonstrate meaningful use, as discussed later. Starting in 2015, eligible professionals who have not successfully demonstrated meaningful use are penalized by Medicare. They are subject to payment reductions starting at 1 percent and increasing each year that they fail to demonstrate meaningful use, but payments cannot be reduced by more than 5 percent.[5]

Under the Medicaid program, eligible professionals[6] can earn payments of up to $63,750 over six years, and participation years need not be consecutive. However, eligible professionals must begin participation by 2016.

In the first year of Medicaid program compliance, eligible professionals can receive an incentive payment just for adopting, implementing, or upgrading

---

[4] Eligible professionals are doctors of medicine or osteopathy, doctors of dental surgery or dental medicine, doctors of podiatry, doctors of optometry, and chiropractors. Centers for Medicare and Medicaid Services, "Eligibility"; available at: www.cms.gov/Regulations-and-Guidance/Legislat ion/EHRIncentivePrograms/eligibility.html#BOOKMARK1 (accessed August 25, 2015).

[5] Centers for Medicare and Medicaid Services, "Medicare and Medicaid EHR Incentive Program Basics"; available at: www.cms.gov/Regulations-and-Guidance/Legislation/EHRInc entivePrograms/Basics.html (accessed August 25, 2015).

[6] Eligible professionals are physicians (primarily doctors of medicine and osteopathy), nurse practitioners, certified nurse-midwives, dentists, and physician assistants who treat patients in federally qualified health centers or rural health clinics led by physician assistants. Eligible professionals also must meet one of the following criteria: (1) have a minimum 30 percent Medicaid patient volume, (2) be pediatricians and have a minimum 20 percent Medicaid patient volume, or (3) practice predominantly in a federally qualified health center or rural health center and have a minimum 30 percent patient volume consisting of economically disadvantaged individuals. Centers for Medicare and Medicaid Services, "Eligibility."

certified EHR technology. In later years, they can obtain payments for successfully demonstrating meaningful use, as discussed later.

The incentive payments are significant, but they may not cover all expenses associated with EHR implementation. A 2011 study estimated that, on average, a five-physician practice in North Texas would spend $162,000 on implementation plus $85,500 on maintenance costs in the first year. In addition, implementation teams would need 611 hours, on average, to prepare to go live, and the practice would spend 134 hours per physician to train staff to use EHR systems.[7] A government resource, HealthIT.gov, states that the "cost of purchasing and installing an electronic health record (EHR) ranges from $15,000 to $70,000 per provider," averaging $33,000 per provider in up-front costs and $4,000 per provider in annual costs.[8] Likewise, a 2015 article in *JAMA Ophthalmology* concluded that "meaningful use" incentive payments did not offset the costs of implementing the technology in a large ophthalmology practice.[9]

2.1.2 *Eligible Hospitals and CAHs*

Unlike eligible professionals, eligible hospitals and CAHs[10] can simultaneously participate in both the Medicare and Medicaid programs. Eligible hospitals and CAHs qualify for Medicare incentive payments if they demonstrate meaningful use of certified EHR technology, and they could receive payments from federal fiscal year (FY) 2011 to FY 2016,[11] but payments will decrease for hospitals and CAHs that start receiving payments in 2014 and later. Incentive payments are based on a number of factors, and the initial base payment is $2 million.[12] Eligible facilities that fail to demonstrate meaningful

---

7   Neil S. Fleming et al., "The Financial and Nonfinancial Costs of Implementing Electronic Health Records in Primary Care Practices," *Health Affairs* 30, no. 3 (2011): 481.

8   HealthIT.gov, "How Much Is This Going to Cost Me?"; available at: www.healthit.gov/providers-professionals/faqs/how-much-going-cost-me (accessed November 17, 2015).

9   Rishi P. Singh et al., "The Practice Impact of Electronic Health Record System Implementation within a Large Multispecialty Ophthalmic Practice," *JAMA Ophthalmology* 133, no. 6 (2015): 668.

10   Eligible hospitals are the following: (1) "Subsection (d) hospitals" in the fifty states or DC that are paid under the Inpatient Prospective Payment System, (2) CAHs, and (3) Medicare Advantage Hospitals. CAHs are facilities that have been certified as such under section 1820 (c) of the Social Security Act.

11   While professionals participate according to the calendar year, hospitals participate according to the federal fiscal year, which spans from October 1 to September 30.

12   The calculation is somewhat different for CAHs. Centers for Medicare and Medicaid Services, "Critical Access Hospitals Electronic Health Record Incentive Payment Calculations," last updated May 2013; available at: www.cms.gov/Regulations-and-Guidance/Legislation/EHRIncentivePrograms/Downloads/MLN_TipSheet_CriticalAccessHospitals.pdf (accessed August 25, 2015).

use of certified EHR technology are subject to penalties in the form of Medicare payment adjustments that began in FY 2015.

Under the Medicaid EHR Incentive Program, eligible hospitals[13] can qualify for incentive payments if they "adopt, implement, upgrade or demonstrate meaningful use of certified EHR technology during the first participation year or successfully demonstrate meaningful use of certified EHR technology in subsequent participation years." Eligible hospitals could begin receiving incentive payments in any year from (FY) 2011 to FY 2016. The Medicaid program does not establish penalties for those who fail to demonstrate meaningful use.[14]

2.1.3 *Program Participation*

Even though healthcare providers have much to gain financially from participating in the Medicare or Medicaid incentive programs, not all have rushed to do so. One study that was published in *Health Affairs* examined participation rates among New York physicians in 2011 and 2012. It found that in 2011, only 8.1 percent participated in the Medicare program, and 6.1 percent participated in the Medicaid program. In 2012, the numbers grew to 23.9 and 8.5 percent, respectively.[15] As of 2015, according to the Office of the National Coordinator for Health Information Technology (ONC), 95 percent of hospitals and CAHs and 56 percent of office-based physicians had demonstrated meaningful use and were participating in the federal incentive program.[16]

Why would any physician opt out of the incentive programs? Some implement EHR systems but do not wish to comply with what they consider to be burdensome regulatory requirements. Others do not accept Medicare or Medicaid patients and thus are not eligible for the incentive programs.

Still others do not wish to adopt EHR systems at all and prefer to retain old-fashioned paper records. For some older physicians, the transition to complex EHR systems late in their careers is simply too daunting. In the alternative, doctors may wish to avoid computerization because of privacy concerns.

---

[13] Eligible hospitals are acute-care hospitals with at least a 10 percent Medicaid patient volume and all children's hospitals regardless of whether they have Medicaid patients. CAHs are considered to be acute-care hospitals for purposes of Medicaid. CMS, *supra* n. 9.

[14] Centers for Medicare and Medicaid Services, "Eligible Hospital Information"; available at: www.cms.gov/Regulations-and-Guidance/Legislation/EHRIncentivePrograms/Eligible_Hospital_Information.html (accessed January 24, 2016).

[15] Hye-Young Jung et al., "Growth of New York Physician Participation in Meaningful Use of Electronic Health Records Was Variable, 2011–2012," *Health Affairs* 34, no. 6 (2015): 1035.

[16] HealthIT.gov, "Health IT Quick Stats"; available at: http://dashboard.healthit.gov/quickstats/quickstats.php (accessed December 28, 2015).

A psychiatrist once told me that she will not adopt an EHR system because she treats many individuals who are themselves healthcare providers and are very concerned about their privacy. She has been successful in attracting these patients because she promises them that their records will not be accessible to any of their colleagues through an EHR system. The patients' records remain locked in her office file cabinets that only she can open.

Physicians who accept Medicare payments and do not adopt EHR systems are subject to payment reductions, but these are relatively small (capped at 5 percent). Thus there are doctors who feel that the benefit of avoiding the costs, training, and headaches associated with EHR implementation outweigh the Medicare penalties.

2.2 THE REGULATORY FRAMEWORK

To be eligible for incentive payments, healthcare providers must demonstrate that they are "meaningful users" of certified EHR technology. This section will explain the meaningful use and certification regulations.

2.2.1 *The Meaningful Use Regulations*

CMS is rolling out the meaningful use regulations in three stages. Stage 1 meaningful use regulations became effective in 2011, and stage 2 went into effect in 2014. Stage 3 will be optional in 2017 and become mandatory in 2018.[17]

Healthcare providers begin to participate in the incentive programs by meeting the stage 1 meaningful use requirements for ninety days in their first year of participation and for a full year in their second year. Then they must meet stage 2 requirements for two full years.[18]

Under stage 1, eligible professionals are required to meet fifteen core objectives and to select five of ten "menu objectives." Eligible hospitals have to meet fourteen core objectives and to choose five of ten menu objectives.[19] In stage 2, eligible professionals must meet seventeen core objectives and three of six menu objectives, and eligible hospitals must meet sixteen core objectives and three of six menu objectives.[20]

The seventeen stage 2 core objectives for eligible professionals are

---

[17] 42 CFR § 495.24 (2015).

[18] HealthIT.gov, "Health IT Regulations: Meaningful Use Regulations"; last updated March 20, 2015; available at: www.healthit.gov/policy-researchers-implementers/meaningful-use-regula tions (accessed August 25, 2015).

[19] 42 CFR § 495.6(a)–(g) (2015).

[20] 42 CFR § 495(h)–(m) (2015).

1. Use computerized provider order entry (CPOE) for medication, laboratory, and radiology orders.
2. Generate and transmit permissible prescriptions electronically (eRx).
3. Record demographic information.
4. Record and chart changes in vital signs.
5. Record smoking status for patients thirteen years old or older.
6. Use clinical decision support to improve performance on high-priority health conditions.
7. Provide patients with the ability to view online, download, and transmit their health information.
8. Provide clinical summaries for patients for each office visit.
9. Protect electronic health information created or maintained by the certified EHR technology.
10. Incorporate clinical laboratory test results into certified EHR technology.
11. Generate lists of patients by specific conditions to use for quality improvement, reduction of disparities, research, or outreach.
12. Use clinically relevant information to identify patients who should receive reminders for preventive/follow-up care.
13. Use certified EHR technology to identify patient-specific education resources.
14. Perform medication reconciliation.
15. Provide a summary-of-care record for each transition of care or referral.
16. Submit electronic data to immunization registries.
17. Use secure electronic messaging to communicate with patients on relevant health information.

The six menu objectives for eligible professionals are

1. Submit electronic syndromic surveillance data to public health agencies.
2. Record electronic notes in patient records.
3. Make imaging results accessible through certified EHR technology.
4. Record patient family health history.
5. Identify and report cancer cases to a state cancer registry.
6. Identify and report specific cases to a specialized registry (other than a cancer registry).[21]

---

[21] Centers for Medicare and Medicaid Services, "Stage 2 Overview Tipsheet"; last updated August, 2012; available at: www.cms.gov/Regulations-and-Guidance/Legislation/EHRIncentiv ePrograms/Downloads/Stage2Overview_Tipsheet.pdf.

For eligible hospitals and CAHs, the requirements are quite similar, though not identical, and there are only sixteen core objectives.[22]

Note also that beside each criterion, the regulations indicate mandated percentages. Thus, for example, under stage 2, eligible professionals must record more than 60 percent of medication orders, 30 percent of laboratory orders, and 30 percent of radiology orders using computerized physician order entry.[23]

In order to fulfill the meaningful use requirements, eligible professionals and hospitals also must report a certain number of clinical quality measures (CQMs) designed to determine and track the quality of healthcare services.[24]

---

[22] The sixteen core objectives are
  1. Use computerized provider order entry (CPOE) for medication, laboratory, and radiology orders.
  2. Record demographic information.
  3. Record and chart changes in vital signs.
  4. Record smoking status for patients thirteen years old or older.
  5. Use clinical decision support to improve performance on high-priority health conditions.
  6. Provide patients with the ability to view online, download, and transmit their health information within thirty-six hours of discharge.
  7. Protect electronic health information created or maintained by the certified EHR technology.
  8. Incorporate clinical laboratory test results into certified EHR technology.
  9. Generate lists of patients by specific conditions to use for quality improvement, reduction of disparities, research, or outreach.
  10. Use certified EHR technology to identify patient-specific education resources and provide those resources to patients if appropriate.
  11. Perform medication reconciliation.
  12. Provide a summary-of-care record for each transition of care or referral.
  13. Submit electronic data to immunization registries.
  14. Submit electronic data on reportable laboratory results to public health agencies.
  15. Submit electronic syndromic surveillance data to public health agencies.
  16. Automatically track medications with an electronic medication administration record (eMAR).
   In addition, hospitals and CAHs are to select three of six menu objectives:
  1. Record whether a patient sixty-five years old or older has an advance directive.
  2. Record electronic notes in patient records.
  3. Make imaging results accessible through CEHRT.
  4. Record patient family health history.
  5. Generate and transmit permissible discharge prescriptions electronically (eRx).
  6. Provide structured electronic laboratory results to ambulatory providers.
[23] CMS provides detailed comparisons of stage 1 and stage 2 objectives in documents entitled "Stage 1 vs. Stage 2 Comparison Table for Eligible Professionals" and "Stage 1 vs. Stage 2 Comparison Table for Eligible Hospitals and CAHs." Centers for Medicare and Medicaid Services, "Stage 1 vs. Stage 2 Comparison Table for Eligible Hospitals and CAHs"; last updated August 2012; available at: www.cms.gov/Regulations-and-Guidance/Legislation/EHRIncentiv ePrograms/Downloads/Stage1vsStage2CompTablesforHospitals.pdf (accessed August 25, 2015).
[24] Eligible professionals must report nine and eligible hospitals must report sixteen out of a large menu of clinical quality measures (CQMs). Centers for Medicare and Medicaid Services, "An

For example, providers may report the percentage of patients fifty to seventy-five years of age who had appropriate screening for colorectal cancer or the percentage of patients sixty-five years of age and older who have received a pneumonia vaccine. In 2014, CMS established that the selected quality measures had to cover at least three of six available National Quality Strategy (NQS) domains. These are

1. Patient and family engagement
2. Patient safety
3. Care coordination
4. Population/public health
5. Efficient use of healthcare resources
6. Clinical process/effectiveness[25]

In October 2015 CMS proposed a final rule for meaningful use stage 3.[26] The rule strives to simplify and streamline the regulatory requirements, replacing the core and menu objectives with a "single set of objectives and measures."[27] There are eight objectives that all eligible professionals, eligible hospitals, and CAHs must meet in order to comply with the meaningful use mandate. Stripped to their essence, they are

1. Protect electronic health information.
2. Engage in electronic prescribing.
3. Provide clinical decision support.
4. Use computerized provider order entry.
5. Enable patient electronic access to health information.
6. Coordinate care through patient engagement.
7. Facilitate health information exchange.
8. Report public health and clinical data to appropriate authorities.[28]

Introduction to EHR Incentive Programs for Eligible Professionals: 2014 Clinical Quality Measure (CQM) Electronic Reporting Guide"; last updated September 2014; available at: www.cms.gov/Regulations-and-Guidance/Legislation/EHRIncentivePrograms/Downloads/CQM2014_GuideEP.pdf (accessed December 28, 2015).

[25] Centers for Medicare and Medicaid Services, "2014 Clinical Quality Measures"; last modified July 22, 2014; available at: www.cms.gov/Regulations-and-Guidance/Legislation/EHRIncentivePrograms/2014_ClinicalQualityMeasures.html (accessed August 25, 2015); see also Centers for Medicare and Medicaid Services, eCQM Library, "Annual Updates eCQM Electronic Specifications"; available at: www.cms.gov/Regulations-and-Guidance/Legislation/EHRIncentivePrograms/eCQM_Library.html (accessed April 8, 2016).

[26] *Fed. Reg.* 80: 62761 (Oct. 16, 2015); 42 CFR § 495.24 (2016).

[27] *Fed. Reg.* 80: 62761, 62765.

[28] Department of Health and Human Services Centers for Medicare and Medicaid Services, "Medicare and Medicaid Programs: Electronic Health Record Incentive Program – Stage 3," *Fed. Reg.* 80: 16732, 16743 (March 30, 2015).

In order to receive meaningful use payments, eligible professionals and hospitals must provide attestation regarding their compliance with the regulatory requirements. Each year, they must register with CMS, use certified technology, complete an online attestation module, and retain relevant documentation for purposes of potential audits.[29]

After the Medicare incentive program expires in 2016, CMS will retain oversight over physicians' use of EHR systems through the Medicare Access and CHIP Reauthorization Act of 2015 (MACRA).[30] MACRA adjusts the way in which Medicare pays providers who care for Medicare patients. To that end, MACRA establishes the Merit-Based Incentive Payment System (MIPS).[31] Under MIPS, eligible professionals will be measured on four elements for purposes of payment: (1) quality, (2) resource use, (3) clinical practice improvement, and (4) meaningful use of certified EHR technology.[32] CMS will begin measuring performance for doctors and other clinicians through MIPS in 2017 and commence paying them based on those measures in 2019.[33] MACRA will affect only Medicare payments to physicians and will not apply to hospitals or change the Medicaid Meaningful Use program.[34]

2.2.2 *Certification Criteria*

Incentive payments are awarded only to those who use certified EHR systems. The certification process is overseen by ONC, a division of the US Department of Health and Human Services.

---

[29] Centers for Medicare and Medicaid Services, "EHR Incentive Programs: Getting Started"; last modified March 11, 2015; available at: www.cms.gov/Regulations-and-Guidance/Legislation/ EHRIncentivePrograms/Getting_Started.html (accessed August 25, 2015).

[30] Pub. L. No. 114–10, 129 Stat. 87 (2015).

[31] *Ibid.*, at § 101(b).

[32] Centers for Medicare and Medicaid Services, "Quality Payment Program: Delivery System Reform, Medicare Payment Reform, and MACRA: The Merit-Based Incentive Payment System (MIPS) and Alternative Payment Models (APMs)"; available at: www.congress.gov/11 4/plaws/publ10/PLAW-114publ10.pdf (accessed July 13, 2016); Centers for Medicare and Medicaid Services, "Notice of Proposed Rulemaking Medicare Access and CHIP Reauthorization Act of 2015 Quality Payment Program," 2; available at: www.cms.gov/Medic are/Quality-Initiatives-Patient-Assessment-Instruments/Value-Based-Programs/MACRA-MIP S-and-APMs/NPRM-QPP-Fact-Sheet.pdf (accessed July 13, 2016).

[33] Mike Miliard, "MACRA Proposed Rule Published by HHS, Streamlining Federal Programs Including Meaningful Use," *HealthcareITNews*; available at: www.healthcareitnews.com/news/ macra-proposed-rule-published-hhs-streamlining-federal-programs-including-meaningful-use (accessed July 13, 2016); Pub. L. No. 114–10 § 101(c)(5)(B).

[34] Miliard, "MACRA Proposed Rule Published by HHS, Streamlining Federal Programs Including Meaningful Use."

The certification criteria parallel the meaningful use requirements.[35] EHR systems are eligible for certification if they enable healthcare providers to fulfill the meaningful use objectives. To illustrate, one certification criterion is that the EHR system enable users to "electronically record, change, and access" medication, laboratory, and radiology or imaging orders.[36] CMS provides useful charts mapping the certification criteria to meaningful use stage 1 and 2 requirements.[37] Certification criteria are adjusted or supplemented by ONC periodically.[38]

2.2.3 *Certification Process*

While ONC oversees the certification process, it delegates the actual work of certification to other entities. ONC appoints one Approved Accreditor (ONC-AA) to accredit Authorized Certification Bodies (ONC-ACBs). The American National Standards Institute (ANSI) was appointed to serve as the ONC-AA for two terms: 2011–2014 and 2014–2017.

ONC has also designated the National Voluntary Laboratory Accreditation Program (NVLAP) to accredit testing laboratories (ATLs), of which there were five in 2015.[39] The NVLAP is administered by the National Institute of Standards and Technology (NIST).

---

[35] As of 2014, ONC's certification criteria for health information technology (IT) products cover seven general categories:

Clinical (e.g., recording data during a patient visit, CPOE, CDS);
Care coordination (relating to transitions of care and the ability to receive, display, and incorporate transition of care/referral summaries);
Clinical quality measures;
Privacy and security safeguards;
Patient engagement tools (e.g., ability to view and download records, secure messaging);
Public health (ability to report and transmit data to public health authorities); and
Utilization (miscellaneous requirements). 45 CFR § 170.314 (2015).

[36] 45 CFR § 170.314(a)(1) (2015).

[37] Centers for Medicare and Medicaid Services, "2014 Edition EHR Certification Criteria Grid Mapped to Meaningful Use Stage 1"; available at: www.healthit.gov/sites/default/files/2014editio nehrcertificationcriteria_mustage1.pdf (accessed August 25, 2015); Centers for Medicare and Medicaid Services, "2014 Edition EHR Certification Criteria Grid Mapped to Meaningful Use Stage 2"; available at: www.healthit.gov/sites/default/files/2014editionehrcertificationcriteria_mu stage2.pdf (accessed August 25, 2015).

[38] See Office of the National Coordinator for Health Information Technology (ONC), Department of Health and Human Services (HHS), "2015 Edition Health Information Technology (Health IT) Certification Criteria, 2015 Edition Base Electronic Health Record (EHR) Definition, and ONC Health IT Certification Program Modifications," *Fed. Reg.* 80(16804): 16804 (March 30, 2015); available at: www.federalregister.gov/articles/2015/03/30/2015–06612/2015-edition-health-in formation-technology-health-it-certification-criteria-2015-edition-base (accessed August 25, 2015).

[39] As of 2016, the following were the accredited ATLs: Drummond Group, ICSA Labs, InfoGard Laboratories, Inc., and SLI Global Solutions. HealthIT.gov, " ONC Health IT Certification

EHR manufacturers and vendors who wish to have their products certified must first contact an ATL for testing. Testing is accomplished through submission of mock patient data.[40] Each ATL uses its own test scripts, but the scripts are all based on specific test methods and requirements provided by ONC detailing the activities in which ATLs must engage for each test element.[41]

The testing criteria are still evolving, and ONC changes them from time to time. As of 2014, EHR vendors must include evidence of user-centered design and usability test results in their certification submissions.[42] *User-centered design* is a process that prioritizes the cognitive and information needs of all users, and *usability* is "the extent to which the technology helps users achieve their goals in a satisfying, effective, and efficient manner within the constraints and complexities of their work environment."[43] When the vendor conducts usability testing, it recruits participants to engage in representative tasks relating to eight EHR capabilities, and the vendor measures the amount of time it takes to complete the task, the number and types of errors found, and subjective user satisfaction with the way the EHR system operated. The results are presented in a standardized format, required by ONC, and are publicly available.[44]

Once the product has been tested and deemed satisfactory, the manufacturer or vendor can contact an ONC-ACB to obtain certification. The ONC-ACB reviews the testing results as well as a number of other items relating to product design, functionality, and security, all of which can be done remotely.

Program"; last updated August 5, 2016; available at: www.healthit.gov/policy-researchers-imple menters/certification-bodies-testing-laboratories (accessed August 16, 2016).

[40] 45 CFR § 170.207 (2015).

[41] Office of the National Coordinator for Health Information Technology, "2014 Edition Test Procedure Overview," December 14, 2012; available at: www.healthit.gov/sites/default/files/20 14_edition_test_procedure_overview.pdf (accessed September 28, 2015).

[42] 45 CFR § 170.314(g)(3) (2015); Office of the National Coordinator for Health Information Technology, "2014 Edition Test Procedure for § 170.314(g)(3) Safety-Enhanced Design"; available at: www.healthit.gov/sites/default/files/170-314g3safetyenhanceddesign_2014_tp_ap provedv1.4.pdf (accessed December 19, 2014).

[43] Raj M. Ratwani et al., "Electronic Health Record Vendor Adherence to Usability Certification Requirements and Testing Standards," *Journal of the American Medical Association* 314, no. 10 (2015): 1070.

[44] Robert M. Schumacher and Svetlana Z. Lowry, "Customized Common Industry Format Template for Electronic Health Record Usability Testing," *NISTIR* 7742, November 2010; available at: www.nist.gov/itl/hit/upload/LowryNISTIR-7742Customized_CIF_Template_fo r_EHR_Usability_Testing_Publicationl_Version-doc.pdf (accessed September 28, 2015). See, e.g., Drummond Group, "Test Results Summary for 2014 Edition EHR Certification"; avail-able at: www.drummondgroup.com/images/ehr_pdf/IntegratedDocumentAbbaDoxEHR14 _CompAmb12302014-2855-8.pdf (accessed September 28, 2015).

ONC-ACBs issue certifications and submit certified products to ONC each week to be posted on the certified Health IT Product List.[45] As of 2016, there were three ONC-ACBs: Drummond Group, ICSA Labs, and InfoGard Laboratories, Inc.[46] These bodies can certify both complete EHRs and EHR modules, which are products that meet at least one certification criterion but do not feature all capabilities required for complete EHRs.[47] In August 2016, 3,873 certified products were included on the ONC list.

2.3 CRITIQUE AND RECOMMENDATIONS

The meaningful use and certification regulations are lengthy, and much thought has been invested in developing them. Nevertheless, they leave considerable room for further improvement. This section critiques the regulations and offers several recommendations for amendment.

2.3.1 *The Meaningful Use Regulations Are Too Burdensome and Not Aligned with Clinical Realities*

Some clinicians consider the meaningful use regulations to be a hindrance rather than a means to advance patient care. They complain that the regulations place excessive burdens on providers and fail to align with clinical realities.

In his well-received book, *The Digital Doctor: Hope, Hype, and Harm at the Dawn of Medicine's Computer Age*, Professor Robert Wachter writes that "many of the new mandates [of the stage 2 regulations] depended on a clinical ecosystem and healthcare culture that did not yet exist."[48] For example, they require that more than 5 percent of patients "view, download, and transmit" their electronic health information to third parties. This compels physicians to put pressure on patients to engage in activities in which patients often have no interest and awkwardly makes regulatory compliance depend on the behavior of third parties.

In addition, the regulations require hospitals to transmit discharge summaries electronically to other facilities. They do not, however, mandate that these

---

[45] Office of the National Coordinator for Health Information Technology, "Certified Health It Product List"; available at: https://chpl.healthit.gov/#/search (accessed August 16, 2016).

[46] HealthIT.gov, " ONC Health IT Certification Program."

[47] HealthIT.gov, "Health IT Certification Programs: Frequently Asked Questions"; last updated January 18, 2013; available at: www.healthit.gov/policy-researchers-implementers/standards-certification-regulations-faqs (accessed August 25, 2015).

[48] Robert Wachter, *The Digital Doctor: Hope, Hype, and Harm at the Dawn of Medicine's Computer Age* (New York: McGraw Hill Education, 2015), 209.

summaries be useful to the recipients. Consequently, some providers are randomly sending discharge summaries to other hospitals for no reason other than to "check a box on ... [their] Stage 2 scorecard."[49]

As a third example, Dr. Wachter cites the requirement that doctors give educational materials to 10 percent of their patients, prompted by their EHR. Doctors who have routinely given useful information sheets concerning diagnoses and treatments to their patients are not deemed in compliance. They must find a way to be *prompted* by their EHR systems. According to the author, the regulations are so problematic that some clinicians refer to them as "Meaningless Abuse."[50]

Other commentators echo Dr. Wachter's concerns. They also posit that the meaningful use criteria should focus on measures that are specific to particular medical specialties rather than establish requirements that are uniformly imposed on all healthcare providers. Dr. Peter Basch and EHR expert Thomson Kuhn characterize meaningful use stage 2 as "one size fits none" regulations.[51]

2.3.2 *Lack of Clinical Safety Testing*

Meticulous testing of EHR products is critical to their safety. Current testing methods are insufficiently stringent. For example, while ONC has endorsed guidelines providing that usability testing should include at least fifteen participants, one group of researchers found that 63 percent of the vendors they studied failed to meet this standard.[52] In addition, there is no prohibition on including participants who are the vendor's own employees.[53] Yet the vendor's employees may have conflicts of interest if they serve as testers. They may hesitate to criticize the product out of loyalty to their employer or anxiety about their job security. Furthermore, coupling EHR certification criteria with meaningful use requirements limits the extent of EHR system scrutiny. As the American Medical Association and many other professional organizations wrote in a 2015 letter to Dr. Karen DeSalvo, National Coordinator for Health Information Technology, "certification should not

---

[49] *Ibid.*

[50] *Ibid.*, 210.

[51] Peer Basch and Thomson Kuhn, "It's Time to Fix Meaningful Use," *Health Affairs Blog*, January 14, 2016; available at: http://healthaffairs.org/blog/2016/01/14/its-time-to-fix-meaningful -use/ (accessed April 17, 2016).

[52] Ratwani et al., "Electronic Health Record Vendor Adherence to Usability Certification Requirements and Testing Standards," 1071.

[53] See ONC, HHS, "2015 Edition Health Information Technology (Health IT) Certification Criteria, 2015 Edition Base Electronic Health Record (EHR) Definition, and ONC Health IT Certification Program Modifications."

only show that an EHR can meet MU [meaningful use] objectives and measures but that tested systems can support interoperability and ensure patient safety."[54]

Before EHR systems are certified, they should be carefully monitored during clinical use at several facilities over an extended period of time. The certification regulations should specify the evaluation methodology, including the types of system failures and adverse events to be considered; how they should be detected, reported, and confirmed; and what failure rates and adverse-event rates are unacceptable (rates of zero are not realistic).

As a first step, EHR systems could be tested more extensively through simulations, as is done in the field of aviation.[55] Simulations do not require that a product be installed in a medical facility but rather ask it to perform various functions when hypothetical patient information is entered.

Unlike pilots, though, EHR system users will be extremely diverse, with very different educations, skill levels, and capabilities. Simulations are necessarily based on particular assumptions about users and use environments, and these will be accurate in only limited circumstances. They would not be able to anticipate all of the problems, complications, and mistakes that could arise in real clinical settings. As the American Medical Association and other prominent experts have noted, EHR systems "deployed in dynamic clinical settings do not always mirror the laboratory testing environment of the ONC Certification Program."[56] Hence EHR systems also need to be launched in their natural environments for testing.

Admittedly, clinical evaluation of new products would pose significant challenges. First, with only five ATLs and three ONC-ACBs, an extensive testing process would impose a very high burden on an inadequate number of oversight bodies. Most likely, additional testers and certifiers would have to be appointed. Second, healthcare facilities at which EHR systems are assessed would have to implement systems that are not fully approved and thus may be more problematic than other products. ONC and the EHR system industry would need to create incentives to encourage providers to agree to test EHR products and find ways to minimize the difficulties providers face in so doing.

However, certification of technology that has not been thoroughly evaluated is no more responsible than approval of a drug that has not undergone

---

54 American Medical Association et al., "Joint Letter to ONC on EHR Certification," January 21, 2015; available at: www.aafp.org/dam/AAFP/documents/advocacy/health_it/emr/LT-ONC-EHRCertification-012115.pdf (accessed September 28, 2015).

55 Wachter, *The Digital Doctor*, 269.

56 American Medical Association et al., "Joint Letter to ONC on EHR Certification," January 21, 2015; available at: www.aafp.org/dam/AAFP/documents/advocacy/health_it/emr/LT-ONC-EHRCertification-012115.pdf (accessed January 7, 2016).

comprehensive clinical testing. Certifiers must assume that providers will use whatever system they purchase for many years and that the system will affect the care of thousands of patients. After investing substantial money, time, and effort in purchasing and adopting a particular system, it is often too difficult for providers to switch products even if significant flaws are discovered. Diligent and thorough clinical testing of EHR systems is therefore critical to patient welfare.

2.3.3 *Continuing Review and Adverse-Event Reporting*

The regulations focus primarily on initial certification of EHR systems. Unfortunately, they largely ignore an equally important component of oversight – continued monitoring after approval. One provision calls for ONC-ACBs to "[s]ubmit an annual surveillance plan to the National Coordinator and annually report to the National Coordinator its surveillance results."[57] However, it provides no further details and establishes no sound mechanism to ensure that EHR systems operate as expected when they are placed in real clinical settings and used by busy providers with different levels of technical skill.

ONC has issued short guidance documents regarding surveillance, but these provide few specifics.[58] Thus far, surveillance is generally reactive, triggered by user complaints and feedback. ONC does not publicize the number of surveys that have been conducted. Because there are only three ONC-ACBs, it is safe to assume that the number is not large. Vendors, however, should be cautioned that in September 2015, ONC reported that it stripped two EHR products of certification because their producers failed to respond to and participate in surveillance requests.[59]

Another glaring omission is that there is no mandate that adverse events be reported and documented. ONC guidance leaves it up to EHR system developers to establish their own complaint mechanisms, and the agency verifies their existence only if the developer is subject to an ONC survey.[60] ONC-ACBs also may scrutinize vendor complaint processes. For example,

---

[57] 45 CFR 170.523(i) (2015).

[58] See, e.g., Office of the National Coordinator for Health Information Technology, "ONC HIT Certification Program, Program Policy Guidance #14–01"; available at: www.healthit.gov/sites/default/files/onc-acb_cy15annualsurveillanceguidance.pdf (accessed August 26, 2015).

[59] Akanksha Jayanthi, "2 EHRs stripped of ONC certification," *Becker's Health IT & CIO Review*, September 2, 2015; available at: www.beckershospitalreview.com/healthcare-information-technology/2-ehrs-stripped-of-onc-certification.html (accessed January 7, 2016).

[60] Office of the National Coordinator for Health Information Technology, "ONC HIT Certification Program, Program Policy Guidance #13–01"; available at: www.healthit.gov/sites/default/files/onc-acb_cy15annualsurveillanceguidance.pdf (accessed August 26, 2015).

Drummond Group requires each applicant to submit a complaint process summary and vendors to disclose customer complaints on request. Surprisingly, Drummond reported that there were only "14 complaints submitted on certified EHR systems during CY [calendar year] 2014."[61] ONC also makes complaint forms available through the Internet but instructs that they should be filled out only by users who failed to have their concerns addressed by their vendors and ONC-ACBs.[62]

This relatively lenient regulatory approach is very different from the one that applies to privacy and security breaches under the Health Insurance Portability and Accountability Act (HIPAA), discussed in Chapter 3. Such breaches must be reported to the government, and breaches affecting 500 or more individuals are publicized on a website.[63] It is also noteworthy that drugs and devices are subject to continued review and adverse-event reporting.[64] It makes no sense to have a radically different oversight standard for EHR systems, which manage so many aspects of patient care. Without postlaunch monitoring, the government cannot intervene if a product turns out to be defective despite certification.

The absence of publicly available adverse-event reports is also problematic for consumers. Those interested in particular products cannot easily research the product's performance history. Instead, in selecting products, they often must rely on vendors' presentations and word-of-mouth recommendations. Thus future purchasers may not be able to make sufficiently educated decisions about which products have the strongest safety records.

CMS also must recognize that providers can customize and configure EHR systems differently. Consequently, a system that works well at one facility can experience safety problems when customized by other users.

To ensure that EHR systems are safe throughout their product lifetimes, CMS must include provisions for enhanced surveillance and adverse-event reporting in its certification criteria. Special attention should be paid to customization of EHR systems.

Adverse-event reporting can operate much as HIPAA breach reporting does. Vendors should be required to report safety problems of sufficient

---

[61] "Drummond Group 2014 Surveillance Plan Audit Report" (author's copy).

[62] "Health IT Complaint Form," HealthIT.gov; available at: www.healthit.gov/healthitcom plaints (accessed September 28, 2015).

[63] US Department of Health and Human Services Office for Civil Rights, "Breaches Affecting 500 or More Individuals"; available at: https://ocrportal.hhs.gov/ocr/breach/breach_report.jsf (accessed August 26, 2015).

[64] See Sharona Hoffman and Andy Podgurski, "Finding a Cure: The Case for Regulation and Oversight of Electronic Health Record Systems, *Harvard Journal of Law & Technology* 22, no. 1 (2008): 147–50.

significance, as determined by CMS. Vendors should bear reporting responsibility because users will presumably contact vendors in order to have problems fixed, and thus they will be aware of all difficulties that require professional intervention. Moreover, vendors will be able to judge whether the problem was caused by user error, is trivial, or is indicative of an actual EHR system flaw. CMS should develop guidelines that will set standards for making this determination. Vendors would have incentive to be honest in their reporting because dishonesty could be detected through continuing review surveillance. To that end, ONC-ACBs could periodically audit vendors' internal records of customer complaints and send surveys to a random sampling of EHR system customers.

The Transparent Ratings on Usability and Security to Transform Information Technology Act, a bipartisan bill that was introduced by Senators Bill Cassidy and Sheldon Whitehouse in October 2015, would require ONC to establish a ratings system for EHR systems. The ratings would be based on confidential assessments that physicians would submit concerning the quality and performance of their EHR systems.[65] Though the bill is unlikely to be enacted, creation of a publicly available rating system would be a welcome development.

At the very least, CMS should compile a list of adverse events, including the vendor, product, date, and a short description of the incident and post the list on its website. Publication of the data would serve as a powerful incentive for vendors to produce high-quality products with minimal flaws. Publication also would enable the healthcare community to research EHR products more thoroughly prior to purchase and not rely solely on vendor presentations and word-of-mouth recommendations.

2.3.4 *Interoperability*

Many agree that the benefits of the transition to EHR systems will not be maximized until we have a national health information network. With interoperability, medical records no longer would be fragmented among different facilities. Authorized individuals in any hospital or medical office would be able to access a patient's complete record when they need it for treatment purposes. Providers could more easily and cheaply switch from an EHR system that is a poor fit for them to a better one because data could simply be transferred to the new product. In addition, technological innovations could benefit all providers more quickly because they could sync with all EHR systems.[66]

---

[65] Section 2141: Transparent Ratings on Usability and Security to Transform Information Technology Act of 2015, 114th Cong. (2015).

[66] Wachter, *The Digital Doctor*, 215.

Interoperability will not happen without regulatory intervention. Vendors are not motivated to promote interoperability because it will increase the likelihood that dissatisfied customers will jettison their existing EHR systems and switch to new ones made by different manufacturers.[67] Likewise, large hospitals are unenthusiastic about sharing information with competing and unaffiliated healthcare providers because doing so may result in loss of revenue and market dominance.[68]

Thus far, the meaningful use and certification regulations have done little more than pay lip service to interoperability. They include requirements that clinicians be able to report certain information to public health authorities and transmit discharge summaries to other facilities. The regulations do not mandate more comprehensive interoperability that could allow widespread information sharing and save many lives.[69]

In 2014, ONC issued a ten-year road map for achieving interoperability called "Connecting Health and Care for the Nation: A 10-Year Vision to Achieve an Interoperable Health IT Infrastructure."[70] Whether this plan has any real-world impact has yet to be seen, but ONC's focus on the interoperability issue is encouraging.

The meaningful use and certification regulations are a solid first step toward achieving quality control for EHR products. However, they approach testing too much as though EHR systems are ordinary computer products rather than an integral and critical part of patient care. The testing and certification process is too brief and insufficiently rigorous. The ONC-ACBs provide no information as to whether any products are ever denied certification,[71] so it is impossible to tell whether any applicants fail to obtain approval. More work must be done in the regulatory arena. It is only with sufficient oversight that EHR systems will fulfill their promise of dramatically improving health outcomes.

[67] *Ibid.*

[68] Office of the National Coordinator for Health Information Technology (ONC), "Report to Congress: Report on Health Information Blocking (April 2015)," 16, 18; available at: www.hea lthit.gov/sites/default/files/reports/info_blocking_040915.pdf (accessed August 26, 2015).

[69] ONC, "Report to Congress: Report on Health Information Blocking," 22, 31.

[70] Office of the National Coordinator for Health Information Technology, "Connecting Health and Care for the Nation: A 10-Year Vision to Achieve an Interoperable Health IT Infrastructure"; available at: www.healthit.gov/sites/default/files/ONC10yearInteroperabilityC onceptPaper.pdf (accessed August 26, 2015).

[71] See Enesha Cobb and Kori Sauser, "Case Study 3: Electronic Health Records," in *Redirecting Innovation in US Health Care: Options to Decrease Spending and Increase Value*, ed. by Steven Garber et al. (Santa Monica, CA: Rand Corporation, 2014), 30; available at: www.rand.org/co ntent/dam/rand/pubs/research_reports/RR300/RR308/RAND_RR308.casestudies.pdf (accessed August 26, 2015).

3

EHR Data Security

Once health data are computerized, they become more vulnerable to data breaches. Computer systems can be hacked, computer equipment containing thousands of records can be stolen or misplaced, e-mail can be sent to the wrong recipient, medical employees can view charts that they should not be accessing from the privacy of their office computers, and many other electronic mishaps can occur. This chapter is dedicated to analysis of electronic health record (EHR) data security threats and the regulations that the federal government has implemented to address them.

I pause here for a brief introductory discussion of privacy terminology. The concept of privacy was first articulated in the legal literature in a 1890 *Harvard Law Review* article written by Samuel Warren and Louis Brandeis. The two scholars proposed that *privacy* is "the right to be let alone."[1] Thereafter, the Supreme Court found that the Constitution embodies the right to privacy even though the word appears nowhere in the document. For example, in the 1965 contraception case *Griswold* v. *Connecticut*, the Court declared that "the First Amendment has a penumbra where privacy is protected from governmental intrusion."[2] Similarly, in the now-famous 1973 case *Roe* v. *Wade*, the Court determined that the right to privacy encompasses a woman's decision to terminate her pregnancy, with some limitations.[3]

This chapter is based in part on Sharona Hoffman and Andy Podgurski, "In Sickness, Health, and Cyberspace: Protecting the Security of Electronic Private Health Information," *Boston College Law Review* 48, no. 2 (2007): 331.

[1] Samuel D. Warren and Louis D. Brandeis, "The Right to Privacy," *Harvard Law Review* 4 (1890): 193.

[2] *Griswold* v. *Connecticut*, 381 US 479, 483, 485–6 (1965).

[3] *Roe* v. *Wade*, 410 US 113, 153 (1973).

Today, three separate terms relate to what are commonly known as privacy concerns. In the EHR context, the term "privacy" refers to the collection, storage, and use of patients' health information. Thus privacy has to do with whether information can be acquired and used, by whom, and under what circumstances. "Confidentiality" is the principle that clinicians must maintain secrecy concerning patient information and should not disclose data without patient authorization. The "security" of medical records, which is the subject of this chapter, relates to technical measures and procedures that protect records from being inappropriately accessed or disclosed by hacking or other means.[4]

The risks associated with the electronic storage and transmission of personal information in general and health data in particular are grave. A research letter published in the prestigious *Journal of the American Medical Association* stated the following:

> Between 2010 and 2013, data breaches reported by HIPAA-covered entities increased, involving 29 million records. Most data breaches resulted from overt criminal activity. The persistent threat of theft and the increase in hacking raise serious security concerns.[5]

The authors noted that their study was limited to reported breaches that affected 500 or more individuals. It thus did not include smaller and unacknowledged breaches.

The "Fifth Annual Benchmark Study on Privacy and Security of Healthcare Data," conducted by the Ponemon Institute in 2015, found that over 90 percent of study participants had a data breach, and 40 percent experienced over five breaches during the preceding two years.[6] The researchers estimated that, on average, a data breach costs healthcare organizations $2.1 million. Criminal attacks were the most common cause of breaches, and their number grew by 125 percent since 2010.

---

[4] Committee on Health Research and the Privacy of Health Information: The HIPAA Privacy Rule; Board on Health Sciences Policy; Board on Health Care Services; Institute of Medicine, *Beyond the HIPAA Privacy Rule: Enhancing Privacy, Improving Health through Research*, ed. by Sharyl J. Nass, Laura A. Levit, and Lawrence O. Gostin (Washington, DC: National Academies Press, 2009), 76.

[5] Vincent Liu, Mark A. Musen, and Timothy Chou, "Data Breaches of Protected Health Information in the United States," *Journal of the American Medical Association* 313, no. 14 (2015): 1472.

[6] Ponemon Institute, "Fifth Annual Benchmark Study on Privacy and Security of Healthcare Data," May, 2015, 1; available at: www2.idexpertscorp.com/fifth-annual-ponemon-study-on -privacy-security-incidents-of-healthcare-data (accessed August 24, 2015). The study included 178 entities, 90 of which were healthcare providers and 88 of which were business associates of providers.

Cloud-based EHRs may raise particular concerns. Privacy breaches can occur during the process of transferring information to the cloud. Moreover, healthcare providers must trust third-party cloud operators to maintain security at the highest level, and a single breach may affect numerous healthcare providers using the same cloud. Finally, the information's availability through the Internet might make it all the more vulnerable to privacy threats.[7] At the same time, data storage on the cloud may be more secure than in-house storage. Cloud operators can have more resources to invest in security than small healthcare providers, and hackers may have more difficulty attacking remote server farms and identifying the data they want in a cloud setting.[8]

Accessing health records can enable perpetrators to engage in identity theft, insurance fraud, or credit-card theft. It can also allow entities with a financial stake in individuals' health status, such as employers or marketers of health-related products, to make decisions that can yield significant financial gain. The following is a partial list of large breaches detected in March through May 2015 in the United States:

- Employees at Boston-based Partners HealthCare were duped by "phishing" e-mails and may have exposed records of 3,300 patients.
- Hackers may have accessed data belonging to as many as 39,000 patients of the Seton Family of Hospitals, based in Austin, Texas.
- Oregon's Advantage Dental notified 151,626 patients that their data may have been compromised through a breach.
- Premara Blue Cross in Washington reported a cyberattack that exposed the data of 11 million customers, employees, and business affiliates.
- Sacred Heart Health System in Florida reported that one of its third-party vendors had suffered a "phishing" attack that potentially compromised the data of 14,000 patients.[9]

One of the largest data breaches in US history was detected in July 2015. Hackers, probably from China, obtained data from government computer systems that related to 19.7 million people who had undergone federal

7   Joel J. P. C. Rodrigues et al., "Analysis of the Security and Privacy Requirements of Cloud-Based Electronic Health Records Systems," *Journal of Medical Internet Research* 15, no. 8 (2013): e186; available at: www.ncbi.nlm.nih.gov/pmc/articles/PMC3757992/; Assad Abbas and Samee U. Khan, "A Review on the State-of-the-Art Privacy-Preserving Approaches in the e-Health Clouds," *Biomedical and Health Informatics* 18, no. 4 (2014): 1431–41.
8   Alice Noblin, Kendall Cortelyou-Ward, and Rosa Servan, "Cloud Computing and Patient Engagement: Leveraging Available Technology," *Journal of Medical Practice Management* 30, no. 2 (2014): 89–93.
9   Akanksha Jayanthi, "9 Latest Data Breaches," *Becker's Health IT & CIO Review*, May 12, 2015; available at: www.beckershospitalreview.com/healthcare-information-technology/9-latest-data-breaches-5-12-15.html (accessed August 24, 2015).

background checks and 1.8 million other individuals. The stolen information included health histories.[10]

The United States is not alone in suffering data breaches. For example, in 2014, 17 million records belonging to the Korean Medical Association, the Association of Korean Medicine, and the Korean Dental Association were exposed through an identity-theft attack.[11] In a 2013 incident in Canada, a laptop with the unencrypted data of 620,000 patients in Alberta was stolen.[12] A 2014 BBC News report asserted that the United Kingdom's National Health Service had almost 2,500 confidentiality breaches per year, involving problems such as data being misplaced or stolen, posted on social media, accidentally published online, or inappropriately shared with others by e-mail, letter, or fax.[13] In one particularly blatant breach, an online pharmacy in the United Kingdom sold customer information to marketing companies.[14]

3.2 DATA SECURITY BACKGROUND

3.2.1 *Reasons for Concern*

Trafficking in protected health information (PHI) poses a significant risk to the public. PHI is medical information that is protected by Health Insurance Portability and Accountability Act of 1996 (HIPAA) regulations and is defined as "individually identifiable health information" that is transmitted or maintained electronically or in any other form.[15]

Why would anyone want to obtain the health information of others? The reasons are numerous, with the following as just a few illustrations:

- Criminals may be interested in accessing EHRs for purposes of identity theft, credit-card use, medical insurance fraud, blackmail, and other illicit purposes.

[10] Julie Hirschfeld Davis, "Hacking of Government Computers Exposed 21.5 Million People," *New York Times*, July 9, 2015; available at: www.nytimes.com/2015/07/10/us/office-of-personnel -management-hackers-got-data-of-millions.html?_r=1 (accessed August 24, 2015).

[11] Gemalto, "2014 Year of Mega Breaches and Identity Theft: Findings from the 2014 Breach Level Index," February 2015; available at: http://breachlevelindex.com/pdf/Breach-Level -Index-Annual-Report-2014.pdf (accessed January 7, 2016).

[12] "Laptop Stolen with Health Information of 620,000 Albertans," *CBC News*, January 22, 2014; available at: www.cbc.ca/news/canada/edmonton/medicentres-data-breach-spurs-changes-to -privacy-laws-1.2635950 (accessed January 7, 2016).

[13] "NHS Has Repeated Data Breaches," *BBC News*, November 14, 2014; available at: www.bbc .com/news/health-30037938 (accessed January 7, 2016).

[14] "Online Pharmacy Fined for Selling Customer Data," *BBC News*, October 21, 2015; available at: www.bbc.com/news/technology-34570720 (accessed January 7, 2016).

[15] 45 CFR 160.103 (2015).

- Employers may be interested in the health information of applicants and employees in order to retain the best workers possible. Such information may help employers to avoid absenteeism, productivity problems, and high health insurance costs.
- Financial institutions may be interested in individuals' health status in order to identify investors and borrowers who will likely work for a long time and be able to accrue significant wealth or pay off their loans.
- Advertisers and marketers wish to tailor their material to the needs and wants of consumers. They thus have much to gain from learning about individuals' health problems and habits.
- Life, disability, and long-term care insurers customarily assess applicants' health status in order to make determinations about policy issuance and premium prices.[16]
- The media are interested in medical news about celebrities and in other interesting health-related stories.
- Parties involved in custody battles may wish to use adverse health information to argue that their opponents are not physically or mentally fit to care for a child.
- Those seeking a spouse or romantic partner may want to learn about their dates' current medical problems and potential health vulnerabilities in order to find a healthy mate and to have healthy, attractive, and/or successful children.[17]

Americans are aware of these dangers. A "Health Information National Trends Survey" conducted in 2011–2012 revealed that two-thirds of the almost 1,500 respondents were concerned that a breach in security might occur when their medical records were transferred by fax or electronically. Furthermore, over 12 percent admitted that they had withheld medical information from a clinician because of privacy and security concerns.[18]

The medical community is likewise well aware of data security risks, and the insurance industry has responded by developing "cyberinsurance" products.

---

[16] By contrast, health insurers' underwriting decisions are rigorously governed by HIPAA and the Affordable Care Act. *See* 29 USC § 1182 (2010); 42 US Code §§ 300gg–300gg-8 (2010).

[17] Hoffman and Podgurski, "In Sickness, Health, and Cyberspace," 334–5; Charles Ornstein, "Your Health Records Are Supposed to Be Private. They Aren't," *Washington Post*, January 3, 2016; available at: www.washingtonpost.com/posteverything/wp/2015/12/30/your-health-records-are-supposed-to-be-private-they-arent/?hpid=hp_no-name_opinion-card-a%3Ahomepage%2Fstory. (accessed January 7, 2016).

[18] Israel T. Agaku et al., "Concern about Security and Privacy, and Perceived Control over Collection and Use of Health Information Are Related to Withholding of Health Information from Healthcare Providers," *Journal of the American Medical Informatics Association* 21, no. 2 (2014): 375.

Increasingly, healthcare providers are purchasing cyberinsurance policies in order to protect themselves against damages arising from data breaches. Coverage, however, may be contingent on the purchaser's implementation of adequate security measures.[19]

3.2.2 *International Data Security Mandates*

The European Union has issued several documents that emphasize the importance of data security. Directive 95/46/EC of the European Parliament and of the Council of 24 October 1995 on the Protection of Individuals with regard to the Processing of Personal Data and on the Free Movement of Such Data includes Article 17 on "Security of Processing."[20] A second document published two years later, the Council of Europe's Recommendation No. R (97) 5 on the Protection of Medical Data, likewise includes Section 9 on security. This provision requires that "[a]ppropriate technical and organisational measures ... be taken to protect personal data ... against accidental or illegal destruction, accidental loss, as well as against unauthorised access, alteration, communication or any other form of processing."[21]

A decade later, in 2007, the European Union's Working Party on the Protection of Individuals with regard to the Processing of Personal Data, which was established pursuant to Directive 95/46/EC, issued a third key document. The "Working Document on the Processing of Personal Data Relating to Health in Electronic Health Records" outlines data security requirements in a variety of provisions. It addresses identification and authentication of patients and healthcare professionals, authorization for accessing EHRs, privacy-enhancing technologies, data-protection auditing, and more. The Working Document stresses that the "integrity of the system must be guaranteed by making use of the knowledge and instruments representing the present state of the art in computer science and information technology."[22]

---

[19] Alex Ruoff, "Legal Dispute between Provider, Cyberinsurer Exposes Uncertain Liability Protection Regime," *BNA's Health Law Reporter* 24, no. 29 (2015): 953.

[20] Directive 95/46/EC of the European Parliament and of the Council of 24 October 1995 on the Protection of Individuals with regard to the Processing of Personal Data and on the Free Movement of Such Data, EUR-Lex – 31995L0046; available at: http://eur-lex.europa.eu/Lex UriServ/LexUriServ.do?uri=CELEX:31995L0046:en:HTML (accessed January 7, 2016).

[21] Council of Europe, Recommendation No. R (97) 5 of the Committee of Ministers to Member States on the Protection of Medical Data, Strasbourg, February 13, 1997 8.1 and 8.3; available at: https://wcd.coe.int/ViewDoc.jsp?id=407311&Site=CM&BackColorInternet=C3C3C3&BackCo lorIntranet=EDB021&BackColorLogged=F5D383 (accessed December 6, 2015).

[22] European Commission Article 29 Data Protection Working Party, "Working Document on the Processing of Personal Data Relating to Health in Electronic Health Records," February 15,

In Canada, the Personal Information Protection and Electronic Documents Act (PIPEDA) regulates privacy in the private sector.[23] Schedule 1 of PIPEDA lists ten principles to which organizations must adhere when collecting, processing, or disclosing personal information for purposes of business activities. These include a mandate that "[p]ersonal information shall be protected by security safeguards appropriate to the sensitivity of the information."[24]

3.2.3 *US State and Federal Privacy Regulations*

Traditionally, the states have regulated the privacy and security of health information through constitutional provisions, common law, and statutes.[25] For example, most states protect information about cancer, genetic testing, HIV/AIDS, mental health, and sexually transmitted diseases and require disclosure of medical data breaches that involve personal information.[26] However, the state regulatory schemes form a patchwork with broad variance among different state provisions.

In order to address concerns about the privacy of medical records more uniformly, in 2003, the US Department of Health and Human Services (HHS) enacted a set of regulations called the "HIPAA Privacy Rule."[27] HHS was authorized to promulgate these regulations by the 1996 HIPAA statute.[28] The HIPAA Privacy Rule governs the use and disclosure of electronic and hardcopy medical information. Key provisions establish that, with some exceptions, regulated entities must obtain patients' permission to disclose their medical information to third parties,[29] must furnish patients with notices of their privacy practices,[30] and must allow patients to review their medical records and request that they be amended or used restrictively.[31]

2007, 20; available at: http://ec.europa.eu/justice/policies/privacy/docs/wpdocs/2007/wp131_en .pdf (accessed December 6, 2015).

[23] Canada Personal Information Protection and Electronic Documents Act (PIPEDA), SC 2000, c.5; available at: http://laws-lois.justice.gc.ca/eng/acts/P-8.6/index.html (accessed January 7, 2016).

[24] PIPEDA, Sch. 1, cl. 4.7, SC 2000, c.5.

[25] Joy L. Pritts, "Altered States: State Health Privacy Laws and the Impact of the Federal Health Privacy Rule," *Yale Journal of Health Policy, Law, and Ethics*, 2, no. 2 (2002): 327.

[26] Patient Privacy Rights Foundation, State Law Information; available at: https://patientprivacy rights.org/state-law-information/ (accessed July 31, 2016).

[27] 45 CFR §§ 160.101–534 (2015).

[28] 42 USC §§ 1320d-d-8 (2010).

[29] 45 CFR §§ 164.508–510 (2015).

[30] 45 CFR § 164.520(a) (2015).

[31] 45 CFR §§ 164.520, 164.522 (2015).

A subsequent set of regulations, the "HIPAA Security Rule,"[32] is less well known than the Privacy Rule but equally important. The Security Rule took effect on April 20, 2005, for most covered entities. These regulations and the protections they do and do not afford are vitally important for all EHR data. The remainder of this chapter will analyze and critique the HIPAA Security Rule.

3.3 THE HIPAA SECURITY RULE

The HIPAA Security Rule establishes general security requirements and provides regulated entities with broad discretion to choose appropriate technologies with which to implement the standards.[33] The Security Rule establishes four general requirements. Covered entities must (1) ensure the "confidentiality, integrity, and availability" of electronic health information that they produce, obtain, maintain, or transmit; (2) protect the data against reasonably anticipated threats to its security or integrity; (3) safeguard against impermissible use or disclosure of the information; and (4) ensure that their employees comply with the rule.[34] The details of the security mandate are discussed next.

3.3.1 *HIPAA Security Requirements*

The HIPAA Security Rule features "standards" and "implementation specifications" that provide instructions concerning how to fulfill the obligations outlined in the rule. There are two types of implementation specifications: "required" and "addressable."[35] Required implementation specifications are mandatory.[36] By contrast, implementers may respond to an addressable implementation specification in one of three ways: (1) by implementing it, (2) by implementing an "equivalent alternative measure," or (3) by doing neither because implementation would not be "reasonable and appropriate."[37] A covered entity that does not implement an implementation specification

---

[32] 45 CFR §§ 164.302–18 (2015).

[33] 45 CFR §§ 164.302–18. See also Health Insurance Reform: Security Standards; Final Rule, *Fed. Reg.* 68: 8336 (2003) (stating that the final rule was written "to frame the standards in terms that are as generic as possible and which, generally speaking, may be met through various approaches or technologies").

[34] 45 CFR § 164.306(a) (2015). Permissible and impermissible uses of private health information are described in Subpart E of the HIPAA Privacy Rule, 45 CFR §§ 164.500–534 (2015).

[35] 45 CFR § 164.306(d) (2015).

[36] 45 CFR § 164.306(d)(2) (2015).

[37] 45 CFR § 164.306(d)(3) (2015).

must document its justification for not doing so,[38] and all covered entities must review their compliance and modify their security measures as needed.[39]

3.3.1.1 Administrative Safeguards

Several required implementation specifications establish administrative safeguards.[40] Covered entities must conduct risk assessments in order to determine what their security vulnerabilities are. They then must institute risk-management practices. Covered entities are also required to impose sanctions on noncompliant employees and to review information system activities.[41] In addition, covered entities must identify a "security official" who is responsible for compliance with the Security Rule and establish procedures whereby only authorized individuals have access to electronic protected health information.[42] In order to achieve workforce security, a covered entity should implement authorization and supervision standards, workforce clearance procedures, and procedures to terminate authorization, but these are considered "addressable" implementation specifications.[43]

In addition, covered entities should implement security awareness and training programs for their workforces along with measures such as security reminders, mechanisms that protect against malicious software, log-in monitoring, and password management.[44] The Security Rule mandates response and reporting mechanisms for security incidents[45] and contingency plans that focus on data backup, disaster recovery, emergency-mode operation, testing and revision procedures, and analysis of the criticality of the affected data and applications.[46] The Security Rule also instructs that covered entities should perform periodic evaluations of their compliance[47] and may enter into written contracts or other arrangements with business associates[48] to

[38]   45 CFR § 164.306(d)(3)(ii)(B)(1) (2015).
[39]   45 CFR § 164.306(e) (2015).
[40]   45 CFR § 164.308(a) (2015).
[41]   45 CFR § 164.308(a)(1)(ii) (2015).
[42]   45 CFR § 164.308(a)(2)–(3)(i) (2015).
[43]   45 CFR § 164.308(a)(3)(ii) (2015).
[44]   45 CFR § 164.308(a)(5) (2015). These are addressable implementation specifications.
[45]   45 CFR § 164.308(a)(6) (2015).
[46]   45 CFR § 164.308(a)(7) (2015). The development of testing and revision procedures and applications and data criticality analysis are addressable implementation specifications. The other safeguards are required.
[47]   45 CFR § 164.308(a)(8) (2015).
[48]   "Business associates" are persons or entities that provide services to other covered entities that involve the use or disclosure of PHI. Examples are claims processors, accountants, lawyers,

handle electronic protected health information as long as the associates provide satisfactory assurances that they will appropriately safeguard the data.[49] The Security Rule, however, does not apply to the transmission of electronic protected health information to another healthcare provider who is treating the patient, to a group health plan sponsor, or to agencies determining eligibility for government programs providing public benefits.[50]

3.3.1.2 Physical Safeguards

The HIPAA Security Rule next establishes physical safeguards aimed at thwarting unauthorized access to electronic information systems and the facilities in which they are housed while ensuring access to authorized personnel.[51] The facility access control subsection describes several "addressable" implementation specifications, which include designing contingency operations, facility security plans, and access control and validation procedures and maintaining records concerning repairs and modifications to security-related components of the physical plant.[52] Next, covered entities are required to maintain workstation security[53] and to establish procedures that govern the movement of hardware that contains electronic protected health information within and out of the facility in question.[54] These procedures should address electronic media disposal, removal of protected health information in cases in which equipment will be reused for other purposes, maintenance of records of the hardware's whereabouts and who is responsible for it, and data backup and storage prior to moving equipment.[55]

3.3.1.3 Technical Safeguards

The required and addressable technical safeguards detailed by the HIPAA Security Rule are designed to ensure that only authorized personnel have

---

transcriptionists, and consultants. 45 CFR § 160.103 (2015); US Department of Health and Human Services, "Health Information Privacy: Business Associates"; available at: www.hhs.gov /ocr/privacy/hipaa/understanding/coveredentities/businessassociates.html (accessed August 24, 2015).

[49] 45 CFR § 164.308(b)(1), (3), and (4) (2015). See also 45 CFR § 164.314 (2015) for specifications regarding business associate contracts and other arrangements.

[50] 45 CFR § 164.308(b)(2) (2015); 45 CFR § 164.502(e)(1)(ii)(C) (2015).

[51] 45 CFR § 164.310(a)(1) (2015).

[52] 45 CFR § 164.310(a)(2) (2015).

[53] 45 CFR § 164.310(b) and (c) (2015).

[54] 45 CFR § 164.310(d)(1) (2015).

[55] 45 CFR § 164.310(d)(2) (2015). The implementation specifications for disposal and media reuse are required, while the record-keeping and data backup and storage requirements are addressable.

access to electronic protected health information.[56] These safeguards include assigning unique user identification names or numbers, establishing emergency access procedures, having an automatic logoff after a specific period of inactivity, and implementing encryption and decryption mechanisms.[57] The technical safeguards provision also discusses audit controls, authentication mechanisms for electronic protected health information and for users who want access to it, and measures to ensure security when protected health information is transmitted electronically.[58]

3.3.2 *Enforcement*

The HIPAA legislation authorizes both civil and criminal penalties.[59] Covered entities that disclose health information in an unauthorized manner or that fail to implement appropriate security measures can be investigated and penalized.

3.3.2.1 Complaint Investigation and Penalties

The HIPAA regulations establish a primarily complaint-driven enforcement scheme for privacy violations.[60] Persons[61] who believe that a violation has occurred may submit a complaint to HHS.[62] Between October 2014 and March 2015, HHS received approximately 940 complaints relating to HIPAA Security Rule violations.[63] The HHS Office of Civil Rights (OCR), which administers the Security Rule, is tasked with investigating complaints and attempting to resolve cases of noncompliance through voluntary compliance, corrective action, and/or resolution agreements.[64] If the noncompliant

[56] 45 CFR § 164.312(a)(1) (2015).

[57] 45 CFR § 164.312(a)(2) (2015). Unique user identification and emergency access procedures are required, while automatic logoff and encryption and decryption are addressable implementation specifications.

[58] 45 CFR § 164.312(b)–(e) (2015). Mechanisms for information authentication and integrity controls for the transmission of data are designated "addressable."

[59] 42 USC §§ 1320d-5 and 1320d-6 (2010).

[60] *Fed. Reg.* 70: 20226 (2005). The regulations, however, also provide that HHS may conduct compliance reviews without receiving a complaint. *Id.*; 45 CFR § 160.308 (2015).

[61] A "person" is defined as a "natural person, trust or estate, partnership, corporation, professional association or corporation, or other entity, public or private." 45 CFR § 160.103 (2015).

[62] 45 CFR § 160.306(a) (2015).

[63] US Department of Health and Human Services, "Health Information Privacy: Enforcement Highlights"; available at: www.hhs.gov/ocr/privacy/hipaa/enforcement/highlights/index.html (accessed August 24, 2015).

[64] US Department of Health and Human Services, "How OCR Enforces the HIPAA Privacy and Security Rules"; available at: www.hhs.gov/ocr/privacy/hipaa/enforcement/process/howocrenforces.html (accessed August 24, 2015).

party is uncooperative, OCR may impose civil monetary penalties for non-compliance that are tiered based on the violator's blameworthiness. The maximum penalty amount is a hefty $50,000 per violation "except that the total amount imposed on the person for all such violations of an identical requirement or prohibition during a calendar year may not exceed $1,500,000."[65] A respondent may request a hearing before an administrative law judge (ALJ).[66] As is typical in administrative proceedings, only limited discovery is permitted,[67] and the ALJ is generally not bound by the Federal Rules of Evidence.[68] OCR does not have authority to impose criminal penalties, and therefore it refers cases involving potential criminal violations to the Department of Justice.[69]

OCR does not often impose monetary penalties, but when it does, the punishment is not trivial. As of June 2015, OCR collected a total of only twenty-four fines.[70] However, during the first ten months of 2014, OCR reportedly levied five fines in the following amounts: $215,000, $3.3 million, $1.5 million, $1,725,220, and $250,000.[71] In addition, covered entities that suffer a breach often spend many millions on their own incident investigations, notification of patients, and risk-mitigation activities. For example, in 2012, Blue Cross and Blue Shield of Tennessee paid HHS $1.5 million to settle a case growing out of a 2009 breach that affected over 1 million individuals. However, its total cost for the breach was approximately $18.5 million.[72]

3.3.2.2 Lawsuits by State Attorneys General

The HIPAA statute also authorizes state attorneys general to sue HIPAA Privacy and Security Rule violators whose misconduct harms or threatens the welfare of state residents.[73] Attorneys general may obtain injunctive relief or civil damages not to exceed $25,000 per calendar year for "all violations of an identical requirement" by a person.

[65] 42 USC § 1320d-5 (2010).

[66] 45 CFR § 160.526(a) (2015).

[67] 45 CFR § 160.538 (2015).

[68] 45 CFR § 160.558(b) (2015).

[69] See 42 USC § 1320d-6 (2010).

[70] Bernadette M. Broccolo and Edward G. Zacharias, "US Privacy and Security Compliance Enforcement in the Health Care Industry: Recent Developments and Trends," *BNA's Health Law Reporter* 24, no. 25 (2015): 801, 802.

[71] Daniel Solove, "The Brave New World of HIPAA Enforcement (Part 4)," *SafeGov*, October 20, 2014; available at: www.safegov.org/2014/10/20/the-brave-new-world-of-hipaa-enforcement-(part-4) (accessed August 24, 2015).

[72] Kim Baldwin-Stried Reich, "Trends in e-Discovery: Four Cases Provide a Glimpse of Healthcare Litigation's Future," *Journal of AHIMA* 83, no. 5 (2012): 44, 45.

[73] 42 USC A § 1320d-5(d) (2010).

As of 2015, the attorneys general of Connecticut, Vermont, Minnesota, Massachusetts, Illinois, Indiana, New York, and California brought enforcement actions, though they often sue under both HIPAA and state privacy or consumer protection laws.[74] For example, the Massachusetts attorney general sued South Shore Hospital under the state Consumer Protection Act and HIPAA after it shipped 473 unencrypted backup computer tapes with 800,000 individuals' readable PHI to a third-party vendor who was to erase the data and resell the tapes. The tapes included names, Social Security numbers, account numbers, and medical diagnoses. The hospital did not inform the vendor that the tapes contained PHI and did not ensure that the vendor would handle this sensitive information appropriately. Worse yet, only one of the three shipped boxes arrived at the vendor's facility, and the other two were never recovered, though there is no evidence that anyone obtained the missing data. South Shore Hospital agreed to pay $750,000 to settle the case in 2012.[75]

3.3.2.3 Breach Notification Requirements and Audits

Two other enforcement mechanisms are noteworthy. First, under HIPAA's breach notification provisions, covered entities must report security breaches both to affected individuals and to OCR.[76] Entities must inform individuals within sixty days of discovering the breach but can report to OCR annually. However, if the breach affects 500 or more individuals in a particular state or jurisdiction, the entity must inform HHS within sixty days and also notify prominent media outlets so that the occurrence can be publicized.[77] OCR also posts a list of breaches affecting 500 or more people on its website.[78]

Second, by law, OCR is required to perform periodic audits of covered entities' compliance with the HIPAA Privacy, Security, and Breach Notification Rules.[79] To that end, OCR established a pilot audit program in

[74] Solove, "The Brave New World of HIPAA Enforcement (Part 4)"; Broccolo and Zacharias, "US Privacy and Security Compliance Enforcement in the Health Care Industry," 808; James Swann, "University of Rochester Hospital Reaches HIPAA Settlement with NY Attorney General," *BNA's Health Law Reporter* 24, no. 47 (2015): 1615.

[75] Attorney General of Massachusetts, "South Shore Hospital to Pay $750,000 to Settle Data Breach Allegations," May 24, 2012; available at: www.mass.gov/ago/news-and-updates/press-releases/2012/2012-05-24-south-shore-hospital-data-breach-settlement.html (accessed August 24, 2015).

[76] 45 CFR §§ 164.400–14 (2015).

[77] US Department of Health and Human Services, "Breach Notification Rule"; available at: www.hhs.gov/ocr/privacy/hipaa/administrative/breachnotificationrule/ (accessed August 24, 2015).

[78] US Department of Health and Human Services Office for Civil Rights, "Breaches Affecting 500 or More Individuals"; available at: https://ocrportal.hhs.gov/ocr/breach/breach_report.jsf (accessed August 24, 2015).

[79] 42 USC § 17940 (2010).

2011 and assessed 115 covered entities. The office then instituted a formal evaluation of its audit program's effectiveness.[80] In 2016, OCR launched phase two of its audit program, through which it plans to audit 350 covered entities.[81]

3.4 HIPAA SECURITY RULE COMPLIANCE

3.4.1 *Flexibility or Inadequate Guidance?*

The Security Rule leaves the mechanisms of implementing the outlined security standards to the discretion of the covered entity.[82] For example, a provision entitled "Flexibility of Approach" states: "Covered entities may use any security measures that allow the covered entity to reasonably and appropriately implement the standards and implementation specifications."[83] The regulations elaborate on the "reasonably and appropriately" standard only by instructing covered entities to take into account the entity's size, complexity, capabilities, and technical infrastructure; the security measures' costs; and the "probability and criticality of potential risks to electronic protected health information."[84] This language does not explain the term "criticality" and fails to provide guidance concerning how to identify "potential risks." Likewise, in its "Administrative Safeguards" section, the Security Rule requires covered entities to "[c]onduct an accurate and thorough assessment of the potential risks and vulnerabilities to the confidentiality, integrity, and availability of electronic protected health information."[85] No further details are provided concerning how the complex and critical task of risk analysis is to be accomplished.

A flexible approach eases compliance burdens for covered entities. They are free to adopt security mechanisms of their choice as long as these are effective. Moreover, the approach is sensitive to the fact that technology is ever changing and must continuously evolve to respond to increasingly sophisticated forms of hacking or other attacks. It would be impractical, therefore, for the rule to

[80] US Department of Health and Human Services, "HIPAA Privacy, Security, and Breach Notification Audit Program"; available at: www.hhs.gov/ocr/privacy/hipaa/enforcement/audit/index.html (accessed August 24, 2015).

[81] Broccolo and Zacharias, "US Privacy and Security Compliance Enforcement in the Health Care Industry," 802; US Department of Health and Human Services, "OCR Launches Phase 2 of HIPAA Audit Program" HHS.gov; available at: www.hhs.gov/hipaa/for-professionals/compliance-enforcement/audit/phase2announcement/index.html (accessed March 24, 2016).

[82] 45 CFR § 164.306(b) (2015).

[83] 45 CFR § 164.306(b)(1) (2015).

[84] 45 CFR § 164.306(b)(2) (2015).

[85] 45 CFR § 164.308(a)(1)(ii)(A) (2015).

dictate that particular technologies or security products be used because these might quickly become outdated.

Yet, while flexibility is a desirable quality, it can also be hazardous in the regulatory context because it can leave those subject to regulation without sufficient guidance as to how to comply with legal requirements. Of particular concern is the fact that the Security Rule omits an explicit requirement that covered entities, perhaps with the assistance of consultants or vendors, identify the relevant *best current security practices* of the health informatics and computer security communities. Such a requirement is needed to ensure that covered entities are knowledgeable about sound security practices and emergent security risks and their countermeasures. The rapid exploitation of newly discovered vulnerabilities in software systems and applications by attackers makes it essential that covered entities be extremely diligent in learning about and responding to these vulnerabilities.

3.4.2 *Compliance Resources*

Cybersecurity experts Lisa Gallagher and Michael Garvin advise healthcare providers to spend an initial 40 percent of their information technology (IT) budgets to implement data security measures and thereafter 10 percent of budget to maintain security.[86] In reality, however, on average, covered entities spend approximately 3 percent of their IT budgets on security, an alarmingly inadequate amount. According to a Ponemon Institute study, over half of respondents believed that their organizations were underfunded to address security concerns, and a majority failed to perform risk assessments despite the HIPAA Security Rule's mandate.[87]

Detailed suggestions regarding technical security solutions are beyond the scope of this book. I leave those to the capable hands of an emerging industry of security experts that offers consulting services to healthcare providers. Among them are powerhouses such as Symantec and Northrop Grumman, as well as small boutique operations. The International Association of Privacy Professionals has 20,000 members and is growing at 25 percent a year.[88]

---

[86] Arthur Allen, "Health Care Spending Billions to Protect the Records It Spent Billions to Install," *Politico*, June 1, 2015; available at: www.politico.com/story/2015/06/health-care-spending-billions -to-protect-the-records-it-spent-billions-to-install-118432.html (accessed August 24, 2015).

[87] Ponemon Institute, "Fifth Annual Benchmark Study on Privacy and Security of Healthcare Data," 2.

[88] Allen, "Health Care Spending Billions to Protect the Records It Spent Billions to Install."

Indeed, healthcare providers most often turn to vendors to implement appropriate security measures.[89]

A large number of resources are available to covered entities and their agents. HHS has a webpage dedicated to "Security Rule Guidance Material."[90] It has created a "Security Rule Educational Paper Series" with papers addressing administrative, physical, and technical safeguards, risk analysis, implementation by small providers, and other matters. HHS has also developed security guidance regarding risk analysis and remote access and use of PHI. Finally, the HHS website provides links to a number of very useful National Institute of Standards and Technology (NIST) publications regarding risk management and security data safeguards. In addition, other reputable industry organizations such as the International Organization for Standardization (ISO), the Computer Emergency Readiness Team, and the National Information Assurance Partnership all produce and disseminate relevant and useful information.[91]

Numerous other resources can readily be found on the Internet. For example, The Doctors Company, a medical malpractice insurer, offers these sound tips:

- Identify all areas of potential vulnerability. Develop secure office processes, such as
  - Sign-in sheets that ask for only minimal information.
  - Procedures for the handling and destruction of paper records.
  - Policies detailing which devices are allowed to contain PHI and under what circumstances those devices may leave the office.
- Encrypt all devices that contain PHI (laptops, desktops, thumb drives, and centralized storage devices). Make sure that thumb drives are encrypted and that the encryption code is not inscribed on or included with the thumb drive. Encryption is the best way to prevent a breach.

---

[89] Deloitte and Oracle, "Securing Electronic Health Records (EHRs) to Achieve 'Meaningful Use' Compliance, Prevent Data Theft and Fraud," March 2011, 1; available at: www.oracle.com/us/industries/healthcare/oracle-deloitte-secure-ehr-wp-454659.pdf (accessed August 24, 2015).

[90] US Department of Health and Human Services, "Health Information Privacy: Security Rule Guidance Material"; available at: www.hhs.gov/ocr/privacy/hipaa/administrative/securityrule/securityruleguidance.html (accessed August 24, 2015).

[91] See International Organization for Standardization; available at: www.iso.org/iso/home.html (accessed August 24, 2015); United States Computer Emergency Readiness Team; available at: www.us-cert.gov/ (accessed August 24, 2015); and the National Information Assurance Partnership; available at: https://www.niap-ccevs.org/ (accessed August 24, 2015).

- Train your staff on how to protect PHI. This includes not only making sure policies and procedures are HIPAA compliant but also instructing staff not to openly discuss patient PHI.
- Audit and test your physical and electronic security policies and procedures regularly, including what steps to take in case of a breach. The OCR audits entities that have had a breach, as well as those that have not. The OCR will check if you have procedures in place in case of a breach. Taking the proper steps in the event of a breach may help you to avoid a fine.
- Insure. Make sure that your practice has insurance to assist with certain costs in case of a breach.[92]

Many of these recommendations are echoed by health law experts. McDermott Will & Emery's Bernadette Broccolo and Edward Zacharias write that a "key ingredient in a HIPAA compliance formula is conducting periodic, comprehensive HIPAA Security Rule risk analyses, documenting them, developing a remediation plan to address the findings, and executing on that plan."[93] They note that almost 70 percent of OCR's first-round audits revealed that the audited entity did not conduct an acceptable risk analysis. Broccolo and Zacharias also recommend that covered entities be scrupulous about encryption and prepare for breaches through tabletop exercises.

Cloud-based EHR systems require the same security measures as those operating out of healthcare providers' servers. However, healthcare providers must ensure that cloud operators adhere to HIPAA Security Rule mandates, especially if they also store nonmedical information that does not require HIPAA safeguards. Cloud operators with diverse data collections may not be fully familiar with regulatory security requirements or may have difficulty tracking which data are and are not subject to compliance.[94] In addition, healthcare providers using the cloud are advised to retain backup copies of patient health information in different data centers.[95]

[92] David McHale, "Be Cybersecure: Protect Patient Records, Avoid Fines, and Safeguard Your Reputation," *Michigan Medicine* 113, no. 5 (2014): 9; available at: www.thedoctors.com/Kno wledgeCenter/PatientSafety/articles/Be-Cybersecure-Protect-Patient-Records-Avoid-Fines -and-Safeguard-Your-Reputation (accessed August 24, 2015).
[93] Broccolo and Zacharias, "US Privacy and Security Compliance Enforcement in the Health Care Industry," 808–9.
[94] Cloud operators will be considered business associates that are covered under HIPAA, so they could be subject to penalties for security violations about which OCR learns.
[95] Noblin, Cortelyou-Ward, and Servan, "Cloud Computing and Patient Engagement," 68; Rodrigues et al., "Analysis of the Security and Privacy Requirements of Cloud-Based Electronic Health Record Systems."

3.5 RECOMMENDED HIPAA SECURITY RULE REVISIONS

I turn now back to the text of the law and regulations. To enhance the efficacy of the HIPAA Security Rule, I offer two further recommendations: (1) expand the definitions of "covered entity" and "health information" and (2) establish a private cause of action for aggrieved individuals.

3.5.1 *The Narrow Definition of Covered Entities*

3.5.1.1 Critique

The HIPAA Security Rule governs the behavior of only a fraction of persons and entities that handle personal health information. The rule targets those who most obviously process high volumes of health information on a daily basis. Presumably, legislators did not want to impose heavy compliance burdens on data holders that are not in the business of healthcare. However, their exclusion may pose serious privacy risks to the public.

The regulations define "covered entities" as including health plans, health-care clearinghouses,[96] healthcare providers who transmit health information electronically for purposes of HIPAA-relevant transactions, and their business associates.[97] Consequently, doctors, hospitals, pharmacists, health insurers, and health maintenance organizations (HMOs) must comply with the HIPAA privacy standards, but not all parties possessing identifiable health data are covered. Thus websites selling nonprescription medications or dispensing medical advice, employers handling applicants' and employees' medical records, marketers, and many other business entities that obtain health data are not bound by the requirements of the HIPAA Security Rule. The rule's narrow scope of coverage compromises its ability to protect Americans against misuse of their medical information. It leaves the vast amount of health information that is stored on systems maintained by noncovered entities especially vulnerable to theft, leaks, destruction, or alteration.

3.5.1.2 Solution: Expanding the Regulatory Scope

COVERED ENTITIES. Because healthcare providers, insurers, clearinghouses, and their business associates are by no means the only entities that maintain

---

[96] "Healthcare clearinghouses" are "entities that process nonstandard health information they receive from another entity into a standard (i.e., standard electronic format or data content), or vice versa." US Department of Health and Human Services, "Health Information Privacy: For Covered Entities and Business Associates"; available at: www.hhs.gov/ocr/privacy/hipaa/understanding/coveredentities/ (accessed August 24, 2015).

[97] 45 CFR §§ 160.102–103 (2015); 42 USC § 17934 (2010).

and transmit PHI, it is illogical to limit the jurisdiction of the Security Rule in particular and the privacy regulations in general to these types of entities. Consequently, the term "covered entity" in the HIPAA Privacy Rule should be significantly expanded. Federal legislators need not struggle to formulate a novel definition. Rather, they could adopt the broad language of the very strong Texas health privacy law, which provides

> "Covered entity" means any person who:
>
> (A) for commercial, financial, or professional gain, monetary fees, or dues, or on a cooperative, nonprofit, or pro bono basis, engages, in whole or in part, and with real or constructive knowledge, in the practice of assembling, collecting, analyzing, using, evaluating, storing, or transmitting protected health information. The term includes a business associate, health care payer, governmental unit, information or computer management entity, school, health researcher, health care facility, clinic, health care provider, or person who maintains an Internet site;
>
> (B) comes into possession of protected health information;
>
> (C) obtains or stores protected health information under this chapter; or
>
> (D) is an employee, agent, or contractor of a person described by Paragraph (A), (B), or (C) insofar as the employee, agent, or contractor creates, receives, obtains, maintains, uses, or transmits protected health information.[98]

A broad definition such as that of the Texas statute would offer much more comprehensive privacy protection to the American public without being inappropriately restrictive. Because of the qualifying language at the beginning of subsection (A), the term "covered entities" would not, for example, capture private citizens who e-mail each other about a friend's medical problem out of concern for his or her welfare. Thus the proposed definition would not constitute unwarranted government intrusion on purely private matters.

HEALTH INFORMATION. The recommended change to the definition of "covered entity" will necessitate an expansion of the meaning of "health information," which is found in the privacy regulations' "Definition" section as well as in HIPAA's "Statutory Definitions" section.[99] "Health information" currently means:

any information, whether oral or recorded in any form or medium, that –

---

[98] Tex. Health & Safety Code Ann. 181.001(b)(2) (West).

[99] 45 CFR § 160.103 (2015); 42 USC § 1320d(4) (2000).

(A) is created or received by a health care provider, health plan, public health authority, employer, life insurer, school or university, or health care clearing-house; and

(B) relates to the past, present, or future physical or mental health or condition of an individual, the provision of health care to an individual, or the past, present, or future payment for the provision of health care to an individual.

This definition excludes PHI that is handled by parties not specified in the provision, such as financial institutions, marketers, website operators, and other parties with an interest in individuals' electronic PHI. An expansion of the concept of "covered entities" will necessitate a parallel expansion in the meaning of "health information." "Health information" should mean "any information, recorded in any form or medium, that relates to the past, present, or future physical or mental health or condition of an individual, the provision of healthcare to an individual, or the past, present, or future payment for the provision of healthcare to an individual." This language does not limit "health information" based on who its creator or recipient is.

3.5.2 *The Absence of a Private Cause of Action*

The HIPAA Security Rule does not provide for a private cause of action.[100] A private cause of action would have surely faced enormous resistance from regulated entities who feel that the HIPAA Privacy and Security Rules are extremely burdensome even without the threat of private litigation. A few state courts have accepted plaintiffs' arguments that HIPAA should inform the standard of care in negligence cases relating to privacy breaches.[101] However, the Privacy Rule itself can be enforced only through administrative procedures, hearings before an ALJ, and state attorneys general actions.

3.5.2.1 Critique

Under the enforcement system established by the regulations, any aggrieved individual has a right to file a complaint with OCR.[102] Even if OCR imposes a fine, however, the money is deposited in the US Treasury and is not given to

---

[100] See 45 CFR §§ 160.300–552 (2015).

[101] See, e.g., *RK v. St. Mary's Med. Ctr. Inc.*, 735 S.E.2d 715 (W.Va. 2012); *I.S. v. Wash. Univ.*, No. 4:11-cv-235SNLJ, 2011 US Dist. LEXIS 66043 (E.D. Mo. June 14, 2011); *Harmon v. Maury Cnty. Tenn.*, No. 1:05-cv-26, 20015 US Dist. LEXIS 48094 (M.D. Tenn. August 31, 2005); *Yath v. Fairway Clinics NP*, 767 N.W.2d 34 (Minn. Ct. App. 2009); *Acosta v. Byrum*, 638 S.E.2d 246 (N.C. Ct. App. 2006); *Byrne v. Avery Center for Obstetrics and Gynecology, P.C.*, 102 A.3d 32 (Conn. 2014).

[102] 45 CFR § 160.306(c) (2015).

the complainant.[103] At the request of the covered entity, a hearing may be held before an ALJ, but the only parties to participate in the hearing process are the accused offender and HHS personnel.[104] Likewise, the states rather than private individuals receive damages recovered in state attorneys general actions.[105]

By contrast to the HIPAA Privacy and Security Rules, many other American privacy laws establish a private cause of action. These include the Privacy Act of 1974, the Cable Communications Policy Act, the Electronic Communications Privacy Act, the Video Privacy Protection Act of 1988, and the Driver's Privacy Protection Act of 1994.[106] The laws provide explicitly for a right to recover attorneys' fees and costs so that even plaintiffs with minimal damages resulting from inappropriate disclosure are likely to find attorneys who are willing to litigate their cases.

Without a private cause of action, aggrieved individuals obtain no relief no matter how severe the HIPAA violation is. Moreover, private litigation is often needed as an adjunct to administrative procedures for deterrence purposes. Aggressive pursuit of governmental enforcement actions may depend on political priorities and pressures or on budgetary and resource-allocation constraints. Thus clear violations that affect only a small number of people could be ignored, and cases that would not set important precedents might not be litigated by the government no matter how justified prosecution would be. Such inevitable resource-rationing decisions can leave a significant deterrence void, which can only be filled through private enforcement.

Arguably, several causes of action relating to privacy violations already exist in tort law and could be used by victims of HIPAA Security Rule violations. In truth, however, common-law theories will be of limited help in HIPAA breach cases. The tort of public disclosure of private facts consists of four elements: (1) public disclosure, (2) of a private fact, (3) that would be objectionable and offensive to a reasonable person, and (4) that is not of legitimate public concern.[107] Most courts have found that in order to support this theory of liability, plaintiffs must prove widespread dissemination of personal information to the public and have deemed this tort theory to fit mostly cases

---

[103] 45 CFR § 160.424(a) (2015); US Department of Health and Human Services, "How OCR Enforces the HIPAA Privacy and Security Rules"; available at: www.hhs.gov/ocr/privacy/hipaa/enforcement/process/howocrenforces.html (accessed August 24, 2015).

[104] 45 CFR § 160.504(a) (2015).

[105] 42 USC § 1320d-5(d) (2010).

[106] 5 USC § 552a(g) (2010); 47 USC § 551(f)(1) (2010); 18 USC § 2520 (2010); 18 USC § 2710(c) (2010); and 18 USC § 2724 (2010).

[107] See *Diaz* v. *Oakland Tribune*, 139 Cal.App.3d 118, 126 (1983).

involving publication through the media.[108] In the context of HIPAA violations, however, PHI will generally be obtained by hackers or thieves and will not be distributed to the general public, and thus the tort of public disclosure of private facts will be inapplicable.

A more fruitful tort theory for plaintiffs might be breach of confidentiality.[109] Courts have based the patient's right of confidentiality on a variety of sources, including privilege statutes protecting physician–patient communications, licensing statutes prohibiting the disclosure of patient information without authorization, and medical ethics principles articulated in the Hippocratic Oath and other sources. In *Horne* v. *Patton*,[110] for example, the court found that a physician breached his duty of confidentiality by disclosing medical information to the patient's employer. The court ruled that a doctor has a duty not to disclose patient information obtained in the course of treatment and that a private cause of action exists in cases where the duty is breached.[111] An action for breach of confidentiality can be maintained regardless of the degree to which the information has been publicly distributed or of its offensiveness, and there is no requirement to prove the intent of the perpetrator.[112]

Nevertheless, in general, the tort of breach of confidentiality can be established only when the perpetrator and the victim of the breach of confidentiality had a direct relationship, such as that of a clinician and patient.[113] Plaintiffs have also occasionally prevailed against third parties who knowingly induced physicians to reveal confidential information in violation of physician–patient confidentiality responsibilities, but here too the improper disclosure was made by the doctor.[114] The breach of confidentiality tort, therefore, will not extend to cases of hacking, theft, or disclosure by anyone who did not have a relationship with the patient. In addition, because breach of confidentiality is a common-law tort, the standard for establishing liability

---

[108] Peter K. Winn, "Confidentiality in Cyberspace: The HIPAA Privacy Rules and the Common Law," *Rutgers Law Journal* 33 (2002): 653; Daniel Solove, *The Digital Person: Technology and Privacy in the Information Age* (New York: New York University Press, 2006), 60. See *Satterfield* v. *Lockheed Missiles and Space Co.*, 617 F. Supp. 1359, 1369 (S.C. 1985); *Beard* v. *Akzona, Inc.*, 517 F. Supp. 128, 132 (E.D. Tenn. 1981); *Tollefson* v. *Price*, 430 P.2d 990 (Ore. 1967); *Vogel* v. *W. T. Grant Co.*, 327 A.2d 133, 137 (Pa. 1974); *Swinton Creek Nursery* v. *Edisto Farm Credit*, 514 S.E.2d 126, 131 (S.C. 1999).

[109] See Winn, "Confidentiality in Cyberspace," 652–8.

[110] *Horne* v. *Patton*, 287 So.2d 824 (Ala. 1973).

[111] *Ibid.*, 829–30.

[112] Winn, "Confidentiality in Cyberspace," 657–8.

[113] *Ibid.*, 662; *Humphers* v. *First Interstate Bank*, 696 P.2d 527, 530 (Or. 1985).

[114] Winn, "Confidentiality in Cyberspace," 661–5. See *Hammonds* v. *Aetna Casualty & Surety Co.*, 243 F. Supp. 793 (N.D. Ohio 1965); *Alberts* v. *Devine*, 479 N.E.2d 113 (Mass. 1985); *Morris* v. *Consolidation Coal Co.*, 446 S.E.2d 648 (W.Va. 1994); *Biddle* v. *Warren General Hospital*, 715 N.E.2d 518 (Ohio 1999).

can vary from state to state. Without a federal statutory cause of action, plaintiffs have few options to litigate privacy breach cases, and their success may depend on the state in which the case was brought.

3.5.2.2 Solution: Bolstering Enforcement through a Private Cause of Action

The HIPAA Privacy and Security Rules' lack of a private cause of action diminishes their deterrent and remedial powers. Thus the privacy regulations should adopt the approach of many of the other US privacy laws and establish a private cause of action.[115]

The HIPAA Privacy and Security Rules' administrative penalties should be retained alongside a private right of litigation. This approach will allow for governmental intervention even when no individuals suffer injury, such as in cases in which electronic security is inadequately maintained but unauthorized third parties do not access or misuse data. At the same time, it will introduce the threat of private enforcement in cases that the government does not pursue, which may be the vast majority of breaches.

Borrowing from the private cause of action provisions found in other privacy legislation, the HIPAA statute and regulations should include the following language[116]:

1. Any person aggrieved by any act of a covered entity in violation of this section may bring a civil action in a US District Court.[117]
2. The court may award –
   (a) actual damages, but not less than liquidated damages in the amount of $2,500;
   (b) punitive damages upon proof of willful or reckless disregard of the law;
   (c) reasonable attorneys' fees and other litigation costs reasonably incurred; and
   (d) such other preliminary and equitable relief as the court determines to be appropriate.[118]

---

[115] It is well established that defendants can be subjected to both criminal penalties and civil damages for the same wrong. See *US* v. *Bajakajian*, 524 US 321, 331 (1998); *Tuttle* v. *Raymond*, 494 A.2d 1353, 1357–8 (Maine 1985).

[116] The private cause of action should be added to both the administrative regulations and the federal statute because the means of enforcement are authorized under the statute itself. See 42 USC §§ 1320d-5 and 1320d-6 (2003).

[117] See Privacy Act of 1974, 5 USC § 552a(g)(1)(D) (2010); Cable Communications Policy Act, 47 USC § 551(f)(1).

[118] See Driver's Privacy Protection Act of 1994, 18 USC § 2724 (2010), for identical language.

To limit the burden such a cause of action would impose on the courts, Congress might consider requiring aggrieved parties to exhaust administrative remedies before filing lawsuits in court. This mechanism has been embraced by several employment discrimination laws, which establish that potential plaintiffs must file charges of discrimination with the Equal Employment Opportunity Commission and receive a determination and/or a right to sue letter before filing a lawsuit in court.[119] Presumably, such a system would filter out many of the weakest cases because lawyers and potential litigants would be discouraged by negative administrative agency findings and would not pursue frivolous cases. However, effective administrative review would only be possible if OCR were adequately resourced and staffed to process a large volume of claims.

In addition, a private cause of action is unlikely to open the floodgates of litigation because plaintiffs would need to have suffered provable damages in order to sue. Specific injury will not be provable in the routine cases in which computer systems are hacked but there is no evidence that the perpetrators used the information in a way that harmed specific individuals. Plaintiffs would have standing only if they could show harm such as use of their credit-card numbers, reputational harm, or loss of opportunities because their sensitive medical information was disclosed to third parties.

The security of EHR systems is critical to protecting patient welfare and winning public trust in the new digitized world of medical care. The HIPAA Security Rule provides a solid foundation for regulating EHR system security and establishing sound security standards. Technical experts and policy-makers, however, must remain ever vigilant and continue to strive to improve security through all possible regulatory and technical means.

---

[119] See, e.g., Title VII of the Civil Rights Act of 1964, 42 USC §§ 2000e-5(b) and (f)(1) (2010).

4

EHR Systems and Liability

The 2012 case of *Burkett* v. *Advocate Health & Hosp.*[1] involved an infant who received an intravenous solution that was prepared with over sixty times the appropriate amount of sodium and, as a result, died a few hours later. The immediate cause of the death was that a technician typed incorrect information into an electronic health record (EHR) data field. However, several other problems related to the EHR system contributed to the tragedy as well. Automated alerts on the intravenous (IV) compounding machine that could have identified the error were not activated. In addition, a lack of interoperability prevented the doctor's order from being transmitted electronically to the automated compounding system for IV bags. Therefore, a technician had to read the order and enter the information, and an opportunity for human error was created.[2] The case settled for $8.25 million.[3]

While advocates fervently hope that EHR system adoption will significantly reduce medical errors and related medical malpractice lawsuits, it is not at all clear that this hope has been fulfilled thus far. The many EHR shortcomings that were discussed in Chapter 1 might make clinicians just as vulnerable to malpractice suits as they were in the paper era, if not more so. In addition, working with complex EHRs rather than traditional paper files might make the litigation process more cumbersome and difficult.

This chapter is based in part on the following articles: Sharona Hoffman and Andy Podgurski, "E-Health Hazards: Provider Liability and Electronic Health Record Systems," *Berkeley Technology Law Journal* 24, no. 4 (2009): 1523; Sharona Hoffman, "Medical Big Data and Big Data Quality Problems," *Connecticut Insurance Law Journal* 21, no. 1 (2015): 289.

[1] *Burkett* v. *Advocate Health & Hosp.*, No. 11 L 3535, 2012 WL 1795177 (Ill. Cir. Ct. April 5, 2012) (verdict and settlement summary).

[2] Judith Graham and Cynthia Dizikes, "Baby's Death Spotlights Safety Risks Linked to Computerized Systems," *Chicago Tribune*, June 27, 2011; available at: http://articles.chicago tribune.com/2011–06-27/news/ct-met-technology-errors-20110627_1_electronic-medical-record s-physicians-systems (accessed August 19, 2015).

[3] *Burkett*, 2012 WL 1795177.

Liability concerns have arisen in both the United States and elsewhere. An independent European advisory body issued a report entitled "Working Document on the Processing of Personal Data Relating to Health in Electronic Health Records" in 2007. The report includes a section entitled "Liability Issues." It urges European states that are implementing EHR systems to conduct "in-depth, expert civil and medical law studies and impact assessments to clarify the new liability issues likely to arise." These issues may involve the "accuracy and completeness" of EHR data, the extent to which treating physicians must study patients' EHRs, technical failures that prevent clinicians from accessing EHRs, and more.[4]

This chapter is dedicated to an exploration of the liability and litigation implications of EHR systems. These complex systems, on which physicians rely to manage so many aspects of their daily work, will influence not only clinical care but also any litigation associated with it. How this new technology might alter medical malpractice litigation is a question that is of great interest to healthcare providers and health law attorneys alike.

4.1 LIABILITY RISKS

Chapter 1 detailed the many shortcomings of contemporary EHR systems and the many problems that can arise from their use. These can include

- Data-entry errors,
- Inaccuracies caused by copying and pasting information without editing it carefully,
- Information overload,
- Difficulty navigating the EHR because of data display flaws,
- The challenges of decision support,
- Software defects,
- Computer shutdowns,
- EHR system inflexibility,
- Time constraints and EHR system demands,
- Lack of interoperability,
- Interference with the doctor–patient relationship, and
- Data security breaches.

---

[4] European Commission Article 29 Data Protection Working Party, "Working Document on the Processing of Personal Data Relating to Health in Electronic Health Records," February 15, 2007, 20; available at: http://ec.europa.eu/justice/policies/privacy/docs/wpdocs/2007/wp131_en.pdf (accessed December 6, 2015).

Given all these potential pitfalls, a natural question follows: will EHR systems make healthcare providers more vulnerable to liability claims? Surprisingly, thus far EHR systems are rarely the subject of reported medical malpractice cases. Perhaps, however, they are a bigger factor in the vast majority of cases that are not published or reported electronically or that are settled with confidentiality provisions.[5] It is also noteworthy that only a small percentage of patients who are negligently injured file medical malpractice claims (perhaps 2 to 10 percent),[6] and thus a paucity of lawsuits should not necessarily lead to an inference that EHR-related harm is uncommon. As more patients and attorneys become familiar with the technology, it is likely that litigants will increasingly focus on EHR systems in malpractice cases.

In the United States there are no laws that specifically address EHR-related liability. Consequently, attorneys will rely on traditional causes of action. The same is generally true in Europe, though a few countries, including Croatia, Finland, and Sweden, have adopted laws that explicitly treat EHR data errors and erasures.[7] The following section explores the various liability theories that are available to US litigants.

4.1.1 Clinician Negligence

Plaintiffs who feel their caregivers were negligent in treating them may assert medical malpractice claims. To prove that medical malpractice has occurred, a plaintiff must establish the four elements of negligence: (1) a duty of care owed by the defendant to the plaintiff, (2) breach of that duty through conduct that fails to meet the applicable standard of care, (3) harm or injury, and (4) a causal link between the injury and the breach of duty.[8] The standard of care in each case is determined based on an assessment of whether the defendant "proceed[ed] with such reasonable caution as a prudent man would have

[5] See A. Benjamin Spencer, *Civil Procedure: A Contemporary Approach*, 4th edn. (St. Paul, MN: West Academic Publishing, 2014), 779 (stating that only 1.2 percent of cases filed in federal court during the period March 2012 through March 2013 were resolved with trials).

[6] Christopher M. Burkle, "Medical Malpractice: Can We Rescue a Decaying System?," *Mayo Clinic Proceedings* 86, no. 4 (2011): 327–9; David A. Hyman and Charles Silver, "Medical Malpractice Litigation and Tort Reform: It's the Incentive Stupid," *Vanderbilt Law Review* 59 (2006): 1089–91.

[7] Milieu Law and Policy Consulting, *Overview of the National Laws on Electronic Health Records in the EU Member States and Their Interaction with the Provision of Cross-Border eHealth Services: Final Report and Recommendations*, Contract 2013 63 02 (Brussels, 2014), 44; available at: http://ec.europa.eu/health/ehealth/docs/laws_report_recommendations_en.pdf (accessed January 4, 2016).

[8] William Lloyd Prosser et al., eds., *Prosser and Keeton on the Law of Torts*, 5th edn. (St. Paul: West Publishing Co., 1984), 164–8.

exercised under such circumstances."[9] Thus, in medical malpractice cases, plaintiffs must prove that "the professional failed to conform to the generally recognized and accepted practices in his [or her] profession."[10] The standard of care is generally determined through expert witness testimony.[11]

4.1.1.1 Negligence Associated with Medical Treatment Mistakes

Clinicians could be sued and judged to have committed medical malpractice because of a variety of EHR-related mistakes. For example, in *K.N. v. Dr. B. Residents and Hospital*, a patient sued for complications that followed her bariatric surgery.[12] A key question in the case, which settled for $1.3 million, was whether the plaintiff's laboratory test results were present and accessible within the EHR.

Clinicians may be reassured, however, by the dearth of EHR-generated cases filed thus far. A 2012 study of 394 malpractice claims in Colorado found that none arose because of EHR systems.[13] The Doctors Company, the largest physician-owned US medical malpractice insurer, conducted a review of malpractice claims from 2007–2014 and found that only 0.9 percent (ninety-seven) were EHR related.[14] Hospitals experienced more EHR claim events than any other type of medical facility (43 percent of the EHR-related claims), and problems were attributed to technology, design, and user factors. Examples include incorrect data input, incorrect copy and paste, insufficient area for documentation in the EHR, lack of EHR training, lack of an EHR alert, alert fatigue, and more.

The Harvard-affiliated firm CRICO reviewed and analyzed 200 legal claims in which EHRs were a factor. It concluded that while EHR glitches occurred, they "rarely led directly to patient harm."[15]

---

[9] *Vaughn v. Menlove*, (1837) 132 Eng. Rep. 490, 492 (C.P.) (affirming a jury verdict for the plaintiff who was injured when a fire that began in the defendant's haystack burned down his house).

[10] *Doe v. American Red Cross Blood Serv.*, 377 S.E.2d 323, 326 (1989).

[11] Maxwell J. Mehlman, "Professional Power and the Standard of Care in Medicine," *Arizona State Law Journal* 44, no. 3 (2012): 1166, 1184–6.

[12] *K.N. v. Dr. B. Residents and Hospital*, 26 Nat. J.V.R.A. 4:3, 2010 WL 9447001 (Minn. Dist. Ct. Sep. 8, 2010) (verdict and settlement summary).

[13] Michael S. Victoroff et al., "Impact of Electronic Health Records on Malpractice Claims in a Sample of Physician Offices in Colorado: A Retrospective Cohort Study," *Journal of General Internal Medicine* 28, no. 5 (2012): 640.

[14] David B. Troxel, "Analysis of EHR Contributing Factors in Medical Professional Liability Claims," The Doctors Company; available at: www.thedoctors.com/KnowledgeCenter/Publi cations/TheDoctorsAdvocate/CON_ID_006908 (accessed August 19, 2015).

[15] Arthur Allen, "Electronic Record Errors Growing Issue in Lawsuits," *Politico*, May 4, 2015; available at: www.politico.com/story/2015/05/electronic-record-errors-growing-issue-in-law suits-117591.html (accessed August 19, 2015).

Nevertheless, healthcare providers should not be complacent. It is possible that the scarcity of cases is rooted simply in the novelty of EHR products. Many providers did not adopt EHR systems until after 2010,[16] and plaintiffs' lawyers may still not be accustomed to investigating whether EHRs played some part in the alleged poor treatment outcome. Moreover, cases can take five or six years to be fully litigated, so many of those that are now in process will not come to light for some time.[17]

4.1.1.2 Managing Online Communication with Patients

SECURE MESSAGING. EHR systems allow patients to communicate with physicians through secure messaging, which is less vulnerable to privacy breaches than ordinary e-mail. Such electronic communication can increase clinicians' accessibility and patients' perception that their doctors are responsive to them. It also can promote convenience and efficiency by reducing the need for telephone calls and ambulatory care visits. In many instances, online contact can enhance the clinician–patient relationship and improve patients' engagement, trust, and satisfaction.[18]

Nevertheless, online messaging creates new liability concerns because its mishandling can lead to patient harm and, ultimately, to litigation.[19] A patient, for example, might send a message to her doctor stating that she is experiencing chest pain, expecting an immediate response. If she hears nothing from the physician, she might wrongly assume that the doctor does not think that the pain is serious and does not want her to go to the emergency room. If the patient is in fact having a heart attack, her reliance on electronic communication and misplaced faith that her doctor is checking it constantly

---

[16] See Introduction.

[17] Allen, "Electronic Record Errors Growing Issue in Lawsuits."

[18] Yi Yvonne Zhou et al., "Patient Access to an Electronic Health Record with Secure Messaging: Impact on Primary Care Utilization," *American Journal of Managed Care* 13, no. 7 (2007): 424 (concluding that patients using electronic messaging had 6.7 to 9.7 percent fewer outpatient primary care visits than others); Kim M. Nazi, "The Personal Health Record Paradox: Health Care Professionals' Perspectives and the Information Ecology of Personal Health Record Systems in Organizational and Clinical Settings," *Journal of Medical Internet Research* 15, no. 4 (2013): e70; J. Herman Blake et al., "The Patient-Surgeon Relationship in the Cyber Era: Communication and Information," *Thoracic Surgery Clinics* 22, no. 4 (2012): 532–3.

[19] Madhavi R. Patt et al., "Doctors Who Are Using E-Mail with Their Patients: A Qualitative Exploration," *Journal of Medical Internet Research* 5, no. 2 (2003): e9 (stating that doctors are concerned about e-mails reaching them in a timely fashion); Paul Rosen and C. Kent Kwoh, "Patient-Physician E-Mail: An Opportunity to Transform Pediatric Health Care Delivery," *Pediatrics* 120, no. 4 (2007): 705 (stating that e-mail communication might produce anxiety about increased liability). While these articles address regular e-mail use, the same concerns apply to secure messaging.

might have catastrophic consequences. Clinicians who do not educate patients about proper and improper secure messaging use or do not have a qualified staff member read messages frequently, thus might face malpractice claims.

Doctors who encourage patients to use secure messaging but fail to respond to electronic communication may be more likely to be sued than doctors who do not enable its use at all. Multiple studies have shown that patients most often decide to sue when they are displeased with the quality of the physician–patient relationship, including their communication experiences.[20]

No reported medical malpractice case involving secure messaging or even regular e-mail could be found as of 2015. However, doctors have been sued for failure to respond appropriately to phone calls.[21] It is only a matter of time before similar claims involving electronic messages will arise.

PERSONAL HEALTH RECORDS. Many EHR systems offer personal health records (PHRs) that enable patients to view part of their medical records.[22] In some cases, PHRs, which are also called "patient portals," are tethered to the EHR system and are automatically populated with information, including problem lists, allergies, laboratory test results, appointment schedules, and more. Patients may also be allowed to enter information into the PHR, such as results of blood sugar tests, blood pressure checks, or other procedures that they conduct on their own at home.[23] In other cases, the PHR is not tethered to the EHR system, so all information is self-entered by the patient or drawn from sources such as laboratories, pharmacies, or insurers, with the patient's permission.[24]

Studies of patients in the United States and the United Kingdom show that they are often enthusiastic about PHRs. PHRs can enhance patients' access to their data and help them to feel more empowered in their relationship with healthcare providers.[25]

[20] Beth Huntington and Nettie Kuhn, "Communication Gaffes: A Root Cause of Malpractice Claims," *Baylor University Medical Center Proceedings* 16, no. 2 (2003): 157–60.

[21] *Kaznowski v. Biesen-Bradley*, No. C063872, 2012 WL 5984491 (Cal. Ct. App. Nov. 30, 2012); *Lemlek v. Israel*, 161 A.D.2d 299, 301 (1990), modified, 577 N.E.2d 1041 (1991).

[22] See Chapter 1.

[23] Taya Irizarry et al., "Patient Portals and Patient Engagement: A State of the Science Review," *Journal of Medical Internet Research* 17, no. 6 (2015): e148.

[24] Ibid.; N. Archer et al., "Personal Health Records: A Scoping Review," *Journal of the American Medical Informatics Association* 18, no. 4 (2011): 515.

[25] Simon de Lusignan et al., "Patients' Online Access to Their Electronic Health Records and Linked Online Services: A Systematic Interpretative Review," *BMJ Open* 4, no. 9 (2014): e006021; Kim M. Nazi et al., "Evaluating Patient Access to Electronic Health Records: Results from a Survey of Veterans," *Medical Care* 51, no. 3 (Suppl. 1) (2013): S52–6.

Clinicians, for their part, approach PHRs with different philosophies. Some believe that all health information belongs to the patient and should be released as soon as possible, even if it is bad news.[26] Indeed, a patient who can digest bad news and formulate appropriate questions before seeing her doctor might have a less emotional and much more productive discussion during the office visit.

Other clinicians worry that access to certain information might have adverse consequences for the physician–patient relationship. For example, patients who learn of abnormal test results or serious diagnoses by logging onto the computer at home rather than through a conversation with a clinician could be traumatized, misunderstand their diagnoses, or feel angry or hopeless.[27] Such patients might be too frightened to pursue appropriate medical care, become discouraged and stop complying with their treatment protocols, and suffer clinical setbacks. Similarly, if providers share candid psychiatric problem lists and complete progress notes, including personal impressions, with patients, patients could become less cooperative or trusting of their doctors.[28] They may also become less candid with their doctors and withhold certain types of information. Doctors' behavior may itself be influenced by the fact that patients can see their notes. They may write their assessments with their audience in mind and compose more guarded, "watered down" notes than they otherwise would.[29]

Information that is entered by patients themselves may raise additional concerns about accuracy. Patients may misunderstand instructions regarding data entry, measure values incorrectly, or have confusion or dementia that affects their ability to work with PHRs. Physicians who rely on self-entered information must keep these possibilities in mind.

Physicians' PHR policies and data disclosure practices can have wide-ranging impacts on the physician–patient relationship and the quality of documentation, which, in turn, can raise liability concerns. These policies therefore require careful thought.[30]

---

[26] Sarah A. Collins et al., "Policies for Patient Access to Clinical Data via PHRs: Current State and Recommendations," *Journal of the American Medical Informatics Association* 18 (Suppl. 1) (2011): i2, i5.

[27] Ellen M. Friedman, "You've Got Mail" *JAMA* 315, no. 21 (2016): 2275–6.

[28] John Halamka, Kenneth D. Mandl, and Paul C. Tang, "Early Experiences with Personal Health Records" *Journal of the American Medical Informatics Association* 15 (2008): 3–5.

[29] Jan Walker et al., "The Road toward Fully Transparent Medical Records," *New England Journal of Medicine* 370, no. 1 (2014): 6–8.

[30] Joanne Callen et al., "Emergency Physicians' Views of Direct Notification of Laboratory and Radiology Results to Patients Using the Internet: A Multisite Survey," *Journal of Medical Internet Research* 17, no. 3 (2015): e60; Traber Davis Giardina et al., "Releasing Test Results

4.1.2 *Healthcare Entities' Liability: Corporate Negligence and Vicarious Liability*

Hospitals, clinics, and other healthcare organizations with EHR systems might be sued for corporate negligence.[31] Healthcare organizations can be held liable for failing to safeguard their patients' safety and welfare.[32] Hospitals have the following four duties:

> (1) a duty to use reasonable care in the maintenance of safe and adequate facilities and equipment; (2) a duty to select and retain only competent physicians; (3) a duty to oversee all persons who practice medicine within ... [their] walls ... and (4) a duty to formulate, adopt and enforce adequate rules and policies to ensure quality care for the patients.[33]

In establishing a prima facie case of corporate negligence, plaintiffs must show that (1) the hospital deviated from the standard of care, (2) the hospital has actual or constructive knowledge of the flaws or procedures that caused the injury, and (3) a causal link between the conduct and the harm exists.[34]

Organizations can also be liable for the actions of their employees through the vicarious liability theory of *respondeat superior*. The doctrine of *respondeat superior*, literally, "let the superior answer," establishes that employers are responsible for the wrongful acts of their employees committed within the scope of their employment.[35] Thus hospitals may be held liable for inappropriate EHR system use by nurses, residents, interns, and other health professionals. In many instances, physicians are considered independent contractors rather than employees, and this status shields hospitals from liability for their acts.[36] Nevertheless, courts have found that a hospital's imposition of workplace rules and regulations

---

Directly to Patients: A Multisite Survey of Physician Perspectives," *Patient Education and Counseling* 98, no. 6 (2015): 788–96.

[31] *Darling* v. *Charleston Community Mem'l Hosp.*, 211 N.E.2d 253 (Ill. 1965) (recognizing a cause of action for corporate negligence).

[32] *Thompson* v. *Nason Hosp.*, 591 A.2d 703, 707 (Pa. 1991).

[33] *Ibid.*

[34] *Rauch* v. *Mike-Mayer*, 783 A.2d 815, 827 (Pa. Super. 2001).

[35] Bryan A. Garner et al., eds., *Black's Law Dictionary*, 10th edn. (St. Paul, MN: Thomson West, 2014), 1505

[36] See, e.g., *Kashistan* v. *Port*, 481 N.W.2d 277, 280 (Wis. 1992) (holding that even though a physician was a member of the hospital's staff and was required to comply with hospital policies, no master–servant relationship existed); *Albain* v. *Fowler Hosp.*, 553 N.E.2d 1038, 1044 (Ohio 1990) (finding that the physician's staff privileges did not make the hospital vulnerable to *respondeat superior* liability for his actions).

on staff physicians is enough to undercut the doctors' independent contractor status and expose the hospital to liability.[37]

Hospitals and other healthcare entities have indeed been subject to claims involving EHR systems. In one case, a physician hand wrote a potassium prescription for a dialysis patient with an unclear dosage amount. The pharmacist and nurses administered a fatal dose of 120 millimoles rather than the intended 20 millimoles. The catastrophic error would have been avoided had the clinicians heeded the EHR system's alert that the dosage needed to be confirmed. The hospital entered into a confidential settlement before trial. The physician proceeded to trial, and the jury assigned him 10 percent of the fault, with a verdict of almost $38,000.[38]

In another case, a patient in a residential care facility received a daily dose of methotrexate for rheumatoid arthritis rather than a weekly dose because of the pharmacy's computer software error. The overdose was fatal, and the facility settled for $1.5 million.[39]

4.1.3 EHR Vendor Liability

Very few EHR vendors have been sued thus far. Nevertheless, analysts predict that this trend will change with time as the technology becomes more established and plaintiffs' lawyers become more accustomed to considering EHR problems in constructing their liability theories.[40] In fact, it is possible that in the future EHR vendors will routinely be added as defendants to medical malpractice lawsuits. EHR systems are involved in numerous aspects of patient care, and their use will often be integral to the story of how a physician handled the case in question. Attorneys may posit that fault lies not only with the healthcare providers but also with the technology they used, and they may well consider vendors to be deep pockets who will add to the settlement value of the case.

---

[37] *Mduba v. Benedictine Hosp.*, 384 N.Y.S.2d 527, 529 (App. Div. 1976) (finding that a physician was a hospital employee rather than an independent contractor because the hospital controlled the way he operated its emergency room). See generally Martin C. McWilliams, Jr., and Hamilton E. Russell, III, "Hospital Liability for Torts of Independent Contractor Physicians," *South Carolina Law Review* 47 (1996): 431–74.

[38] *Martha G. Garcia, Judith Rocha, et al. v. Baptist Health System, d/b/a VHS San Antonio Partners L.P. d/b/a Northeast Baptist Hospital and Flavio Alvarez MD*, 2012-CI-10242, 2013 Jury Verdicts LEXIS 13176 (Bexar County District Court, TX, Oct. 3, 2013) (verdict summary). The verdict against the physician was originally $379,122.39 but was reduced by the court to $37,912.24.

[39] *Plaintiff Estate of Patient Doe v. Defendant Medical Facility*, 30 N.Eng. J.V.R.A. 7:2, 1000 WL 184840 (Unknown State Ct. Mass.) (verdict and settlement summary).

[40] Allen, "Electronic Record Errors Growing Issue in Lawsuits."

Inclusion of EHR vendors as defendants will make cases more complex and expensive. Furthermore, proving technical failures might be very difficult and require highly skilled experts. Experts might need to be capable of detecting defects that involve only one line of code among many thousands.[41] Hiring such individuals may be financially out of reach for many parties.

4.1.3.1 Litigation Theories

CONTRACT THEORIES. At least one large case has already been filed against a vendor, and it has garnered considerable attention. It is a class action brought by the Pain Clinic of Northwest Florida in late 2012 against Allscripts Healthcare Solutions, which was still in the midst of litigation in 2015.[42] Allscripts sold an EHR product called "MyWay" in 2009 to approximately 5,000 physicians in small practices throughout the United States who implemented it at a cost of $40,000 per doctor. When MyWay proved to be defective, Allscripts withdrew it from the market in 2012 and offered "free upgrades" to its customers. In truth, what the company offered was the "Professional Suite Electronic Health Records System" with completely different software that was not a good fit for small practices. It was also more complex and expensive to maintain, and its adoption required considerable staff training and effort.[43]

The plaintiffs alleged breach of warranty and unjust enrichment. Plaintiffs can prevail on a breach of warranty claim by showing that (1) they received an express or implied warranty for the product, (2) the product was defective when it left the defendant's control, and (3) the defect proximately caused their damages, though the specific elements of proof vary from state to state.[44] The unjust enrichment claim was asserted because purchasers paid Allscripts money for MyWay, Allscripts retained and benefited from that money, and the company failed to deliver a quality product to the doctors.[45]

Other contract lawsuits have been filed against vendors as well. As early as 2007, a dermatology practice sued an EHR vendor after experiencing numerous problems with the product it purchased. The plaintiff alleged breach of contract, breach of warranty, fraud in the inducement, negligent

---

[41] Sharona Hoffman and Andy Podgurski, "Finding a Cure: The Case for Regulation and Oversight of Electronic Health Record Systems," *Harvard Journal of Law & Technology* 22, no. 1 (2008): 125.

[42] *Allscripts v. Pain Clinic of Northwest Florida, Inc.*, 158 So.3d 644 (3rd D. Ct. App. Fl. 2014).

[43] Ibid., 645; *Pain Clinic of Northwest FL, Inc. v. Allscripts Healthcare Solutions, Inc.*, No. 12-49371CA40 (Fla. Cir. Ct. 11th Cir. Dec. 20, 2012), class action complaint, filed Dec. 20, 2012.

[44] See UCC Art. 2, §§ 2-314 and 2-315.

[45] See *Pain Clinic of Northwest FL, Inc.*, class action complaint.

misrepresentation, unjust enrichment, and violation of the Connecticut Unfair Trade Practices Act, though it ultimately lost the case on appeal.[46]

More recently, in 2014, an obstetrics and gynecology practice sued its EHR system vendor, claiming that the system "supplied incorrect diagnostic and procedure codes on automatically generated insurance billings, randomly deleted treatment notes, and assigned patient charts randomly to the wrong files."[47] It asserted a variety of theories, among which were fraud, misrepresentation, breach of warranty, and breach of contract. These cases may not be isolated. Given the volume of physicians' complaints about their EHR systems, vendors may find themselves increasingly embroiled in litigation brought by dissatisfied customers.

CLAIMS FOR DESIGN, MANUFACTURING, AND INFORMATION DEFECTS. The contract-based causes of action are available only to purchasers of a product, in this case, healthcare providers who bought EHR systems. Other claims against EHR vendors are also available to providers and, in some cases, to patients as well.[48] Plaintiffs can assert product liability claims for three different types of defects: (1) manufacturing defects, (2) design defects, and (3) information defects.[49]

Manufacturing defect cases are strict liability claims. "Strict liability" means that a defendant can be held liable without proof of fault, negligence, or ill intent as long as the product is in fact defective.[50] A plaintiff will prevail on a manufacturing defect claim if he can establish that the product is not consistent with the manufacturer's own specifications. In these cases, the product's design is not problematic, but some of the products were allegedly manufactured with flaws. Plaintiffs also have to establish a causal link between the defects and their injuries.[51]

Plaintiffs bring design defect cases when they believe that there is an inherent flaw in the design of the product at issue. Patients have been allowed to sue manufacturers of surgical equipment for design defects even though they did not purchase or use the devices themselves but rather were allegedly

---

[46] *Western Dermatology Consultants, P.C. v. VitalWorks, Inc.*, 146 Conn. App. 169 (2013).

[47] *East Bay Women's Health, Inc. v. Glostream, Inc.*, No. 14–11586, 2015 WL 71830 (E.D. MI 2015, Jan. 6, 2015).

[48] David C. Vladeck, "Machines without Principals: Liability Rules and Artificial Intelligence," *Washington Law Review* 89, no. 1 (2014): 132.

[49] *Ibid.*, 127.

[50] American Law Institute, *Restatement of the Law Second Torts* (Philadelphia: American Law Institute, 1979), § 402A.

[51] *Greenman v. Yuba Power Prods., Inc.*, 377 P.2d 897 (Cal. 1963); American Law Institute, *Restatement of the Law Third Torts*, § 2(a).

affected by their flaws when the equipment was used during surgery.[52] By analogy, patients should be able to sue EHR system vendors for defective design if they believe that the design flaw caused them harm.

Design defects can be proven in one of two ways. In some jurisdictions, an "unreasonably dangerous" defect is one "dangerous to an extent beyond that which would be contemplated by the ordinary consumer who purchases it, with the ordinary knowledge common to the community as to its characteristics."[53] In other jurisdictions, plaintiffs have the more challenging burden of showing that "the foreseeable risks of harm posed by the product could have been reduced by the adoption of a reasonable alternative design."[54]

The third type of defect, informational defects, could be alleged if a vendor neglects to provide users with adequate warnings or instructions about an EHR system's proper use, and this failure leads to harm. Courts are particularly receptive to "duty to train" arguments when the product is sophisticated and complex, as in the case of airplanes.[55] Consequently, plaintiffs may be able to construct compelling arguments regarding vendors' responsibility to provide thorough training and warnings with respect to EHR systems, which are likewise very complicated.

Unlike design and manufacturing defect claims, information defect claims most probably can be brought only by clinicians and not by patients because of the "learned intermediary doctrine." This doctrine was developed to apply to the pharmaceutical industry and has been extended to medical devices such as pacemakers. It provides that manufacturers have a duty to warn physicians regarding the foreseeable risks of a product and provide instructions as to its proper use. If they do so, though, they do not have a further duty to provide warnings to patients.[56] The doctrine's rationale is that physicians, as highly trained and skilled professionals, are in the best position to weigh the benefits and risks of the product for the particular patient and determine whether it should be used. Although EHR systems are not traditional medical devices, the doctrine may well extend to them. Physicians will likely be deemed to be

---

[52] *Vincent v. C.R. Bard, Inc.*, 944 So.2d 1083 (2007); *Schmutz v. Bolles*, 800 P.2d 1307, 1316–17 (Colo. 1990).

[53] *Ibid.*

[54] American Law Institute, ed., *Restatement of the Law Third Torts: Products Liability* (Philadelphia: American Law Institute, 1998), § 2(b); Vladeck, "Machines without Principals," 135.

[55] Vladeck, "Machines without Principals," 140; *Driver v. Burlington Aviation, Inc.*, 430 S.E.2d 476 (N.C. Ct. App. 1993).

[56] *Reyes v. Wyeth Labs.*, 498 F.2d 1264, 1276 (5th Cir. 1974); *Hill v. Searle Lab*, 884 F.2d 1064 (8th Cir. 1989); Thomas R. McLean, "Cybersurgery – An Argument for Enterprise Liability," *Journal of Legal Medicine* 23, no. 2 (2002): 184.

learned intermediaries with respect to EHR systems because patients do not themselves operate the technology.

4.1.3.2 Hold Harmless Clauses

One explanation for the dearth of cases against EHR vendors is that many vendor contracts reportedly include "hold harmless clauses."[57] As the name suggests, these provisions establish that buyers cannot attempt to hold vendors liable for harm to patients no matter what role the EHR system played in the incident in question.[58] If healthcare providers sign contracts containing such provisions at the time of purchase, they must abide by the contract and refrain from suing their EHR vendors.

4.1.3.3 Preemption Concerns

As detailed in Chapter 2, EHR systems undergo a certification process that is overseen by the federal government's Office of the National Coordinator for Health Information Technology (ONC). Potential plaintiffs might be concerned that certification will preempt product liability claims because a certified EHR system will essentially have the government's stamp of approval.[59]

This, however, should not be the case. First, ONC's certification regulations do not explicitly provide that they intend to preempt state law product liability claims. Second, preemption is not implied by the regulatory structure.

The ONC-mandated certification process is of very limited duration and extent. It is designed primarily to verify that EHR systems have particular functions rather than to guarantee that the systems are safe and effective for clinical use.[60] Precedent involving the Food and Drug Administration's

---

[57] Ross Koppel and David Kreda, "Health Care Information Technology Vendors' 'Hold Harmless' Clause," *Journal of the American Medical Association* 301, no. 12 (2009): 1276–8; Institute of Medicine, *Health IT and Patient Safety: Building Safer Systems for Better Care* (Washington, DC: National Academies Press, 2012), 3, 37.

[58] Heather L. Farley et al., "Quality and Safety Implications of Emergency Department Information Systems," *Annals of Emergency Medicine* 62, no. 4 (2013): 399.

[59] Federal preemption doctrine is based in the Supremacy Clause of Article VI of the US Constitution, under which federal laws and regulations override state law. Preemption may be either expressly stated in the text of a law or implied by its structure or purpose. *Jones* v. *Rath Packing Co.*, 430 US 519, 525 (1977). Federal law overrides state law when "(1) Congress expressly preempts state law; (2) Congressional intent to preempt may be inferred from the existence of a pervasive federal regulatory scheme; or (3) State law conflicts with federal law or its purposes." James T. O'Reilly and Katharine A. Van Tassel, *Food and Drug Administration*, 4th edn. (New York: Thomson Reuters, 2015), § 25:5.

[60] See Chapter 2.

(FDA's) approval of medical devices suggests that such a process will not preempt state law claims.

The FDA applies different levels of scrutiny to different classes of devices in different circumstances. The most thorough form of review is premarket approval of Class III devices, which support or sustain human life or pose significant risks.[61] The Supreme Court has held that only this very rigorous premarket approval process has preemptive effect.[62] By extension, the courts should hold that the far less robust EHR system certification process does not preempt design, manufacturing, and information defect claims.

4.1.4 *Privacy Breaches*

Nearly every state now recognizes a cause of action for unauthorized disclosure of private medical data. Many states have passed statutes that specifically provide relief for privacy disclosures.[63] Other states recognize a common-law privacy tort for unauthorized disclosure of medical data.[64] In a third group of states, courts have interpreted state constitutional provisions as establishing an actionable right to privacy of medical data.[65]

---

[61] 21 USCA § 360c(a)(1)(C) (2010).

[62] *Medtronic, Inc.* v. *Lohr*, 518 US 470, 477–9 (1996); *Riegel* v. *Medtronic, Inc.*, 552 US 312, 317–19 (2008).

[63] Ariz. Rev. Stat. Ann. § 12-2292(A) (2005); Ariz. Rev. Stat. Ann. § 36-509 (2015) (limited to mental health–related disclosures); Cal. Civ. Code § 56.35–6 (West 2015); Del. Code Ann. Title 16, § 1208 (West 2012); 410 Ill. Comp. Stat. Ann. 50/3 § 3(d) (2015); Ind. Code Ann. § 16-39-5-3 (West 2015); Me. Rev. Stat. tit. 22, § 1711-C (2014); Md. Code Ann., Health-Gen. § 4-309 (West 2015); Mass. Gen. Laws Ann. ch. 214, § 1B (West 2015); Mass. Gen. Laws Ann. ch. 111, § 70E (West 2015); Minn. Stat. Ann. § 144.298 (West 2015); Mont. Code Ann. § 50-16-553 (West 2015) *amended by* Mont. Laws 2009, ch. 56, § 1827 (2009); N.H. Rev. Stat. Ann. § 151:30 (West 2015); N.J. Stat. Ann. § 26:2H-12.8 (West 2012); N.Y. Pub. Health Law § 18(i) (McKinney 2010); N.D. Cent. Code Ann. § 23-16-09 (West 2015); N.D. Cent. Code Ann. § 23-16-11 (West 2015); Okla. Stat. Ann. Title 63, § 1-502.2(H) (West 2015); Okla. Stat. Ann. Title 36, § 6804(D) (West 2015); Or. Rev. Stat. Ann. § 192.558 (West 2015) *amended by* Laws 2015, c. 473, § 5, eff. June 18, 2015; Or. Rev. Stat. Ann. § 192.571 (West); R.I. Gen. Laws Ann. § 5-37.3–4 (West 2015); S.C. Code Ann. § 44-115-40; Tenn. Code Ann. § 68-11-1504 (West 2015); Tex. Health & Safety Code Ann. § 241.156 (Vernon 2015); Tex. Occ. Code Ann. § 159.009 (Vernon 2015); Vt. Stat. Ann. tit. 18, § 1852 (West 2015); Va. Code Ann. § 32.1–127.1:03 (West 2015); Wash. Rev. Code Ann. § 70.02.170 (West 2015); W. Va. Code Ann. § 33-25A-26 (West 2015); W. Va. Code Ann. § 33-25A-23(6) (West 2015); Wis. Stat. Ann. § 146.84 (West 2015); Wyo. Stat. Ann. § 35-2-616 (West 2015).

[64] See *Weld* v. *CVS Pharmacy, Inc.*, No. CIV. A. 98-0897F, 1999 WL 494114, *3–4 (Mass. Super. Ct. June 29, 1999) (denying the defendant's motion for summary judgment on a pharmacy customer's privacy and confidentiality claims); *Anonymous* v. *CVS Corp.*, 728 N.Y.S.2d 333, 337 (N.Y. Sup. Ct. 2001) (denying a motion to dismiss a common-law claim against a pharmacy that sold an HIV patient's prescription information to a chain drug store without the patient's knowledge or consent), aff'd 739 N.Y.S.2d 565, 565 (N.Y. App. Div. 2002).

[65] *Manela* v. *Superior Court*, 99 Cal. Rptr. 3d 736, 744 (Cal. Ct. App. 2009) (recognizing a constitutional right to privacy in medical records in California); *McEnany I Ryan*, 44 So. 3d

State statutory provisions may provide causes of action that are general, limited to specific types of medical providers, limited to particular conditions, or applicable to certain types of medical data. For example, California allows plaintiffs to sue anyone who negligently releases confidential medical information.[66] By contrast, a West Virginia statute authorizes litigation only against health maintenance organizations (HMOs).[67] As a third example, a Delaware privacy statute applies only to genetic information.[68] States often have numerous different laws that address medical privacy concerns,[69] so attorneys must be diligent in researching state privacy statutes.

Patients can also sue clinicians for privacy breaches under a variety of common-law theories. For example, plaintiffs may assert negligence, breach of contract or implied contract, and infliction of emotional distress.[70] Among the most relevant litigation theories are the torts of invasion of privacy and breach of confidentiality discussed in Chapter 3. Most courts have found that in order to support an invasion of privacy claim, plaintiffs must prove widespread dissemination of personal information to the public and have deemed this tort theory to fit mostly cases involving publication through the media.[71]

245, 247 (Fla. Dist. Ct. App. 2010) (citing *State* v. *Johnson*, 814 So. 2d 390, 393 [Fla. 2002]); *Ussery* v. *Children's Healthcare of Atlanta, Inc.*, 656 S.E.2d 882, 894-5 (Ga. Ct. App. 2008) (recognizing that personal medical records are protected by a Georgia constitutional right to privacy); *Brende* v. *Hara*, 153 P.3d 1109, 1115 (Haw. 2007) (recognizing a privacy right within the Hawaiian state constitution protecting the privacy of highly personal and intimate information contained within medical records); *T.L.S.* v. *Mont. Advocacy Program*, 144 P.3d 818, 824 (Mont. 2006) (recognizing Montana's constitutional right to privacy that protects patients' medical histories).

[66] Cal. Civ. Code § 56.35–6 (West 2015).

[67] W. Va. Code Ann. § 33-25A-26 (West 2015).

[68] Del. Code Ann. Title 16, § 1208 (West 2012) (limited to an individual's genetic information).

[69] "Public Health Departments and State Patient Confidentiality Laws Map," LawAtlas; available at: http://lawatlas.org/preview?dataset=public-health-departments-and-state-patient-confidentiality-laws (accessed August 20, 2015).

[70] Bernadette M. Broccolo and Edward G. Zacharias, "US Privacy and Security Compliance Enforcement in the Health Care Industry: Recent Developments and Trends," *BNA's Health Law Reporter* 24, no. 25 (2015): 805.

[71] Peter A. Winn, "Confidentiality in Cyberspace: The HIPAA Privacy Rules and the Common Law," *Rutgers Law Journal* 33 (2002): 653. See *Satterfield* v. *Lockheed Missiles and Space Co.*, 617 F. Supp. 1359, 1369 (S.C. 1985) (stating that "[c]ommunication to a single individual or to a small group of people" will not support liability under a theory of public disclosure of private facts, which requires publicity rather than publication to a small group of people); *Beard* v. *Akzona, Inc.*, 517 F. Supp. 128, 132 (E.D. Tenn. 1981) (emphasizing that publication to a small number of people will not create liability); *Tollefson* v. *Price*, 430 P.2d 990, 992 (Ore. 1967) (stating that public disclosure occurs only when the information is communicated to the public generally or to a large number of people); *Vogel* v. *W. T. Grant Co.*, 327 A.2d 133, 137 (Pa. 1974) (explaining that the tort is established only if disclosure is made to the public at large or the information is certain to become public knowledge); *Swinton Creek Nursery* v. *Edisto Farm Credit*, 514 S.E.2d 126, 131 (S.C. 1999) (stating that "publicity, as opposed to mere publication, is

The tort of breach of confidentiality also applies only in limited circumstances. Generally, it can be established only when the perpetrator and the
victim of the breach of confidentiality had a direct relationship, such as when
physicians themselves improperly disclose information.[72] Consequently, a
breach of confidentiality cause of action could not be brought in cases of
hacking, theft, or other instances in which the data were not disclosed by a
treating clinician.

4.2 IMPACT ON DISCOVERY

"Discovery" is the phase in litigation in which parties request and obtain
information from one another.[73] Discovery generally includes extensive document production requests. Although it has not yet generated a significant
proliferation of lawsuits, the transition from paper records to EHRs has had
a dramatic impact on medical malpractice litigation. EHRs may bestow
unprecedented amounts of information on litigants, but at the same time,
they can create new discovery obstacles.

4.2.1 *Potential Discovery Advantages*

EHR systems may facilitate discovery of the truth in litigation. Ideally, EHRs
will constitute a complete and comprehensive record of the patient's medical
history, with all information about the patient available from one source. In
the past, physicians jotted down notes or dictated notes to be typed up by
secretaries. How detailed these notes would be was left to the discretion of the
individual doctor. Today's EHR systems, however, demand extensive data
input. If anything, clinicians complain that the records are too lengthy and
even repetitive and thus are cumbersome to navigate.[74] However, exhaustive
documentation, as long as it is accurate, will be of great benefit for purposes of
litigation.

---

what is required to give rise to a cause of action for this branch of invasion of privacy"); Daniel
Solove, *The Digital Person: Technology and Privacy in the Information Age* (New York: New
York University Press, 2006), 60 (explaining that this tort "appears to be designed to redress
excesses of the press").

[72] Solove, *The Digital Person*, 662; *Humphers v. First Interstate Bank*, 696 P.2d 527, 530 (Or. 1985)
(finding that a mother who had given her daughter up for adoption had a cause of action for
breach of confidentiality against a doctor who helped her daughter discover her mother's
identity and explaining that "only one who holds the information in confidence can be charged
with a breach of confidence").

[73] Spencer, *Civil Procedure*, 653.

[74] See Chapter 1.

EHR systems contain not only clinical data but also metadata. "Metadata" are "data about data."[75] According to the *Sedona Conference Glossary*, "Metadata can describe how, when and by whom [information] ... was collected, created, accessed, modified and how it is formatted."[76] Metadata provide details about the content, context, and structure of records. A type of metadata called "audit trails" are particularly useful for discovery. They can show who viewed EHRs, where, for how long, and whether they made any changes to the documentation.[77] All this information can be illuminating and even critical for plaintiffs and defendants alike in medical malpractice cases.[78]

To illustrate, audit trails could reveal whether or not a physician who claimed to have read the results of a diagnostic test actually viewed the report. Metadata have been critical in litigation. In one lawsuit, EHR metadata showed that an anesthesiologist wrote a "postoperative note" stating that the procedure was uncomplicated just minutes after the surgery began and that there was a ninety-minute gap in the log of administered anesthetic gas. Sadly, the patient was rendered a quadriplegic by the operation, and not surprisingly, the anesthesiologist settled the case.[79]

With interoperability,[80] medical records will not be fragmented among different physicians' offices and hospitals but rather could be accessed in their entirety by anyone with proper authorization. Attorneys will no longer have to look at boxes upon boxes of paper documents collected from a multitude of sources. They will need to turn to only one record: the EHR.

Advanced search capabilities may further ease the burdens of discovery. Rather than culling through thousands of printed pages, attorneys, using well-crafted queries, may be able to find the details they seek in computerized records within minutes.

---

[75] Bruce Schneier, *Data and Goliath: The Hidden Battles to Collect Your Data and Control Your World* (New York: W.W. Norton, 2015).

[76] Sherry B. Harris, Paul H. McVoy, and RFP+ Vendor Panel, eds., *The Sedona Conference Glossary: E-Discovery and Digital Information Management*, 3rd edn. (Sedona, AZ: Sedona Conference, 2010), 34; available at: https://thesedonaconference.org/publication/The%20Sed ona%20Conference%C2%AE%20Glossary (accessed August 20, 2015).

[77] Mary Beth Haugen et al., "Rules for Handling and Maintaining Metadata in the EHR," *Journal of AHIMA* 85, no. 5 (2013); available at: http://library.ahima.org/xpedio/groups/public/docu ments/ahima/bok1_050177.hcsp?dDocName=bok1_050177 (accessed August 20, 2015); Danette McGilvray, "Quick References: Definitions of Data Categories," in *Executing Data Quality Projects: Ten Steps to Quality Data and Trusted Information (TM)* (Burlington, MA: Morgan Kaufmann, 2008), 293.

[78] Amalia R. Miller and Catherine E. Tucker, "Electronic Discovery and the Adoption of Information Technology," *Journal of Law, Economics, and Organization* 30, no. 2 (2012): 225.

[79] Thomas R. McLean, "EMR Metadata Uses and E-Discovery," *Annals of Health Law* 18, no. 1 (2009): 117.

[80] See Chapter 2 for a discussion of interoperability.

4.2.2 *Discovery Difficulties*

Reviewing an EHR may nevertheless be far more challenging than reviewing a paper medical record. EHRs are ever evolving. They can be updated by numerous people at numerous times in many places. Therefore, attorneys reviewing EHRs may be uncertain as to whether they have received the complete EHR, when and by whom information was entered, and how the data can be authenticated.[81]

EHRs may be produced in a variety of forms. These include printouts created through a printing function that is built into the system, screenshots, flash drives, or CD-ROMS.[82] These formats, however, do not provide attorneys with access to the many clickable fields that are featured in actual EHRs. For example, printouts do not enable attorneys to click on hyperlinks that lead to other, related parts of the record.[83]

If EHRs are produced without metadata, disputes about authenticity and credibility are likely to arise. Paper records often contain telltale signs of alteration, such as erasure marks, whiteout, and different ink colors. However, a printout or CD-ROM image file of an EHR would divulge no evidence of whether data had been altered or whether clinicians were truthful in their documentation.[84]

The case of *Karam v. Adirondack Neurosurgical Specialists, P.C.*[85] illustrates how EHR technology can complicate discovery. It involved a controversy relating to the time at which a particular nurse's note about the patient's worsening symptoms was entered into the EHR. While the EHR indicated that it had been typed at 11:23 a.m., the emergency room physician testified that he believed that the note had been made at 12:35 p.m. His explanation for why the EHR indicated otherwise was that at times it appeared "as if there were gremlins in [the] computer system."[86] Defendants' attempt to introduce EHR metadata as evidence to support its contention regarding the note's timing was opposed by plaintiff's counsel and denied by the court as "unfair

---

[81] Paul DeMuro and Nick Healey, "Emerging Healthcare Information Technologies and the Legal Challenges They Present," *Wyoming Lawyer* 36 (2013): 24–6.

[82] Jeffrey L. Masor, "Electronic Medical Records and E-Discovery: With New Technology Come New Challenges," *Hastings Science and Technology Law Journal* 5, no. 2 (2013): 245, 250; McLean, "EMR Metadata Uses and E-Discovery," 116–17.

[83] Masor, "Electronic Medical Records and E-Discovery," 251.

[84] McLean, "EMR Metadata Uses and E-Discovery," 116–17; Barbara Drury, Reed Gelzer, and Patricia Trites, "Electronic Health Records Systems: Testing the Limits of Digital Records' Reliability and Trust," *Ave Maria Law Review* 12, no. 2 (2014): 273–4.

[85] *Karam v. Adirondack Neurosurgical Specialists, P.C.*, 93 A.D.3d 1260 (4th Dep't), *reargument denied*, 96 A.D.3d 1513 (4th Dept.), *leave to appeal denied*, 19 N.Y.3d 812 (2012).

[86] *Ibid.*, 1261.

surprise" and "trial by ambush." Anecdotally, courts often do not understand the importance of metadata and deny requests for them, accepting defense counsels' arguments that plaintiffs have all they need once they receive copies of the patient's medical record.

Attorneys will need to recognize that audit trails and other metadata can themselves be deceptive or inaccurate. For example, if a nurse took a patient's temperature at 9:00 a.m. but did not enter the data until 9:30 a.m., the time stamp of 9:30 would be misleading. In addition, one nurse may begin a task with a patient and then be called away so that another nurse must take over. If only the second nurse documents the task in the EHR, the record will be incomplete because it will not indicate who began performing the activity. Furthermore, an audit trail will indicate only the name of the person who entered documentation and will not disclose that other clinicians were in the room at the time, even though their presence could be important for purposes of litigation.[87] Even the terminology present in metadata can be ambiguous. For example, the term "accepted" can mean that an order is pending, filed, shared, or formally accepted by a clinician, and thus a reader may not be able to understand the actual status of the order.[88]

An added complication is the absence of a legal mandate that healthcare providers maintain audit trails. A 2013 report issued by the Department of Health and Human Services found that while almost all hospitals' EHR systems had audit functions, many facilities did not use them to their full extent.[89] Specifically, 44 percent of hospitals studied reported that they could delete their audit logs, 33 percent could disable the audit function, and 11 percent could edit audit logs. Furthermore, the length of time for which audit logs were stored varied widely among hospitals. Therefore, some healthcare providers simply may not have audit trail information to disclose in discovery.

EHR discovery is an area of litigation that is still underdeveloped. In the future, the medical, legal, and vendor communities will need to solve the conundrum of how to produce EHRs during discovery so that plaintiffs' attorneys receive all the information they need but at the same time, EHR system security and other patients' privacy are not compromised.

---

[87] Masor, "Electronic Medical Records and E-Discovery," 251.

[88] *Ibid.*, 255.

[89] Department of Health and Human Services, Office of Inspector, "Not All Recommended Fraud Safeguards Have Been Implemented in Hospital EHR Technology," OEI-01-11-00570 (Dec. 2013); available st: http://oig.hhs.gov/oei/reports/oei-01-11-00570.pdf (accessed August 20, 2015).

4.3 RECOMMENDATIONS

Although healthcare providers have rarely been sued for poor treatment outcomes that are associated with EHR system use, EHR-related liability risks abound. These will diminish only when the technology improves and clinicians can more easily and effectively use their systems. The path ahead may be long and difficult. A 2015 survey found that in the United States, only 52 percent of primary care physicians reported that they are very satisfied or satisfied with their EHR systems.[90]

Clearly, medical and nursing schools and pharmacy degree programs must incorporate EHR system training into their curricula.[91] Training should include actual simulation work so that clinicians become comfortable with the technology, skilled in its use, and sophisticated in determining when to trust and distrust it.[92]

Furthermore, professional associations, government regulators, and healthcare providers should work together to advance EHR technology and respond to liability concerns. Improvements can be achieved through federal regulations, clinical practice guidelines, and creative thinking. A vast literature concerning EHR system problems outlines numerous recommendations, and these cannot all be covered in these pages. Instead, I highlight a sample of promising approaches and develop a number of proposals in three key areas: technology, workplace policy, and regulation.

4.3.1 *Improving Technology*

4.3.1.1 AMA Framework

As a step toward addressing EHR-related concerns, in 2014 the American Medical Association (AMA) released a framework of eight priorities for improving EHR system usability.[93] They are

- Enhance physicians' ability to provide high-quality patient care,
- Support team-based care,

[90] Robin Osborn et al., "Primary Care Physicians in Ten Countries Report Challenges Caring for Patients with Complex Health Needs," *Health Affairs* 34, no. 12 (2015): 2104–12.

[91] Natalie M. Pageler, Charles P. Friedman, and Christopher A. Longhurst, "Refocusing Medical Education in the EMR Era," *Journal of the American Medical Association* 310, no. 21 (2013): 2249.

[92] Robert Wachter, *The Digital Doctor: Hope, Hype, and Harm at the Dawn of Medicine's Computer Age* (New York: McGraw Hill Education, 2015), 270.

[93] "AMA Calls for Design Overhaul of Electronic Health Records to Improve Usability," American Medical Association, September 16, 2014; available at: www.ama-assn.org/ama/pub/news/news/2014/2014-09-16-solutions-to-ehr-systems.page (accessed August 20, 2015).

- Promote care coordination,
- Offer product modularity and configurability,
- Reduce cognitive workload,
- Promote data liquidity,[94]
- Facilitate digital and mobile patient engagement, and
- Expedite user input into product design and postimplementation feedback.

Although these are quite general and do not furnish implementation details, they constitute a sound set of priorities for improving EHR capabilities.

4.3.1.2 Automation

Advances in technology are likely to enhance data accuracy and completeness. Some medical devices that collect patient data could automatically transmit measurements to EHRs without requiring human intermediaries who might mistype information or make other mistakes. Examples are devices that measure vital signs, such as blood pressure, pulse, oxygen rates, and temperature.[95] In addition, high-quality voice-recognition software could reduce the risk of typos and allow users to operate systems more quickly and more safely.[96]

EHRs could further be programmed to generate alerts if implausible or clearly erroneous data are entered.[97] In one study focusing on height and weight measures, researchers had the EHR alert clinicians if they entered figures that deviated by 10 percent or more from height and weight measurements that were previously recorded. Thus, for example, if a patient's weight was recorded as being 150 pounds in one visit and 190 pounds three months later, a message would ask the clinician to check the two entries because it is unlikely that the patient gained forty pounds in such a short period of time.

---

[94] Data are "liquid" when they can move digitally through the healthcare system securely and in a usable format. Thus "the right data is provided to the right person at the right time." Paul T. Courtney, "Data Liquidity in Health Information Systems," *Cancer Journal* 17 no. 4 (2011): 219.

[95] "Partners Healthcare and Center for Connected Health Launch Personal Health Technology Platform to Improve Care," Partners Healthcare, June 20, 2013; available at: http://connected health.partners.org/news-and-events/media-center/announcements/2013/center-for-connec ted-health-launch-personal-health-tech-platform-to-improve-care.aspx (accessed August 20, 2015).

[96] Robert Hoyt and Ann Yoshihashi, "Lessons Learned from Implementation of Voice Recognition for Documentation in the Military Electronic Health Record System," *Perspectives in Health Information Management* 7 (2010): 1e.

[97] Krystl Haerian et al., "Use of Clinical Alerting to Improve the Collection of Clinical Research Data," *AMIA Annual Symposium Proceedings* 2009 (2009): 219–20.

The researchers observed that after the alerts were implemented, EHR error rates fell from 2.4 to 0.9 percent.

4.3.1.3 Decision Support

Decision support should be tailored to particular medical practices to the extent possible. Alerts and reminders should be eliminated if they are not relevant to the specific specialty or patient population.

Alerts should appear in different colors, fonts, or formats depending on their significance. A warning that the clinician is about to administer an excessive dose of a medication that could lead to life-threatening consequences should look very different from an alert that a particular drug causes a mild rash in some people.

4.3.2 *Workforce Policies and Solutions*

4.3.2.1 Data Audits

Healthcare providers should routinely conduct data audits of a random sample of records to assess the accuracy and error rates of EHRs.[98] Data in EHRs, such as diagnoses or treatments, can be substantiated by inspecting source documentation from laboratories or pharmacies, or they can be cross-checked against insurance claims. Experts advise that data audits focus on the following five questions:

1. Are the data complete?
2. Are the data correct?
3. Are there data inconsistencies or contradictions between different elements of the EHR or between the EHR and other source material (e.g., insurance claims)?
4. Does information seem implausible in light of other data about the patient or general scientific knowledge?
5. Is information current (e.g., was it copied and pasted without proper updating)?[99]

Auditors who find that data are incomplete, clearly erroneous, inconsistent, implausible, or outdated can follow up with physicians and require

---

[98] Stephany N. Duda et al., "Measuring the Quality of Observational Study Data in an International HIV Research Network," *PlosOne* 7, no. 4 (2012): e33908.

[99] Nicole Gray Weiskopf and Chunhua Weng, "Methods and Dimensions of Electronic Health Record Data Quality Assessment: Enabling Reuse for Clinical Research," *Journal of the American Medical Association* 20, no. 1 (2013): 145.

explanations and, where appropriate, corrections. If the error rate is high, employees should be required to undergo additional training, and the provider should investigate whether there is a correctable flaw in its EHR system. An additional benefit of audits is their deterrent effect: clinicians who believe they are likely to be audited may be more cautious about EHR data entry.

4.3.2.2 Scribes

One approach that is favored by some clinicians is the use of scribes.[100] Scribes shadow physicians and do the work of entering data into the EHR while the doctor examines the patient. Thus documentation is accomplished by a professional who is devoting all of her attention to the data-entry task.[101] Scribes, who reportedly numbered approximately 10,000 in early 2014, can be hired through companies such as PhysAssist and ScribeAmerica, which provide them with pre-employment training.[102]

Attaching scribes to the medical team, however, may raise its own concerns. Scribes will learn sensitive information about patients and will have to be trusted to maintain confidentiality. In addition, incompetent or careless scribes could add errors to EHRs rather than reduce their frequency. Finally, scribes require salaries, and medical practices must be willing to absorb the cost of hiring them. Nevertheless, many physicians have found that scribes significantly improve their work quality and, consequently, job satisfaction.[103]

4.3.2.3 AMA Guidance Regarding E-Mail

The AMA has issued guidance concerning physicians' use of e-mail, which also applies to secure messaging.[104] In Opinion 5.026, it advises the following:

---

[100] Katie Hafner, "A Busy Doctor's Right Hand, Ever Ready to Type," *New York Times*, January 12, 2014, D1; Scott A. Shipman and Christine A. Sinsky, "Expanding Primary Care Capacity by Reducing Waste and Improving the Efficiency of Care," *Health Affairs* 32, no. 11 (2013): 1993.
[101] Hafner, "A Busy Doctor's Right Hand, Ever Ready to Type."
[102] PhysAssist Scribes; available at: www.iamscribe.com/index.php (accessed August 20, 2015); ScribeAmerica, accessed August 20, 2015, https://www.scribeamerica.com/.
[103] Hafner, "A Busy Doctor's Right Hand, Ever Ready to Type"; Tait D. Shanafelt et al., "Relationship between Clerical Burden and Characteristics of the Electronic Environment with Physician Burnout and Professional Satisfaction," *Mayo Clinic Proceedings* 91, no. 7 (2016): 836, 845.
[104] American Medical Association, "AMA Code of Medical Ethics: Opinion 5.026 – The Use of Electronic Mail"; available at: www.ama-assn.org/ama/pub/physician-resources/medical-eth ics/code-medical-ethics/opinion5026.page (accessed August 20, 2015).

1. The physician–patient relationship should not be established through e-mail communication.
2. Physicians have the same ethical obligations to patients when communicating by e-mail as they do when communicating in person or by phone.
3. Physicians should inform patients of the limitations of e-mail, including privacy risks and likely delays in responding to e-mail.
4. Physicians should obtain patients' consent to communicating by e-mail in light of these limitations.

All these recommendations are sound, and physicians would be wise to embrace them.

4.3.2.4 Decision Support Policies

Decision support will likely raise very interesting questions in litigation. Will complying with decision support prompts constitute a defense for clinicians? Will courts accept an "I was just following orders" (albeit from a computer) defense? Will adhering to alerts and reminders concerning dosage and other matters come to be considered professional custom and the standard of care? The answer will likely depend at least in part on the degree to which regulating authorities oversee clinical decision support and ensure its quality.

At the same time, it is likely that proof that a physician overrode or ignored an alert will constitute powerful evidence of wrongdoing for plaintiffs who claim to be injured by a mistake that could have been avoided through attention to decision support.[105] It would be prudent for healthcare institutions, therefore, to develop guidance concerning the handling of decision support. At the very least, physicians should be very careful to document why they overrode a prompt if doing so could potentially be questioned by patients or their attorneys.

4.3.2.5 PHR Policies

Healthcare providers should develop thoughtful data release policies for their PHRs. Some organizations entirely exclude certain types of information, such as HIV results and psychiatric notes, from PHRs. Others withhold sensitive information for a time in order to allow clinicians to review the information and communicate in person with patients about it. Still others

---

[105] Pat Iyer, "Electronic Medical Records and Lawsuits," part 1, *Medical-Legal Topics*, September 29, 2014; available at: www.medleague.com/blog/2014/09/29/electronic-medical-records-and-lawsuits-part-1/ (accessed August 20, 2015).

release information as soon as it becomes available.[106] The decision to release or withhold information may be left to individual physicians, or there may be an authorized decision maker or committee that establishes institution-wide policies. Thus far no approach has been empirically shown to be superior to others. However, communication is a key component of the physician–patient relationship. How and when diagnoses, test results, and notes are disclosed to patients are serious matters that deserve careful attention.[107]

4.3.2.6 Encouraging Patient Involvement

Healthcare providers should encourage patients to review their records, identify errors, and request corrections. Patients may be able to access their records through PHRs, but even without a PHR, they have a legal right to see their medical records. The Health Insurance Portability and Accountability Act (HIPAA) Privacy Rule furnishes patients with a right to inspect or obtain copies of their records and to request amendments if they detect mistakes.[108] In order to balance patients' rights and providers' needs, the rule allows healthcare providers to charge "reasonable, cost-based" fees for copies of records[109] and to deny requests for amendment on valid grounds, such as a determination that no mistake exists.[110] In addition, providers need only note the amendment once and then supply a link to the amendment's location in other parts of the record that are affected by the change.[111]

European patients have similar rights. The Council of Europe's Recommendation No. R (97) 5 on the Protection of Medical Data provides that all individuals are entitled to access their medical data and to request that inaccurate information be corrected, and many European countries have implemented this right.[112]

Patients could be allowed to submit error reports through their EHR systems' secure messaging feature or through a dedicated website. For their

[106] Sarah A. Collins et al., "Policies for Patient Access to Clinical Data via PHR," 15.
[107] Michael A. Bruno et al., "The 'Open Letter': Radiologists' Reports in the Era of Patient Web Portals," *Journal of the American College of Radiology* 11, no. 9 (2014): 863.
[108] 45 CFR §§ 164.524–6 (2015).
[109] 45 CFR § 164.524(c)(4) (2015).
[110] 45 CFR § 164.526(a)(2) (2015).
[111] 45 CFR § 164.526(c)(1) (2015).
[112] Council of Europe, Recommendation No. R (97) 5 of the Committee of Ministers to Member States on the Protection of Medical Data, Strasbourg, February 13, 1997, 8.1, 8.3; available at: https://wcd.coe.int/ViewDoc.jsp?id=407311&Site=CM&BackColorInternet=C3C3C3&Back ColorIntranet=EDB021&BackColorLogged=F5D383 (accessed December 6, 2015); World Health Organization, "Legal Frameworks for eHealth," *Global Observatory for eHealth Series* 5 (2012): 58; available at: http://apps.who.int/iris/bitstream/10665/44807/1/9789241503143 _eng.pdf (accessed January 7, 2016).

part, clinicians should be obligated to read all error notices, assess them, and make corrections if the patient has in fact found a mistake.[113]

This practice could be lifesaving. For example, if an EHR fails to indicate a prior cancer history, doctors may neglect to conduct appropriate follow-up. A patient who alerts his doctor to the error thus could avoid catastrophic consequences.

Currently, physicians rarely receive requests for amendment.[114] However, if patients more regularly scrutinize their records and ask for corrections, they could add an important layer of data quality oversight without overburdening their physicians. Improved data quality, in turn, could reduce providers' liability exposure.

4.3.3 *Regulatory Interventions*

Another critical component of efforts to enhance EHR data quality is federal regulation. While many in today's political climate are loath to impose regulatory constraints on the free market, regulatory interventions have long been customary in the very complex and critically important realm of health-care. Good data quality can be considered a "positive externality" because those responsible for it, namely, vendors and clinicians, do not reap all the benefits of high EHR quality.[115] Rather, third parties such as patients, insurers, researchers, and others have much to gain from data accuracy and comprehensiveness as well. Because the public's interest is at stake, the government is justified in intervening to induce those who produce and use EHR systems to meet high quality standards. In addition, because the federal government covers over 30 percent of American patients through Medicare, Medicaid, and the Children's Health Insurance Program,[116] it has a direct interest in ensuring that providers do not submit erroneous claims. The federal government could pursue at least two well-established regulatory avenues to address

---

[113] In some cases, patients will be wrong about the existence of an error, and thus clinicians must scrutinize error reports before changing EHR entries.

[114] David A. Hanauer, "Patient-Initiated Electronic Health Record Amendment Requests," *Journal of the American Medical Informatics Association* 21, no. 6 (2014): 992–1000 (finding that "[a]mong all of the patients requesting a copy of their chart, only a very small percentage [~0.2 percent] submitted an amendment request").

[115] Abigail McWilliams, Donald S. Siegel, and Patrick M. Wright., "Guest Editors' Introduction, Corporate Social Responsibility: Strategic Implications," *Journal of Management Studies* 43 (2006): 9 (defining "externality" as "the impact of an economic agent's actions on the well-being of a bystander" and citing innovation as an example of a positive externality because of its general social benefits).

[116] Henry J. Kaiser Family Foundation, "Health Insurance Coverage of the Total Population, 2013"; available at: http://kff.org/other/state-indicator/total-population/ (accessed August 21, 2015).

data quality problems: the "meaningful use" regulations and the HIPAA Security Rule.

4.3.3.1 The Meaningful Use Regulations and Certification Criteria

The meaningful use and certification regulations, discussed in Chapter 2, constitute a good first step toward quality control. However, they do not provide detailed instructions regarding the safety of EHR systems. For example, they provide no guidance regarding copy and paste practices or overruling decision support. In the future, the Centers for Medicare and Medicaid Services (CMS) should continue to develop regulations and guidance that will not only articulate the functions that EHR technology should feature but also help to maximize its benefits and effectiveness and minimize its risks.[117]

4.3.3.2 The HIPAA Privacy and Security Rules

Several provisions of the HIPAA Privacy and Security Rules could serve as additional tools to improve data quality. As already noted, the HIPAA Privacy Rule empowers patients to review their EHRs and to request corrections if they detect errors.[118] In addition, the HIPAA Security Rule's "General Requirements" section states that covered entities bear responsibility for ensuring "the confidentiality, integrity, and availability" of electronic health information that they create, receive, maintain, or transmit.[119] The term "integrity" should be interpreted broadly to include data quality.

The Department of Health and Human Services' Office of Civil Rights (OCR) is authorized to investigate complaints of HIPAA violations filed by complaining parties and to initiate its own investigations as well.[120] To that end, OCR has launched an audit program.[121] The issue of data quality should be among OCR's areas of focus during audits, and the agency should require covered entities to demonstrate that they have implemented measures to verify

---

[117] Department of Health and Human Services, Office of Inspector, "Not All Recommended Fraud Safeguards Have Been Implemented in Hospital EHR Technology," 16.

[118] 45 CFR §§ 164.524–6 (2015).

[119] 45 CFR § 164.306(a)(1) (2015).

[120] 45 CFR §§ 160.306–8 (2015); US Department of Health and Human Services, "How OCR Enforces the HIPAA Privacy and Security Rules"; available at: www.hhs.gov/ocr/privacy/hipaa/enforcement/process/howocrenforces.html (accessed August 20, 2015).

[121] US Department of Health and Human Services, "Audit Program Protocol": available at; www.hhs.gov/ocr/privacy/hipaa/enforcement/audit/protocol.html (accessed August 20, 2015); Patrick Ouellette, "OCR Readies Pre-Audit Survey for HIPAA Covered Entities, BAs," *HealthIT Security*, February 25, 2015; available at: http://healthitsecurity.com/2014/02/25/ocr-readies-pre-aud it-survey-for-hipaa-covered-entities-bas/ (accessed August 20, 2015).

and improve data quality. It should also investigate complaints of pervasive EHR inaccuracies and require covered entities to take corrective action.

Ensuring patients' access to their records and patients' ability to have mistakes corrected in their EHRs should also be enforcement priorities for OCR. OCR indicates that patients' lack of access to their health information is the third most frequently investigated complaint, and in 2015, the Obama administration issued guidelines designed to make it more difficult for providers to refuse patients' requests for their records.[122] Failure to amend records in response to legitimate requests for correction is not listed among the top five complaints, but it is not clear if this is so because providers generally comply with the requests or because patients do not submit such requests frequently. As patients become more educated about EHRs and their HIPAA rights, requests for access and amendments may well increase. The federal government should do its part by making HIPAA enforcement an important component of the data quality enhancement toolkit.

4.3.4 *Discovery*

Plaintiffs should routinely be able to discover metadata. Courts have begun to recognize the importance of this information to a limited extent. In *Peterson* v. *Matlock*,[123] the plaintiff, who alleged that he was injured while in the custody of the New Jersey Department of Corrections (DOC), sought production of his EHR in "native readable format."[124] The plaintiff claimed that the PDF that the DOC produced was too difficult to navigate and understand. He also demanded production of audit trail metadata that would show modifications to the record. The court denied plaintiff's request for "native readable format" production because it would impose undue hardship on the DOC. However, it ordered that the DOC produce the metadata, to which the defendant did not object. The court also stated that the burden "rests with the party objecting to the production of metadata ... to show undue hardship or expense."[125] If, in

---

[122] US Department of Health and Human Services, "Enforcement Highlights," June 30, 2015; available at: www.hhs.gov/ocr/privacy/hipaa/enforcement/highlights/ (accessed August 20, 2015); Robert Pear, "New Guidelines Nudge Doctors on Giving Patients Access to Medical Records," *New York Times*, January 17, 2016, 14.

[123] *Peterson* v. *Matlock*, No. 11–2594, 2014 WL 5475236 (D.N.J. Oct. 29, 2014).

[124] "Native readable format" is "the way [the document] is stored and used in the normal course of business"; *Autotech Technologies Ltd. Partnership* v. *Automationdirect.com, Inc.*, 248 FRD 556, 557 (N.D. Ill. 2008). Attorneys should be able to access documents in native readable format through the software programs on which they were created. *Aguilar* v. *Immigration and Customs Enforcement Div. of US Dept. of Homeland Sec.*, 255 FRD 350, 353 n. 4 (S.D. N.Y. 2008).

[125] *Ibid.*

particular cases, disclosing metadata will be unduly costly or burdensome for the defendant, the court can order cost shifting or carefully tailor the scope of discoverable metadata in its order.

We have only begun to see the impact of EHR systems on medical malpractice litigation. So far digitization seems to make discovery somewhat more difficult, but it has neither generated a plethora of new cases nor reduced the frequency of lawsuit filings. The technology's effects on malpractice insurance are also unclear. Some insurers may have reduced rates for early EHR adopters, but overall, EHR system use does not seem to have perceptibly nudged rates either lower or higher.[126] Only time will tell exactly what the implications of the transition will be in the liability arena.

---

[126] Allen, "Electronic Record Errors Growing Issue in Lawsuits."

PART II

5

Medical Big Data and Its Benefits

The term "big data" is suddenly pervasive. The *New York Times* deemed this the "Age of Big Data" in a 2012 article,[1] and a Google search for the term yields over 50 million hits. "Big data" is difficult to define precisely, but it is characterized by three attributes known as "the three V's": its large volume, its variety, and its velocity, that is, the frequency with which it is generated.[2] Medical big data is a particularly rich but sensitive type of big data, and it holds great promise as a resource for researchers and other analysts. Numerous medical big data initiatives are being launched by public and private enterprises.

The transition from paper medical files to EHR systems has facilitated the creation of large health information databases. Computer processing of digitized records permits fast and relatively inexpensive data analysis and synthesis. These databases, therefore, can serve as invaluable research resources.[3]

This chapter is based in part on the following articles: Sharona Hoffman, "Medical Big Data and Big Data Quality Problems," *Connecticut Insurance Law Journal* 21, no. 1 (2015): 289; Sharona Hoffman and Andy Podgurski, "The Use and Misuse of Biomedical Data: Is Bigger Really Better?," *American Journal of Law & Medicine* 39, no. 4 (2013): 497; Sharona Hoffman and Andy Podgurski, "Balancing Privacy, Autonomy, and Scientific Needs in Electronic Health Records Research," *Southern Methodist University Law Review* 65, no. 1 (2012): 85.

[1] Steve Lohr, "The Age of Big Data," *New York Times*, February 11, 2012; available at: www.nytimes.com/2012/02/12/sunday-review/big-datas-impact-in-the-world.html?pagewanted=all&_r=0 (accessed August 26, 2015).

[2] Philip Russom, *TDWI Best Practices Report: Big Data Analytics* (Renton, WA: TDWI Research, 2011), 6; available at: https://tdwi.org/research/2011/09/best-practices-report-q4-big-data-analytics.aspx?tc=page0 (accessed August 27, 2015).

[3] See Abel N. Kho et al., "Electronic Medical Records for Genetic Research: Results of the eMERGE Consortium," *Science Translation Medicine* 3, no. 79 (2011): 79re1; Mark G. Weiner and Peter J. Embi, "Toward Reuse of Clinical Data for Research and Quality Improvement: The End of the Beginning?," *Annals of Internal Medicine* 151 (2009): 359–60; Charles Safran, "Toward a National Framework for the Secondary Use of Health Data: An American Medical

Medical big data can be derived from other, nontraditional sources as well. Google retains all users' web searches, including those involving medical queries. It can use the data for its own purposes, and at times, the data are requested by government and law enforcement authorities as well. Customer purchasing records, tweets, and Facebook entries can also reveal a great deal of health information.[4] Companies such as Acxiom offer to sell "demographic, behavioral, lifestyle, financial and home data" that they obtain from such sources.[5] This book, however, focuses on medical big data that is derived from electronic health records (EHRs) or from reports submitted by healthcare providers. It does not, therefore, extensively address nontraditional sources of medical big data.

Analysts can access large-scale collections of EHR data in two primary ways. First, health information can be collected into large databases and deidentified to protect patient privacy.[6] Such databases could be limited to particular hospital systems, be expanded to cover entire regions, or even be national in scope. In the alternative, researchers may use a federated system. A "federated network" can be defined as one that "links geographically and organizationally separate databases to allow a single query to pull information from multiple databases while maintaining the privacy and confidentiality of each database."[7] Thus medical institutions manage and maintain control of their own databases, but they allow researchers to submit statistical queries through a standard web service operated by a trusted third party in order to obtain summary statistics for a study population.

Many large EHR databases and federated systems already exist and are used for nontreatment purposes. The use of health information outside the clinical setting for research or other purposes is often called "secondary use."[8] This

Informatics Association White Paper," *Journal of the American Medical Informatics Association* 14 (2007): 2.

[4]   Bruce Schneier, *Data and Goliath: The Hidden Battles to Collect Your Data and Control Your World* (New York: W.W. Norton, 2015): 22–3.

[5]   Acxiom; available at: www.acxiom.com/data-solutions/ (accessed December 6, 2015).

[6]   Hoffman and Podgurski, "Balancing Privacy, Autonomy, and Scientific Needs in Electronic Health Records Research," 128–30.

[7]   Wilson D. Pace et al., *Distributed Ambulatory Research in Therapeutic Network (DARTNet): Summary Report* (Rockville, MD: Agency for Healthcare Research and Quality, July 2009); available at: www.effectivehealthcare.ahrq.gov/ehc/products/53/151/2009_0728DEcIDE_DARTNet.pdf (accessed August 27, 2015); Griffin M. Weber et al., "The Shared Health Research Information Network (SHRINE): A Prototype Federated Query Tool for Clinical Data Repositories," *Journal of the American Medical Informatics Association* 16 (2009): 624.

[8]   Taxiarchis Botsis et al., "Secondary Use of EHR: Data Quality Issues and Informatics Opportunities," *Summit on Translational Bioinformatics* 2010 (2010): 1; Jessica S. Ancker et al., "Root Causes Underlying Challenges to Secondary Use of Data," *AMIA Annual Symposium Proceedings* 2011 (2011): 57.

chapter discusses how EHR data may be used in the realms of biomedical research, quality assessment, public health, and litigation. It also describes a sample of ongoing data-collection initiatives.

5.1 CLINICAL STUDIES VS. OBSERVATIONAL RESEARCH

Before discussing the benefits of medical big data, it is important to review the way medical research has traditionally been conducted and explain the strengths and weaknesses of studies using medical record databases. This section, therefore, compares clinical trials to observational studies.

Randomized, controlled clinical trials are considered to be the gold standard for medical studies.[9] Experimental clinical studies involve "the collection of data on a process when there is some manipulation of variables that are assumed to affect the outcome of a process, keeping other variables constant as far as possible."[10] Thus investigators might design a clinical trial to include two groups to which eligible patients are randomly assigned: one group receives angiotensin-converting enzyme (ACE) inhibitors for heart failure, and the second group receives ACE inhibitors in combination with a different drug for the same condition.[11] The goal of this experimental study would be to determine which treatment is more effective, as reflected by one or more outcome measures.

By contrast, research can also be accomplished through observational studies.[12] One source defines an "observational study" as "an empiric investigation of treatments, policies, or exposures and the effects they cause, but it differs from an experiment in that the investigator cannot control the assignment of treatments to subjects."[13] Rather than conducting a controlled experiment, investigators might review the charts or electronic files of patients receiving different medications or different types of surgery to treat

---

[9] Friedrich K. Port, "Role of Observational Studies versus Clinical Trials in ESRD Research," *Kidney International* 57 (2000): S3. See also Sharona Hoffman, "The Use of Placebos in Clinical Trials: Responsible Research or Unethical Practice?," *Connecticut Law Review* 33 (2001): 452–4.

[10] Bryan F. J. Manly, *The Design and Analysis of Research Studies* (Cambridge University Press, 1992), 1.

[11] Sharona Hoffman, "'Racially-Tailored' Medicine Unraveled," *American University Law Review* 55 (2005): 400–2 (describing a clinical trial for heart failure medication).

[12] Manly, *The Design and Analysis of Research Studies*, 1 (explaining that observational studies involve the collection of data "by observing some process which may not be well-understood"); Charles P. Friedman and Jeremy C. Wyatt, *Evaluation Methods in Biomedical Informatics*, 2nd edn. (New York: Springer, 2006), 369 (defining observational studies as involving an "[a]pproach to study design that entails no experimental manipulation" in which "[i]nvestigators typically draw conclusions by carefully observing ... [subjects] with or without an information resource").

[13] Paul R. Rosenbaum, *Observational Studies*, 2nd edn. (New York: Springer, 2001), vii.

a particular condition in order to determine the efficacy of each approach.[14] Observational studies are often conducted when the Food and Drug Administration (FDA) requires postmarketing studies to verify the safety of drugs.[15]

Observational studies such as reviews of EHR data are vulnerable to several criticisms. These studies are not randomized, and the absence of randomization may introduce biases that skew results.[16] One type of bias occurs if the study population is not representative of the target population, meaning the population that is of interest to researchers conducting the particular study (e.g., women over age fifty, patients with early Parkinson's disease). For example, if investigators review only records that come from a wealthy suburban medical practice, the results derived may not apply to low-income populations with higher levels of stress, poorer diets, and inferior access to medical care. (Note that similar skewing may occur in clinical trials if the subjects are not representative of the target population.) There are, however, ways of mitigating the bias problem in creating (or extracting data from) an EHR database, such as ensuring that the database is large enough and is drawn randomly from the EHRs of a target population.

A second type of bias, known as "confounding bias," occurs if results are confounded by uncontrolled variables because the assignment of different treatments to patients is not randomized.[17] Rather, the treatment has already been given, and analysts review records of existing clinical courses. Therefore, researchers may be unaware that a variety of factors influenced both treatment choice and therapeutic outcomes, such as disease severity or coexisting illnesses. If researchers do not carefully monitor and adjust for these factors, any conclusion concerning the efficacy of the drug at issue is likely to be questionable.[18]

At the same time, observational studies have several advantages over clinical trials.[19] EHR databases could allow researchers to access vast amounts of

[14] Kjell Benson and Arthur J. Hartz, "A Comparison of Observational Studies and Randomized, Controlled Trials," *New England Journal of Medicine* 342, no. 25 (2000): 1879–83.

[15] US Department of Health and Human Services Food and Drug Administration, Center for Drug Evaluation and Research, and Center for Biologics Evaluation and Research, *Guidance for Industry Postmarketing Studies and Clinical Trials – Implementation of Section 505(o)(3) of the Federal Food, Drug, and Cosmetic Act* 7 (Rockville, MD: USDHHS, 2011); available at: www.fda.gov/downloads/Drugs/GuidanceComplianceRegulatoryInformation/Guidances/UCM172001.pdf (accessed August 28, 2015).

[16] Benson and Hartz, "A Comparison of Observational Studies and Randomized, Controlled Trials," 1878; Manly, *The Design and Analysis of Research Studies*, 4–5.

[17] Manly, *The Design and Analysis of Research Studies*, 4–5.

[18] See Chapter 7 for further discussion.

[19] Benson and Hartz, "A Comparison of Observational Studies and Randomized, Controlled Trials," 1878.

information collected over a long period of time about patients with diverse demographics.[20] The data used in observational studies may be far more comprehensive than the data generated by clinical trials, which often include fewer than 3,000 patients and last only one to four years.[21] Record-based studies can also be considerably less costly and time-consuming than experimental research because the data used already exist.[22]

If the researchers' goal is to show whether a specific treatment achieves the desired benefits, they may reasonably choose to conduct a randomized clinical trial to ensure that the study is not confounded by uncontrolled variables.[23] However, observational studies may be needed to determine whether the results of randomized clinical trials that involved only a few thousand patients can be generalized to the patient population at large and to realistic treatment situations rather than carefully controlled ones.[24] Furthermore, observational research based on medical records will often be sufficient to determine a treatment's adverse effects.[25] It is also useful for generating and testing speculative hypotheses that could lead to important insights.[26]

In some cases, it is in fact impossible to conduct clinical trials.[27] This may be because it is too difficult to recruit a large enough subject population to yield statistically significant results, such as when the condition is very rare. It may also be unethical to conduct certain clinical studies. For example, investigators could not examine the outcomes of patients who receive the

[20] Louise Liang, "The Gap between Evidence and Practice," *Health Affairs* 26 (2007): w120; Lynn M. Etheredge, "A Rapid-Learning Health System," *Health Affairs* 26 (2007): w111; James H. Ware and Mary Beth Hamel, "Pragmatic Trials – Guides to Better Patient Care?," *New England Journal of Medicine* 364, no. 18 (2011): 1685.

[21] US Department of Health and Human Services, Office of the Assistant Secretary for Planning and Evaluation, *Examination of Clinical Trial Costs and Barriers for Drug Development* (2014); available at: http://aspe.hhs.gov/report/examination-clinical-trial-costs-and-barriers-drug-development; US Food and Drug Administration, *Step 3: Clinical Research* (2015); available at: www.fda.gov/ForPatients/Approvals/Drugs/ucm405622.htm.

[22] Port, "Role of Observational Studies versus Clinical Trials in ESRD Research," s4; Benson and Hartz, "A Comparison of Observational Studies and Randomized, Controlled Trials," 1878.

[23] Jan P. Vandenbroucke, "The HRT Controversy: Observational Studies and RCTs Fall in Line," *Lancet* 373 (2009): 1234.

[24] Walter F. Stewart et al., "Bridging the Inferential Gap: The Electronic Health Record and Clinical Evidence," *Health Affairs* 26 (2007): w181; Stuart L. Silverman, "From Randomized Controlled Trials to Observational Studies," *American Journal of Medicine* 122 (2009): 114.

[25] Jan P. Vandenbroucke, "Observational Research, Randomised Trials, and Two Views of Medical Science," *PLoS Medicine* 5, no. 3 (2008): e67, 343.

[26] *Ibid.* (asserting that "[m]uch good can come from going down the wrong alley and detecting why it is wrong, or playing with a seemingly useless hypothesis; the real breakthrough might come from that experience").

[27] Benson and Hartz, "A Comparison of Observational Studies and Randomized, Controlled Trials," 1878.

wrong treatment by deliberately giving some individuals incorrect medications. By contrast, review of EHR databases could allow for a broader range of research. Investigators could gain access to patient records all over the country, including those of individuals with very rare illnesses. In addition, researchers could study data relating to actual patients who are treated in clinical settings rather than in the controlled environment of research trials and could analyze care that is of varying quality, some of which is substandard.

It is not anticipated that EHR-based observational studies will replace randomized clinical trials.[28] However, observational studies are an indispensable addition to the research toolkit.[29] In the words of one commentator, EHRs "will offer the capacity for real-time learning from the experience of tens of millions of people and will greatly increase the ability to generate and test hypotheses."[30]

5.2 THE BENEFITS OF MEDICAL BIG DATA

Large-scale EHR databases may be used for many purposes. As suggested earlier, they will surely be used extensively by medical researchers. In addition, they enable healthcare providers to conduct quality assessment and improvement activities, and they assist the FDA in monitoring the safety of drugs and devices on an ongoing basis. EHR databases can also support public health initiatives and allow litigants in tort cases to develop evidence concerning causation and harm.

5.2.1 *Scientific Discovery*

Successful observational studies may fill many existing knowledge gaps. Even today, clinicians practice medicine with an unsettling degree of uncertainty.[31] Despite the abundance of information and medical technology available in

---

[28] Etheredge, "A Rapid-Learning Health System," w108.

[29] *See* Benson and Hartz, "A Comparison of Observational Studies and Randomized, Controlled Trials," 1878, 1884 (concluding, based on a literature review, that "observational studies and randomized controlled trials usually produce similar results"); Port, "Role of Observational Studies versus Clinical Trials in ESRD Research," s5 (arguing that both observational studies and clinical studies have their place and complement each other). But see Gordon H. Guyatt et al., "Randomized Trials versus Observational Studies in Adolescent Pregnancy Prevention," *Journal of Clinical Epidemiology* 53 (2000): 173 (cautioning researchers concerning the risks of observational studies and stating that recommendations should be based on randomized trials whenever possible).

[30] Etheredge, "A Rapid-Learning Health System," w108.

[31] David A. Hyman and Charles Silver, "The Poor State of Health Care Quality in the US: Is Malpractice Liability Part of the Problem or Part of the Solution?," *Cornell Law Review* 90 (2005): 952 (observing that a "great deal of uncertainty exists about the 'best' treatment for

the twenty-first century, "more than half of medical treatments are used without sufficient proof of their effectiveness."[32] For example, experts have recently raised new questions about the efficacy of mammography, a well-established practice that was long considered lifesaving and a key element of preventive medicine.[33] Likewise, although physicians have prescribed and studied hormone-replacement therapy for postmenopausal women for many decades, experts are still unsure as to whether it is advisable or whether its risks outweigh its benefits, at least for some subgroups of patients.[34] A third illustration is a debate over the risks of a particular class of antidepressants called "selective serotonin reuptake inhibitors" (SSRIs) in light of evidence that they may induce suicidal thoughts and behavior in adolescent patients. No consensus has formed regarding this side effect, and further study is necessary. Database proponents believe that records-based research could contribute substantially to the resolution of such uncertainties.[35]

The benefits of observational studies are illustrated by the highly publicized controversy concerning an alleged association between vaccinations and autism. In 1998, Dr. Andrew J. Wakefield and colleagues published a study in the *Lancet* that suggested a link between autism and the measles, mumps, rubella (MMR) vaccination.[36] The findings were based on testing of twelve children with developmental disorders. In 2004, most of the authors "retracted the interpretation placed upon these findings in the paper"[37] after large-scale observational research involving the review of hundreds of records of autistic children in the United Kingdom found no causal association between the MMR vaccine and autism.[38]

---

particular clinical conditions, and about the 'best' way to perform these treatments" and that the "efficacy of most medical treatments has never been proven"); Stewart et al., "Bridging the Inferential Gap: The Electronic Health Record and Clinical Evidence," w181 (discussing the "inferential gap" between "the paucity of what is proved to be effective for selected groups of patients versus the infinitely complex clinical decisions required for individual patients").

[32] Eric B. Larson, "Building Trust in the Power of 'Big Data' Research to Serve the Public Good," *Journal of American Medical Association* 309 (2013): 2444.

[33] Nikola Biller-Andorno and Peter Jüni, "Abolishing Mammography Screening Programs? A View from the Swiss Medical Board," *New England Journal of Medicine* 370, no. 21 (2014): 1965–7.

[34] Herbert I. Weisberg, *Bias and Causation: Models and Judgment for Valid Comparisons* (Hoboken, NJ: Wiley, 2010), 18–21.

[35] Hoffman and Podgurski, "Balancing Privacy, Autonomy, and Scientific Needs in Electronic Health Records Research," 97–102.

[36] Andrew J. Wakefield et al., "Ileal-Lymphoid-Nodular Hyperplasia, Non-Specific Colitis, and Pervasive Developmental Disorder in Children," *Lancet* 351 (1998): 641.

[37] Simon H. Murch et al., "Retraction of an Interpretation," *Lancet* 363 (2004): 750. Dr. Wakefield did not join the retraction.

[38] Brent Taylor et al., "Autism and Measles, Mumps, and Rubella Vaccine: No Epidemiological Evidence for a Causal Association," *Lancet* 353 (1999): 2026–9.

For purposes of genetic research, EHRs can be coupled with genetic samples and data so that analysts can learn more about associations between genetic abnormalities and disease manifestations or responses to various treatments.[39] An increasingly common form of big data observational research is genome-wide association studies (GWASs).[40] GWASs compare the DNA of individuals with a particular disease or condition to the DNA of unaffected individuals in order to find the genes involved in the disease.[41] Critics have noted that although GWASs led to the discovery of many genetic variants that are statistically associated with disease, thus far most of the variants appear to have a minimal effect on disease and explain only a small percentage of heritability.[42] Others assert that many GWASs to date have been compromised by serious design flaws.[43] However, GWASs remain an important scientific endeavor and may well lead to significant discoveries in the future.

A different method of scanning the genome is genome-wide linkage studies (GWLSs). Researchers perform GWLSs when they are focusing on biologically related individuals and a phenotype, such as breast cancer, that some but not all of the family members have.[44] Based on patterns of correlation between alleles[45] and disease found within families, researchers attempt to detect broad DNA regions in which disease-susceptibility loci are most likely to be present.

The federal government and many medical experts have embraced the objective of conducting extensive comparative effectiveness research (CER).[46] The Patient Protection and Affordable Care Act of 2010 defines

[39] Isaac S. Kohane, "Using Electronic Health Records to Drive Discovery in Disease Genomics," *Nature Reviews Genetics* 12 (2011): 417.

[40] Brian D. Juran and Konstantinos N. Lazaridis, "Genomics in the Post-GWAS Era," *Seminars in Liver Disease* 31 (2011): 215; Christophe G. Lambert and Laura J. Black, "Learning from Our GWAS Mistakes: From Experimental Design to Scientific Method," *Biostatistics* 13, no. 2 (2012).

[41] National Cancer Institute at the National Institutes of Health, "Dictionary of Cancer Terms"; available at: www.cancer.gov/dictionary?cdrid=636779.

[42] Juran and Lazaridis, "Genomics in the Post-GWAS Era," 215–16; David J. Hunter, "Lessons from Genome-Wide Association Studies for Epidemiology," *Epidemiology* 23 (2012): 363.

[43] Lambert and Black, "Learning from Our GWAS Mistakes: From Experimental Design to Scientific Method," 2–3.

[44] P. A. Holmans et al., "Genomewide Linkage Scan of Schizophrenia in a Large Multicenter Pedigree Sample Using Single Nucleotide Polymorphisms," *Molecular Psychiatry* 14 (2009): 786–7.

[45] An allele "is one of two or more versions of a gene." Thus the term "allele" is used when there is "variation among genes." National Human Genome Research Institute, "Allele"; available at: www.genome.gov/glossary/?id=4 (accessed September 8, 2015).

[46] 42 USC § 1320e (2010); Institute of Medicine, *Initial National Priorities for Comparative Effectiveness Research* (Washington, DC: National Academies Press, 2009); available at: www.iom.edu/Reports/2009/ComparativeEffectivenessResearchPriorities.aspx (accessed September 8, 2015).

"CER" as "research evaluating and comparing health outcomes and the clinical effectiveness, risks, and benefits of 2 or more medical treatments, services, and items."[47] CER can be conducted in part through observational studies, which can be particularly illuminating because they reflect actual usage of treatments.[48] The outcomes of CER and other observational studies may ultimately enable the healthcare community to alleviate human suffering more effectively, reduce medical costs, and save patients' lives.[49]

5.2.2 *Quality Assessment and Improvement*

Healthcare providers routinely collect quality measures concerning the services they provide.[50] Increasingly, they will use EHR databases to obtain necessary information.[51]

Medical facilities and government authorities conduct a variety of oversight activities. Providers may seek data for internal quality-assessment purposes in order to judge the success of particular initiatives.[52] Insurers may require facilities to submit process and outcome information in the context of pay-for-performance programs.[53] In addition, the Centers for Medicare and Medicaid Services (CMS) and many state governments require quality

---

[47] 42 USC § 1320e(a)(2)(A) (2010).

[48] 42 USC § 1320e(d)(2)(A) (2010). See John Concato et al., "Observational Methods in Comparative Effectiveness Research," *American Journal of Medicine* 123, no. 12 (2010): e16; Vandenbroucke, "Observational Research, Randomised Trials, and Two Views of Medical Science," 340; S. Schneeweiss et al., "Assessing the Comparative Effectiveness of Newly Marketed Medications: Methodological Challenges and Implications for Drug Development," *Clinical Pharmacology and Therapeutics* 90, no. 6 (2011): 777.

[49] 42 USC § 1320e(d)(2)(A) (2010); L. Manchikanti et al., "Facts, Fallacies, and Politics of Comparative Effectiveness Research, Part 1: Basic Consideration," *Pain Physician* 13 (2010): E39; Adam G. Elshaug and Alan M. Garber, "How CER Could Pay for Itself – Insights from Vertebral Fracture Treatments," *New England Journal of Medicine* 364, no. 15 (2011): 1392–3.

[50] Kitty S. Chan, et al., "Electronic Health Records and the Reliability and Validity of Quality Measures: A Review of the Literature," *Medical Care Research and Review* 67, no. 5 (2010): 504.

[51] Joachim Roski and Mark McClellan, "Measuring Health Care Performance Now, Not Tomorrow: Essential Steps to Support Effective Health Reform," *Health Affairs* 3 (2011): 683; Amanda Parsons et al., "Validity of Electronic Health Record-Derived Quality Measurement for Performance Monitoring," *Journal of the American Medical Informatics Association* 19, no. 4 (2012): 609.

[52] Monica M. Horvath et al., "The DEDUCE Guided Query Tool: Providing Simplified Access to Clinical Data for Research and Quality Improvement," *Journal of Biomedical Informatics* 44, no. 2 (2011): 273.

[53] Chan et al., "Electronic Health Records and the Reliability and Validity of Quality Measures," 504; Paul C. Tang et al., "Comparison of Methodologies for Calculating Quality Measures Based on Administrative Data versus Clinical Data from an Electronic Health Record System: Implications for Performance," *Journal of the American Medical Informatics Association* 14, no. 1 (2007): 10.

measurements and public reporting.[54] A prime example is CMS's Hospital Compare, which features publicly available data about the quality of care at over 4,000 hospitals.[55]

5.2.3 *Postmarketing Surveillance of Drugs and Devices*

EHR databases could assist the FDA in regulating drugs and devices.[56] The Food and Drug Administration Amendments Act of 2007 (FDAAA) expanded the FDA's authority to monitor medical products after they have been approved and deployed in the marketplace.[57] Evidence concerning drug safety in the postmarketing period is to be developed in significant part through observational studies.[58]

Congress thus opted to supplement preapproval of clinical trials with postmarketing surveillance. Emerging evidence concerning drug safety problems may save many lives. The FDA may implement regulatory measures to manage drug risks through "risk evaluation and mitigation strategies,"[59] or it may require changes in drug labeling.[60] In cases of imminent public danger, the FDA may also withdraw or suspend its approval of the drug or ask manufacturers to remove drugs voluntarily from the market, as the agency did in 2010 in the case of the pain medication propoxyphene (Darvocet).[61]

[54] Joseph S. Ross et al., "State-Sponsored Public Reporting of Hospital Quality: Results Are Hard to Find and Lack Uniformity," *Health Affairs* 29, no. 12 (2010): 2318–19; Hanys Quality Institute, *Understanding Publicly Reported Hospital Quality Measures: Initial Steps toward Alignment, Standardization, and Value* (Rensselaer, NY: Healthcare Association of New York State, 2007), 1–3; available at: www.hanys.org/publications/upload/hanys_quality_report_card.pdf (accessed August 31, 2015).

[55] US Department of Health and Human Services, "What Is Hospital Compare?"; available at: www.hospitalcompare.hhs.gov/About/WhatIs/What-Is-HOS.aspx (accessed August 31, 2015).

[56] Barbara J. Evans, "Seven Pillars of a New Evidentiary Paradigm: The Food, Drug, and Cosmetic Act Enters the Genomic Era," *Notre Dame Law Review* 85 (2009): 479–85.

[57] Pub. L. No. 110-85, 121 Stat. 823 (codified as amended in scattered sections of 21 USC); 21 USC § 355(o)(3) (2010).

[58] 21 USC § 355(o)(3)(D) (2010); US Food and Drug Administration, "FDA's Sentinel Initiative": available at: www.fda.gov/safety/FDAsSentinelInitiative/ucm2007250.htm (accessed August 31, 2015).

[59] "Risk evaluation and mitigation strategies" are "required risk management plans that use risk minimization strategies beyond the professional labeling to ensure that the benefits of certain prescription drugs outweigh their risks." US Food and Drug Administration, "A Brief Overview of Risk Evaluation and Mitigation Strategies (REMS)"; available at: www.fda.gov/downloads/AboutFDA/Transparency/Basics/UCM328784.pdf (accessed October 23, 2015).

[60] 21 USC §§ 355(o)(4) & 355-1 (2010).

[61] 21 USC § 355(e); US Food and Drug Administration, "Xanodyne Agrees to Remove Propoxyphene from US Market," November 19, 2010; available at: www.fda.gov/NewsEvents/Newsroom/PressAnnouncements/ucm234350.htm (accessed August 31, 2015) (stating that the FDA based its request in part on a review of "postmarketing safety databases").

The need for extensive postmarketing observational studies is demonstrated by the notorious case of the nonsteroidal anti-inflammatory drug Vioxx. The FDA approved Vioxx in 1999, and it was prescribed to tens of millions of people worldwide. However, its manufacturer, Merck, withdrew it from the market sixty-five months later because of concerns that it increased patients' risk of heart attack and stroke. Researchers estimate that Vioxx caused 88,000 to 140,000 cases of serious heart disease. Professor Barbara Evans notes that if the FDA had insurance claims data from 100 million patients, including individuals who both had and had not taken the drug, the problems with Vioxx could have been identified in less than three months.[62]

5.2.4 *Public Health Initiatives*

Federal regulations and ongoing public health projects demonstrate that EHR databases will also be used to promote public health goals. As detailed in Chapter 2, healthcare providers who wish to receive government incentive payments to support EHR system implementation efforts must comply with "meaningful use" regulations that specify the EHR functions they need to be able to perform.[63] These include providing electronic information to immunization registries, cancer registries, and other state entities.[64] Public health authorities are meant to collect the submitted information in databases and use it to conduct disease surveillance and respond to public health threats.[65]

Some public health entities have already launched programs that use electronic data. Examples are programs that track information about vaccine-related adverse events, sexually transmitted diseases (STDs), and HIV/AIDS.

The Centers for Disease Control and Prevention (CDC) is collaborating with nine healthcare organizations to detect adverse events associated with vaccinations.[66] The Vaccine Safety Datalink (VSD) has access to large clinical data repositories that are linked together and provide information about

---

[62] "Up to 140,000 Heart Attacks Linked to Vioxx," *New Scientist*; available at: www.newscientist .com/article/dn6918-up-to-140000-heart-attacks-linked-to-vioxx/ (accessed January 10, 2016); Barbara J. Evans, "Seven Pillars of a New Evidentiary Paradigm: The Food, Drug, and Cosmetic Act Enters the Genomic Era," *Notre Dame Law Review* 85, no. 2 (2010): 419, 456.

[63] Leslie Lenert and David Sundwall, "Public Health Surveillance and Meaningful Use Regulations: A Crisis of Opportunity," *American Journal of Public Health* 102, no. 3 (2012): e1.

[64] 45 CFR §§ 170.205(c)–(d) (2015).

[65] Lenert and Sundwall, "Public Health Surveillance and Meaningful Use Regulations," e1–e2.

[66] Centers for Disease Control and Prevention, "Vaccine Safety Datalink"; available at: www.cdc .gov/vaccinesafety/Activities/VSD.html (accessed August 31, 2015).

almost 2.5 percent of the US population. Information garnered by the VSD could potentially lead to changes in state vaccination laws.[67]

New York City implemented an EHR system in 2004–5 for its ten Department of Health and Mental Hygiene public clinics that treat patients with STDs. The EHRs have enabled the department to analyze the city's clinical services.[68] Several evaluations led the city to alter its policies in order to increase opportunities for STD testing and access to care.

The Louisiana Public Health Information Exchange (LaPHIE) links state-wide public health surveillance information with individual EHR data.[69] LaPHIE alerts clinicians when an HIV-positive patient who has not received HIV care for over twelve months presents at any healthcare facility for any reason so that providers may pursue HIV care for that patient. Such information exchange networks can constitute a valuable tool for combating infectious disease and assist states in fulfilling their public health responsibilities.[70]

5.2.5 *Litigation*

If databases of deidentified EHR information become publicly available for nonclinical purposes, litigants who seek to prove causation or harm in mass tort cases may mine them for evidence. Thus plaintiffs may attempt to prove that a particular product caused certain illnesses. Defendants, for their part, may try to prove that the illness at issue was caused by a different company's product or not by any product at all.

Epidemiological evidence has already been used by litigants in many mass tort cases, such as those alleging harm from "asbestos, Bendectin, electromagnetic radiation, IUDs [intrauterine devices], silicone implants, and tobacco products."[71] Epidemiological data are most often employed with respect to causation, and it is not unusual for the courts to accept them as persuasive.[72]

[67] See Centers for Disease Control and Prevention, "State Vaccination Requirements"; available at: www.cdc.gov/vaccines/imz-managers/laws/state-reqs.html (accessed August 31, 2015); National Vaccine Information Center, "State Law and Vaccine Requirements"; available at: www.nvic.org/vaccine-laws/state-vaccine-requirements.aspx (accessed August 31, 2015).

[68] Rachel Paneth-Pollak et al., "Using STD Electronic Medical Record Data to Drive Public Health Program Decisions in New York City," *American Journal of Public Health* 100, no. 4 (2010): 586.

[69] Jane Herwehe et al., "Implementation of an Innovative, Integrated Electronic Medical Record (EMR) and Public Health Information Exchange for HIV/AIDS," *Journal of the American Medical Informatics Association* 19, no. 3 (2012): 448.

[70] *Ibid.*, 452. Louisiana has developed similar alerts for tuberculosis patients in need of follow-up care.

[71] David L. Faigman et al., *Modern Scientific Evidence: Standards, Statistics, and Research Methods*, Student edn. (Eagan, MN: Thomson West, 2008), 339–40.

[72] *Ibid.*, 341; *Norris v. Baxter Healthcare Corp.*, 397 F.ed 878, 882 (10th Cir. 2005).

In the future, epidemiological evidence may frequently be developed from observational studies based on EHR databases.

While plaintiffs will attempt to prove causation through database analyses, defendants may use the same tool to undermine plaintiffs' claims of causation. For example, defense counsel could argue that plaintiffs' illnesses are linked to genetic factors rather than to the defendants' products.[73] Researchers have found that genetic variants influence conditions that are often at the center of legal disputes. Genetic variants may increase individuals' likelihood of being heavy smokers,[74] of developing lung cancer or chronic obstructive pulmonary disease,[75] and of suffering from carpal tunnel syndrome.[76] Commentators predict that defendants will increasingly attempt to defeat plaintiffs' allegations by arguing that "the genes did it."[77]

The Burlington Northern and Santa Fe Railway Company attempted to use this approach as early as 2002.[78] When several employees claimed that they suffered from carpal tunnel syndrome (CTS) caused by their work, Burlington Northern required them to provide a blood sample that would be tested for a genetic marker believed to be associated with CTS. The case, brought by the

---

[73] See *Bowen v. E.I. Du Pont De Nemours and Co.*, No. Civ. A. 97C-06-194 CH, 2005 WL 1952859, at *4 (Del. Super. Ct. 2005).

[74] Nancy L. Saccone et al., "Multiple Independent Loci at Chromosome 15q25.1 Affect Smoking Quantity: A Meta-Analysis and Comparison with Lung Cancer and COPD," *PLos Genetics* 6, no. 8 (2010): e1001053; Thorgeir E. Thorgeirsson et al., "Sequence Variants at CHRNB3-CHRNA6 and CYP2A6 Affect Smoking Behavior," *Nature Genetics* 42 (2010): 448.

[75] Saccone et al., "Multiple Independent Loci at Chromosome 15q25.1 Affect Smoking Quantity"; Thorgeirsson et al., "Sequence Variants at CHRNB3-CHRNA6 and CYP2A6 Affect Smoking Behavior," 448; Paul Brennan et al., "Genetics of Lung-Cancer Susceptibility," *Lancet Oncology* 12, no. 4 (2011): 402–3; Peter Broderick, "Deciphering the Impact of Common Genetic Variation on Lung Cancer Risk: A Genome-Wide Association Study," *Cancer Research* 69, no. 16 (2009): 6633; Michael H. Cho, "A Genome-Wide Association Study of COPD Identifies a Susceptibility Locus on Chromosome 19q13," *Human Molecular Genetics* 21, no. 4 (2012): 948–9.

[76] Alan J. Hakim et al., "The Genetic Contribution to Carpal Tunnel Syndrome in Women: A Twin Study," *Arthritis & Rheumatism* 47, no. 3 (2002): 277; Santiago Lozano-Calderon, "The Quality and Strength of Evidence for Etiology: Example of Carpal Tunnel Syndrome," *Journal of Hand Surgery* 33, no. 4 (2008): 532–3.

[77] Steve C. Gold, "The More We Know, the Less Intelligent We Are? – How Genomic Information Should, and Should Not, Change Toxic Tort Causation Doctrine," *Harvard Environmental Law Review* 34 (2010): 412; Diane E. Hoffman and Karen H. Rothenberg, "Judging Genes: Implications of the Second Generation of Genetic Tests in the Courtroom," *Maryland Law Review* 66 (2007): 867; Gary E. Marchant, "Genetic Data in Toxic Tort Litigation," *Journal of Law and Policy* 14 (2006): 8; Susan Poulter, "Genetic Testing in Toxic Injury Litigation: The Path to Scientific Certainty or Blind Alley?," *Jurimetrics* 41, no. 2 (2001): 217–20.

[78] *E.E.O.C. v. Burlington Northern and Santa Fe Ry.Co.*, No. 02-C-0456, 2002 WL 32155386 (E.D. Wis. May 8, 2002).

US Equal Employment Opportunity Commission, settled without trial, and Burlington Northern agreed to halt the testing. Likewise, the Cytokine Institute claimed it had developed a proprietary genetic microarray test that "relies on no less than 22,000 DNA-based parameters" to determine whether benzene caused a worker's cancer. The test was apparently used in several worker's compensation cases alleging harm due to benzene exposure.[79] In addition, a study of tobacco manufacturers' defenses in personal injury cases brought by smokers with cancer revealed that in at least one case, *Mehlman v. Philip Morris, Inc.*, a manufacturer cited "heredity" as one of the factors that caused the plaintiff's cancer.[80] A jury found against the plaintiff in 2001.[81]

It is also possible that self-appointed watchdogs will mine public databases to determine whether exposure to particular products or substances results in adverse health consequences. Based on their findings, they could publicize supposed problems, demand government intervention, or encourage lawyers to recruit plaintiffs and initiate litigation.

5.3 ONGOING INITIATIVES TO CREATE EHR DATABASES

The federal government has clearly recognized the usefulness of EHR databases and enthusiastically supports database projects. In 2012, the Obama administration announced an overarching effort called the "Big Data Research and Development Initiative" ("Big Data").[82] The initiative's purposes are to advance cutting-edge technologies needed to gather and process "huge quantities of data"; employ those technologies to promote scientific discovery, improved national security, and education; and expand the workforce skilled in these technologies. Big Data will involve six federal agencies

---

[79] Gary E. Marchant, "The Use and Misuse of Genetic Data," *American Bar Association SciTech Lawyer* 10, no. 1 (2013): 8, 10.

[80] Sharon Milberger et al., "Tobacco Manufacturers' Defense against Plaintiffs' Claims of Cancer Causation: Throwing Mud at the Wall and Hoping Some of It Will Stick," *Tobacco Control* 15 (Suppl. 4) (2006): iv22. The case was *Myron a. Mehlman* v. *Philip Morris, Inc. et al.*, No. L-1141-99 (Sup. Ct. N.J. filed Feb. 4, 1999); available at: http://legacy.library.ucsf.edu/tid/ekz52doo/pdf (accessed August 27, 2015).

[81] *Ibid.*, iv20; Stephen D. Sugarman, "Tobacco Litigation Update (revised as of November 5, 2001): Prepared for the Robert Wood Johnson Foundation's SAPRP Conference," 2; available at: www.law.berkeley.edu/sugarman/tobacco_litigation_upate_october_2001_.doc (accessed August 27, 2015). The decedent, plaintiff's wife, had stopped smoking thirty years before her death.

[82] Office of Science and Technology Policy, Executive Office of the President, "Obama Administration Unveils 'Big Data' Initiative: Announces $200 Million in New R&D Investments," March 29, 2012; available at: www.whitehouse.gov/sites/default/files/microsites/ostp/big_data_press_release_final_2.pdf (accessed August 28, 2015).

and departments and is estimated to cost $200 million.[83] Three years later, in 2015, President Obama announced a $215 million project, the "Precision Medicine Initiative." A key component of the initiative is creation of a "voluntary national research cohort" of patients who will contribute their medical records and other data.[84]

At the same time, many federal entities are independently building health information databases. For example, the Department of Veterans Affairs (VA) is registering volunteers for its "Million Veteran Program" to construct a large research framework that will link "anonymized" blood samples to health information.[85] The VA plans to study how genes affect health and disease.

CMS created a research database called the "Chronic Condition Data Warehouse." This database provides researchers with information about Medicare and Medicaid beneficiaries, claims for services, and assessment data.[86]

In May 2008, the FDA launched the "Sentinel System" to facilitate post-marketing surveillance and early detection of medical products' safety problems.[87] The Sentinel initiative, which began with a pilot project called the "Mini-Sentinel,"[88] aims to enable the FDA to access health information from nearly 180 million individuals.[89] Sentinel is a federated system that allows the FDA to send queries concerning potential product safety problems to data holders, such as Medicare, the VA, and major medical centers. Using special analysis programs, the data holders assess their records and send summary responses to the FDA.[90]

---

[83] *Ibid.* The agencies are the Office of Science and Technology Policy, National Science Foundation, National Institutes of Health, Department of Defense, Department of Energy, and US Geological Survey.

[84] The White House Office of the Press Secretary, "Fact Sheet: President Obama's Precision Medicine Initiative," January 30, 2015; available at: www.whitehouse.gov/the-press-office/2015/01/30/fact-sheet-president-obama-s-precision-medicine-initiative (accessed August 28, 2015).

[85] US Department of Veterans Affairs, "Million Veteran Program: A Partnership with Veterans"; available at: www.research.va.gov/mvp/veterans.cfm (accessed August 28, 2015).

[86] Chronic Condition Data Warehouse, "About Chronic Condition Data Warehouse"; available at: www.ccwdata.org/about/index.htm (accessed August 28, 2015). CCW was created pursuant to Section 723 of the Medicare Modernization Act of 2003.

[87] US Food and Drug Administration, "FDA's Sentinel Initiative"; available at: www.fda.gov/safety/FDAsSentinelInitiative/ucm2007250.htm (accessed August 28, 2015); Deven McGraw et al., "A Policy Framework for Public Health Uses of Electronic Health Data," *Pharmacoepidemiology and Drug Safety* 21 (2012): 18. The Sentinel Initiative was authorized by Congress in the Food and Drug Administration Amendments Act of 2007.

[88] Mini-Sentinel, "Welcome to Mini-Sentinel"; available at: www.mini-sentinel.org/ (accessed August 28, 2015).

[89] Janet Woodcock, "Another Important Step in FDA's Journey towards Enhanced Safety through Full-Scale 'Active Surveillance,'" *FDA Voice*, December 30, 2014; available at: http://blogs.fda.gov/fdavoice/index.php/tag/sentinel-system/ (accessed August 28, 2015).

[90] McGraw et al., "A Policy Framework for Public Health Uses of Electronic Health Data," 19.

A large number of private-sector initiatives are ongoing as well. Geisinger Health Systems in Pennsylvania operates MedMining, a company that extracts EHR data, deidentifies them, and offers them to researchers.[91] The data sets that MedMining delivers to its customers include "lab results, vital signs, medications, procedures, diagnoses, lifestyle data, and detailed costs" from inpatient and outpatient facilities.

Explorys, now an IBM company, formed a large healthcare database derived from financial, administrative, and medical records.[92] It has partnered with major healthcare organizations such as the Cleveland Clinic Foundation and Summa Health System to aggregate and standardize health information from 10 million patients and over 30 billion clinical events. Using a cloud computing platform, it provides customers with big data to use for research and quality-improvement purposes.

The electronic "Medical Records and Genomics Network" (eMERGE) is a consortium of five institutions with DNA repositories linked to EHRs that supply relevant clinical data.[93] The network is supported by the National Human Genome Research Institute and receives additional funding from the National Institute of General Medical Sciences. Each eMERGE center will study "the relationship between genome-wide genetic variation and a common disease/trait" using genome-wide association analysis.[94] A primary purpose of eMERGE is to develop approaches to conducting large-scale genetic research using DNA biobanks that are connected to EHR systems.

The Distributed Ambulatory Research in Therapeutics Network Institute (DARTNet) is a collaboration among nine research networks, including eighty-five healthcare organizations and over 3,000 clinicians across the United States.[95] The first DARTNet federated network, "eNQUIRENet," was created in 2007 and was funded by the Agency for Healthcare Research and Quality. DARTNet members allow data from their EHRs to be captured, deidentified, coded, standardized, and stored in a clinical data repository

---

[91] MedMining, "Welcome to MedMining"; available at: www.medmining.com/index.html (accessed August 28, 2015).

[92] Explorys; available at: www.explorys.com (accessed August 28, 2015).

[93] The eMERGE Network; available at: www.mc.vanderbilt.edu/victr/dcc/projects/acc/index .php/Main_Page (accessed August 28, 2015). The seven sites are Group Health Cooperative with the University of Washington, Geisinger, Marshfield Clinic, Mayo Clinic, Mount Sinai School of Medicine, Northwestern University, and Vanderbilt University.

[94] Catherine A. McCarty et al., "The eMERGE Network: A Consortium of Biorepositories Linked to Electronic Medical Records Data for Conducting Genomic Studies," *BMC Medical Genomics* 4 (2011): 14.

[95] "About DARTNet Institute," DARTNet; available at: www.dartnet.info/AboutDI.htm (accessed August 28, 2015).

(CDR) within each entity that also connects to billing, laboratory, hospital, and prescription databases.[96] CDR data are then transferred to a second database that makes deidentified information available to researchers through a secure web portal.

Other agencies and organizations are building electronic registries and databases that focus on specific disease categories in an effort to promote research and quality-improvement endeavors. These include the "Cancer Biomedical Informatics Grid," the "Interagency Registry for Mechanically Assisted Circulatory Support," the "Extracorporeal Life Support Organization," and the "United Network for Organ Sharing."[97]

The United States is not alone in pursuing big data initiatives, as demonstrated by the following three examples. Canada's "Discharge Abstract Database" (DAD) features administrative, clinical, and demographic information regarding hospital discharges and day surgeries. It receives data from acute care facilities or from the governmental authorities to which they must report.[98] Sweden's "Prostate Cancer Data Base" features over 130,000 prostate cancer cases and is an important national research platform.[99] The "EU-ADR Project" focuses on adverse drug reactions. It involves eight databases containing EHRs from over 30 million Europeans. Researchers exploit these data in order to develop improved mechanisms for early detection of adverse drug events.[100]

---

[96] "Research/Datasets," DARTNet; available at: http://dartnet.info/ResearchAndData.htm (accessed August 28, 2015).

[97] "Cancer Biomedical Informatics Grid (caBIG)," National Cancer Institute, Biorepositories and Biospecimen Research Branch; available at: http://biospecimens.cancer.gov/relatedini tiatives/overview/caBig.asp (accessed October 23, 2015); "About Us," Interagency Registry for Mechanically Assisted Circulatory Support; available at: www.uab.edu/medicine/intermacs/ about-us (accessed August 28, 2015); "ELSO Registry Information," Extracorporeal Life Support Organization; available at: www.elso.org (accessed August 18, 2016); "Data," United Network for Organ Sharing; available at: www.unos.org/donation/index.php?topic= data (accessed August 28, 2015).

[98] "DAD Metadata," Canadian Institute for Health Information; available at: www.cihi.ca/en/ty pes-of-care/hospital-care/acute-care/dad-metadata (accessed December 9, 2015).

[99] "PcBaseSweden – A Platform for Prostate Cancer Research," Karolinska Institutet, Department of Medical Epidemiology and Biostatistics; available at: http://ki.se/en/meb/pcbasesweden -a-platform-for-prostate-cancer-research (accessed January 2, 2016).

[100] José Luis Oliveira et al., "The EU-ADR Web Platform: Delivering Advanced Pharmacovigilance Tools," *Pharmacoepidemiology & Drug Safety* 22, no. 5 (2013): 459–67; EU-ADR, "EU-ADR Project Flyer"; available at: http://synapse-pi.com/new_web/wp-content/upl oads/2013/12/EU-ADR-project_flyer_20111.pdf (accessed January 2, 2016).

Medical big data resources will likely proliferate and become increasingly available in the future. Big data can promote research, quality assessment and improvement, FDA postmarketing surveillance, public health initiatives, and science-based litigation theories. At the same time, however, analysts using EHR databases must proceed with caution. The challenges and complexities of medical big data use are analyzed in detail in the following chapters.

6

Medical Big Data Research
Privacy and Autonomy Concerns

In May 1996, Massachusetts Governor William Weld was hospitalized after losing consciousness because of what turned out to be influenza. In 1997, he received a copy of his hospital records from a graduate student named Latanya Sweeney, who had reidentified them. Ms Sweeney, who is now a Harvard professor, used "anonymized" state employee hospital records that were provided free of charge to researchers by the Massachusetts Group Insurance Commission (GIC). The GIC had removed obvious identifiers such as name and street address, but it had retained the patients' birth dates, sexes, and zip codes. Dr. Sweeney then purchased the complete voter registration records for the city of Cambridge for twenty dollars. She was easily able to identify Governor Weld because "[o]nly six people in Cambridge shared his birth date, only three were men, and of the three, only he lived in his zip code."[1]

Electronic health record (EHR)–based research holds great promise. However, it also raises new questions and concerns. Collection of patient information into large databases poses new risks of privacy breaches that did not exist when paper files were simply locked away in file cabinets.[2] In order to protect patient privacy, database operators generally deidentify information (i.e., they strip away identifying data elements). Yet what

This chapter is based in part on the following articles: Sharona Hoffman and Andy Podgurski, "Balancing Privacy, Autonomy, and Scientific Needs in Electronic Health Records Research," *SMU Law Review* 65, no. 1 (2012): 85; Sharona Hoffman, "Citizen Science: The Law and Ethics of Public Access to Medical Big Data," *Berkeley Technology Law Journal* 30 (2016): 1741.

[1] Paul Ohm, "Broken Promises of Privacy: Responding to the Surprising Failure of Anonymization," *UCLA Law Review* 57, no. 6 (2010): 1709, 1719–20; Kathleen Benitez and Bradley Malin, "Evaluating Re-identification Risks with respect to the HIPAA Privacy Rule," *Journal of the American Medical Informatics Association* 17, no. 2 (2010): 169.

[2] Mark A. Rothstein, "Improve Privacy in Research by Eliminating Informed Consent? IOM Report Misses the Mark," *Journal of Law, Medicine & Ethics* 37, no. 4 (2009): 509–11.

"deidentification" means is often a matter of controversy, and many experts agree that the risk of reidentification can never be fully eliminated.

Research risks such as privacy breaches are traditionally addressed by asking patients to make autonomous decisions about research participation through the informed consent process. Research involving only deidentified information, however, is exempted from informed consent requirements. But should it be?[3]

This chapter focuses on privacy and autonomy concerns in the context of EHR database research. The chapter explores how the potential benefits of EHR database research can be reaped while the privacy and autonomy interests of data subjects are protected.

6.1 THE LEGAL LANDSCAPE

Ordinarily, biomedical research protocols require patient consent and institutional review board (IRB) approval, and patients must authorize the release of identifiable information to researchers under the Health Insurance Portability and Accountability Act (HIPAA) Privacy Rule.[4] By contrast, research using deidentified EHRs can be conducted with few regulatory constraints. Research involving solely deidentified records need not be subject to informed consent requirements or approved by an IRB and is not subject to coverage by the HIPAA Privacy Rule.[5]

---

[3] See Henry T. Greely, "Breaking the Stalemate: A Prospective Regulatory Framework for Unforeseen Research Uses of Human Tissue Samples and Health Information," *Wake Forest Law Review* 34 (1999): 752–8; Franklin G. Miller, "Research on Medical Records without Informed Consent," *Journal of Law, Medicine & Ethics* 36, no. 3 (2008): 564; Fred H. Cate, "Protecting Privacy in Health Research: The Limits of Individual Choice," *California Law Review* 98 (2010): 1798–1801; Committee on Health Research and the Privacy of Health Information: The HIPAA Privacy Rule, Board on Health Sciences Policy, Board on Health Care Services, and Institute of Medicine, *Beyond the HIPAA Privacy Rule: Enhancing Privacy, Improving Health through Research*, ed. by Sharyl J. Nass, Laura A. Levit, and Lawrence O. Gostin (Washington, DC: National Academies Press, 2009) [hereinafter IOM Report], 33–5.

[4] 45 CFR §§ 46.109 & 164.508(b)(3)(1) (2015). According to the FDA, an IRB is "an appropriately constituted group that has been formally designated to review and monitor biomedical research involving human subjects" with "authority to approve, require modifications in (to secure approval), or disapprove research." IRB review is conducted in order to protect "the rights and welfare of human research subjects." US Food and Drug Administration, "Institutional Review Boards Frequently Asked Questions – Information Sheet"; available at: www.fda.gov/regulatoryinformation/guidances/ucm126420.htm.

[5] 45 CFR § 46.101(b)(4) (2015); 45 CFR § 160.103 (2015).

6.1.1 *Federal Research Regulations*

Federal regulations that require IRB review and participant consent, known as the "Common Rule," cover only research on human subjects and define human subject as "a living individual about whom an investigator ... obtains (1) data through intervention or interaction with the individual, or (2) identifiable private information."[6] The regulations specifically exempt research "involving the collection or study of existing data, documents, [or] records ... if the information is recorded by the investigator in such a manner that subjects cannot be identified, directly or through identifiers linked to the subjects."[7] Thus research using a database of EHRs that have been previously deidentified would not be covered by the research regulations.[8] The regulations provide no details as to which identifiers need to be removed to render data deidentified.

In 2015, the US government announced proposed revisions to the Common Rule and issued a Notice of Proposed Rulemaking (NPRM).[9] Under the proposal, research activities that pose no risks other than those related to privacy and that are regulated by the HIPAA Privacy Rule would be excluded from Common Rule coverage. EHR database research that is conducted by HIPAA-covered researchers, consequently, would be governed by the HIPAA Privacy Rule but not the Common Rule even if the records are identifiable.[10] The proposal would also exempt from Common Rule coverage secondary research use of identifiable private information that was acquired for clinical purposes as long as data subjects are given prior notice that their information will be used for specific research projects. In addition, the new rule would allow patients to provide broad, unspecified consent to future research use of their identifiable health data so that they need not be contacted repeatedly and asked to consent to each separate study.[11]

[6] 45 CFR § 46.102 (2015).

[7] 45 CFR § 46.101(b)(4) (2015).

[8] US Department of Health and Human Services, "Frequently Asked Questions: Can I Analyze Data that Are Not Individually Identifiable, Such as Medication Databases Stripped of Individual Patient Identifiers, for Research Purposes without Having to Apply the HHS Protection of Human Subjects Regulations?"; available at: www.hhs.gov/ohrp/policy/faq/qual ity-improvement-activities/analyze-data.html (accessed September 16, 2015).

[9] US Department of Health and Human Services et al., "Federal Policy for the Protection of Human Subjects," *Federal Register* 80, no. 173 (September 8, 2015): 53931–4061; available at: www.hhs.gov/ohrp/regulations-and-policy/regulations/common-rule/ (accessed August 18, 2016).

[10] US Department of Health and Human Services et al., "Federal Policy for the Protection of Human Subjects," 53978; Kathy L. Hudson and Francis S. Collins, "Bringing the Common Rule into the 21st Century," *New England Journal of Medicine* 373, no. 24 (2015): 2293, 2295–6.

[11] US Department of Health and Human Services et al., "Federal Policy for the Protection of Human Subjects," 53966–7.

6.1.2 *The HIPAA Privacy Rule*

The HIPAA Privacy Rule generally prohibits disclosure of individually identifiable health information without patient authorization, unless the information is transmitted for purposes of treatment, payment, or healthcare operations.[12] Research involving identifiable records thus requires patient consent. The Privacy Rule applies to healthcare providers, health insurers, healthcare clearinghouses, and their business associates.[13]

6.1.2.1 Deidentified Information

Like the Common Rule, the HIPAA Privacy Rule covers only "individually identifiable health information."[14] Thus the rule does not prohibit covered entities from disclosing deidentified data to third parties, including researchers. The regulations provide that information can be considered deidentified if an appropriate expert determines that there is only a "very small" risk that the information could be reidentified and documents his or her analysis.[15] This criterion is known as the HIPAA "statistical standard."[16]

The Department of Health and Human Services (HHS) issued guidance that endorsed several deidentification techniques:

1. *Suppression*, which involves redaction of particular data features prior to disclosure (e.g., removing zip codes, birth dates, income);
2. *Generalization*, which involves transforming particular information into less specific representations (e.g., indicating a ten-year age range instead of exact age); and
3. *Perturbation*, which involves exchanging certain data values for equally specific but different values (e.g., changing patients' ages).[17]

---

[12] 45 CFR § 164.506 (2015).
[13] 45 CFR §§ 160.102–3 (2015); 42 USC § 17934 (2010).
[14] 45 CFR § 160.103 (2015).
[15] 45 CFR § 164.514(b)(1) (2015).
[16] Paul Ohm, "Broken Promises of Privacy: Responding to the Surprising Failure of Anonymization," 1737.
[17] US Department of Health and Human Services, "Guidance Regarding Methods for De-identification of Protected Health Information in accordance with the Health Insurance Portability and Accountability Act (HIPAA) Privacy Rule," November 26, 2012; available at: www .hhs.gov/ocr/privacy/hipaa/understanding/coveredentities/De-identification/hhs_deid_guidance .pdf (accessed September 28, 2015) (noting that techniques such as suppression and generalization are often used in combination).

In the alternative, information is deemed automatically deidentified according to the HIPAA Privacy Rule's "safe harbor" provision[18] if the following eighteen identifiers are removed:

(A) Names;

(B) All geographic subdivisions smaller than a State, including street address, city, county, precinct, zip code, and their equivalent geocodes, except for the initial three digits of a zip code if, according to the current publicly available data from the Bureau of the Census:

    (1) The geographic unit formed by combining all zip codes with the same three initial digits contains more than 20,000 people; and

    (2) The initial three digits of a zip code for all such geographic units containing 20,000 or fewer people is changed to 000.

(C) All elements of dates (except year) for dates directly related to an individual, including birth date, admission date, discharge date, date of death; and all ages over 89 and all elements of dates (including year) indicative of such age, except that such ages and elements may be aggregated into a single category of age 90 or older;

(D) Telephone numbers;

(E) Fax numbers;

(F) Electronic mail addresses;

(G) Social Security numbers;

(H) Medical record numbers;

(I) Health plan beneficiary numbers;

(J) Account numbers;

(K) Certificate/license numbers;

(L) Vehicle identifiers and serial numbers, including license plate numbers;

(M) Device identifiers and serial numbers;

(N) Web Universal Resource Locators (URLs);

(O) Internet Protocol (IP) address numbers;

(P) Biometric identifiers, including finger and voice prints;

(Q) Full face photographic images and any comparable images; and

(R) Any other unique identifying number, characteristic, or code.[19]

---

[18] *Fed. Reg.* 67: 53233 (2002).

[19] 45 CFR § 164.514(b)(2)(i) (2015). In addition, information will not be considered deidentified if an entity has "actual knowledge that the information could be used alone or in combination with other information to identify an individual who is a subject of the information." 45 CFR § 164.514(b)(2)(ii).

The requirements for deidentification under this HIPAA provision are far more specific than those of the Common Rule. It is therefore possible that a protocol would be exempt from the current Common Rule's consent mandate because some identifiers are removed but would still require patient authorization under the HIPAA Privacy Rule because not all eighteen safe harbor identifiers are redacted.[20] The proposed regulatory change would eliminate this discrepancy by removing Common Rule jurisdiction over HIPAA-covered EHR studies.

6.1.2.2 Other HIPAA Exemptions

The HIPAA Privacy Rule contains several other exceptions that apply to research use of health data. Covered entities may disclose "limited data sets" without patient consent if recipients sign data use agreements that prohibit reidentification of the data.[21] Limited data sets allow somewhat more liberal disclosures than the safe harbor provision because they make three modifications to the eighteen-factor list. Disclosure of all elements of dates, including exact birth dates, is permitted, and while specific addresses must be withheld, patients' towns or cities and zip codes can be revealed.[22] The limited data set provision also eliminates the catch-all item of "any other unique" identifier.

In addition, the HIPAA Privacy Rule does not protect records of decedents that are used for research purposes.[23] Researchers can obtain further exemptions with approval of an IRB or privacy board in accordance with regulatory guidance.[24]

6.1.3 *State Laws*

All states have recognized a common-law or statutory right to privacy, and all have statutes that address privacy concerns.[25] A thorough analysis of state law is

---

[20] IOM Report, 173.

[21] 45 CFR § 164.514(e)(1) (2015). See 45 CFR § 164.514(e)(4) for details concerning data use agreements.

[22] 45 CFR § 164.514(e)(2) (2015).

[23] 45 CFR § 164.512(i)(1)(iii) (2015).

[24] 45 CFR § 164.512(i)(1)(i) (2015). Identifiable medical records may also be used without patient consent to prepare (but not carry out) research protocols as long as the records do not leave the facility in which they are stored. 45 CFR § 164.512(i)(1)(ii).

[25] Corrine Parver, "Patient-Tailored Medicine, Part Two: Personalized Medicine and the Legal Landscape," *Journal of Health & Life Sciences Law* 2, no. 2 (2009): 32; Americans Health Lawyers Association, *State Healthcare Privacy Law Survey* (2013); "Public Health Departments and State Patient Confidentiality Laws Map," LawAtlas; available at: http://lawatlas .org/preview?dataset=public-health-departments-and-state-patient-confidentiality-laws (accessed September 16, 2015).

beyond the scope of this chapter. In general, though, the state laws are varied and inconsistent, often providing piecemeal protection for some types of data but not others, and these protections may be scattered among multiple laws.[26] Moreover, like the HIPAA Privacy Rule, the states typically allow disclosure of deidentified health information without patient authorization.[27]

6.1.4 *International Law*

The approach of the United States to analysis of health information is consistent with that of the European Union. EU Directive 95/46/EC, "The Data Protection Directive," establishes privacy protections for personal data. In general, the directive prohibits the processing of information concerning health, though it allows its use in limited circumstances, such as with patient consent, for purposes of medical treatment, and otherwise as permitted by national law.[28] The directive defines "personal data" as "information relating to an identified or identifiable natural person ... who can be identified, directly or indirectly, in particular by reference to an identification number or to one or more factors specific to his [or her] physical, physiological, mental, economic, cultural or social identity."[29] Thus deidentified information is exempted from coverage.

6.2 RESEARCH RISKS: PRIVACY AND DIGNITARY HARMS

With this legal background in mind, it is time to assess whether EHR-based research poses any risks to data subjects. The potential privacy and dignitary harms associated with EHR database research are explored next.

---

[26] Deven McGraw et al., "Privacy as an Enabler, Not an Impediment: Building Trust into Health Information Exchange," *Health Affairs* 28 (2009): 420.

[27] Scott Burris et al., "The Role of State Law in Protecting Human Subjects of Public Health Research and Practice," *Journal of Law, Medicine & Ethics* 31 (2003): 656.

[28] Directive 95/46/EC of the European Parliament and of the Council of 24 October 1995 on the protection of individuals with regard to the processing of personal data and on the free movement of such data, EUR-Lex – 31995L0046, Article 5; available at: http://eur-lex.europa .eu/LexUriServ/LexUriServ.do?uri=CELEX:31995L0046:en:HTML (accessed January 7, 2016). For a discussion of the privacy laws that various European nations have adopted, see Milieu Law and Policy Consulting, *Overview of the National Laws on Electronic Health Records in the EU Member States and Their Interaction with the Provision of Cross-Border eHealth Services: Final Report and Recommendations*, Contract 2013 63 02 (Brussels, 2014), 44; available at: http://ec.europa.eu/health/ehealth/docs/laws_report_recommendations_en.pdf (accessed January 4, 2016).

[29] EU Directive 95/46/EC, Article 2(a).

6.2.1 *Privacy*

Big data collections generally consist of deidentified EHRs. Under the HIPAA Privacy Rule, disclosure of fully deidentified EHRs to third parties is not prohibited and does not require patient authorization. Thus many patients will never discover that their records have been incorporated into a database and will have no say in the matter. Deidentification in accordance with the Privacy Rule's guidelines in theory makes it impossible to determine who the data subject is. Yet this is not completely true.

6.2.1.1 The Possibility of Reidentification

In general, deidentification is based on assumptions that third parties do not have certain information about data subjects that may facilitate reidentification. However, adversaries may legally or illegally obtain such information from a variety of sources and then correlate it to deidentified records to achieve reidentification.[30]

Presumably, most EHR databases that are used by professional researchers will be deidentified in accordance with HIPAA guidelines because they will be operated by covered healthcare providers and their business associates. Deidentification in accordance with HIPAA Privacy Rule guidelines is comprehensive. Yet experts have concluded that there remains a small risk that highly skilled and motivated attackers in some circumstances will be able to reidentify records that have been deidentified in compliance with HIPAA guidelines. Reidentification may occur when perpetrators have access to nonmedical open data, such as voter registration records, that they can link to "anonymized" health information. Third parties may also obtain information that could help to reidentify EHRs through records of patients' medication purchases, media stories about accidents and illnesses, Facebook, and other sources.

Dr. Latanya Sweeney, the individual who long ago reidentified Governor Weld's hospital records and who is now a leading authority, asserts that 0.04 percent of records deidentified in compliance with the HIPAA safe harbor provision could be reidentified.[31] A study published in 2010 by Kathleen Benitez and Bradley Malin similarly estimated that when all

---

[30] George T. Duncan, *Statistical Confidentiality* (Berlin: Springer-Verlag, 2011), 37.

[31] National Committee on Vital and Health Statistics, *Report to the Secretary of Health and Human Services on Enhanced Protections for Uses of Health Data: A Stewardship Framework for "Secondary Uses" of Electronically Collected and Transmitted Health Data* (Hyattsville, MD: National Committee on Vital and Health Statistics, 2007), 36, n. 16; available at: www.ncvhs .hhs.gov/wp-content/uploads/2014/05/071221lt.pdf (accessed September 28, 2015).

eighteen HIPAA safe harbor provision identifiers are removed, the percentage of a state's population vulnerable to unique reidentification ranges from 0.01 to 0.25 percent.[32] When the identifiers permitted by HIPAA for limited data sets were added in, the risk rose to between 10 and 60 percent depending on the state. There is wide variance in the risk because the demographic information that is available to the public through voter registration records differs among the states. In 2011, Benitez and Malin published a second paper in which they assessed their own method of deidentification, consistent with HIPAA's statistical standard.[33] They quantified the risk of reidentification in this case as ranging "from 0.01 to 0.19 percent."[34] Although the risk of reidentification seems tiny, it translates into a risk of tens of thousands or even hundreds of thousands of records being reidentified if one thinks in terms of the American population as a whole, consisting of 319 million individuals.[35]

Furthermore, the HIPAA Privacy Rule's safe harbor provision does not ban the disclosure of certain details whose presence could make it easier to identify individuals. For example, according to Dr. Khaled El Emam, if hospital discharge data include length of stay and time since last visit, which are not among the eighteen prohibited identifiers, as many as 16.57 percent of the records could have a high likelihood of reidentification.[36]

If health information is not deidentified in accordance with any HIPAA standard, the risk of reidentification grows exponentially. Dr. Sweeney undertook a research project for which she obtained Washington state hospital discharge data containing many demographic details but not names and addresses, a data set that was available for purchase for fifty dollars.[37] She attempted to match hospitalization records to eighty-one newspaper stories about accidents and injuries in 2011 and was able to determine the name of the patient to whom the records belonged in thirty-five (or 43 percent) of the cases based on the news accounts.[38] A particularly startling estimate is that between

---

[32] Benitez and Malin, "Evaluating Re-identification Risks with respect to the HIPAA Privacy Rule," 176.

[33] Bradley Malin et al., "Never Too Old for Anonymity: A Statistical Standard for Demographic Data Sharing via the HIPAA Privacy Rule," *Journal of the American Medical Informatics Association* 18, no. 1 (2011): 3. The statistical standard is articulated in 45 CFR § 164.514(b)(1).

[34] *Ibid.*, 7.

[35] See US Census Bureau, "US and World Population Clock"; available at: www.census.gov/popclock/ (accessed September 28, 2015).

[36] Khaled El Emam, "Methods for the De-identification of Electronic Health Records for Genomic Research," *Genome Medicine* 3, no. 4 (2011): 27.

[37] The Washington State Department of Health, which provides the data, is not a covered entity under HIPAA and thus does not have to comply with HIPAA deidentification requirements.

[38] Latanya Sweeney, "Matching Known Patients to Health Records in Washington State Data," Data Privacy Lab; available at: http://dataprivacylab.org/projects/wa/1089-1.pdf

63 and 87 percent of the US population could be accurately identified based on the three factors of gender, zip code, and date of birth without any need for details such as name, Social Security number, or precise address.[39]

6.2.1.2 Does Privacy Matter?

This is the era of social media. Many people, especially the young, post their most intimate details on Facebook and other venues for widespread public consumption. Consequently, some might ask whether privacy still matters to Americans.

The answer appears to be yes. Public opinion surveys reveal that Americans still say that they care deeply about privacy. A 2010 Markle survey found that 80 percent of patients and doctors emphasized "the importance of privacy protections as a requirement to ensure that public investment in health IT [information technology] will be well spent."[40] In addition, 90 percent of 4,659 adults surveyed regarding biobank research stated that they would be concerned about privacy if they were research participants.[41]

Studies that focus specifically on social media show that users are very interested in privacy, though they may be naive about the degree to which their privacy is safeguarded online. Facebook users, especially those under age twenty-five, generally believe that its benefits outweigh its privacy risks, but over 60 percent attempt to manage access to their data through privacy settings. Observers also note an emerging trend of "Facebook quitters." Approximately half of those who have closed their Facebook accounts cite privacy concerns as a motivator.[42]

(accessed September 28, 2015); Jordan Robertson, "States' Hospital Data for Sale Puts Privacy in Jeopardy," *BloombergBusiness*, June 5, 2013; available at: http://www.bloomberg.com/news/20 13-06-05/states-hospital-data-for-sale-puts-privacy-in-jeopardy.html (accessed September 28, 2015).

[39] Philippe Golle, "Revisiting the Uniqueness of Simple Demographics in the US Population," in *WPES 2006, Proceedings of the 5th ACM Workshop on Privacy in the Electronic Society* (New York: ACM, 2006), 77; available at: http://crypto.stanford.edu/~pgolle/papers/census .pdf; Latanya Sweeney, "Uniqueness of Simple Demographics in the U.S. Population," *Data Privacy Working Paper* 3 (2000); available at: http://dataprivacylab.org/projects/identifiability/ paper1.pdf.

[40] Markle, "The Public and Doctors Overwhelmingly Agree on Health IT Priorities to Improve Patient Care," January 31, 2011; available at: http://www.markle.org/publications/1461-public-and -doctors-overwhelmingly-agree-health-it-priorities-improve-patient-care (accessed September 28, 2015).

[41] David J. Kaufman et al., "Public Opinion about the Importance of Privacy in Biobank Research," *American Journal of Human Genetics* 85, no. 5 (2009): 645. Biobanks store biological samples such as human tissue for research.

[42] Bernard Debatin et al., "Facebook and Online Privacy: Attitudes, Behaviors, and Unintended Consequences," *Journal of Computer-Mediated Communication* 15, no. 1 (2009): 86, 100;

6.2.1.3 The US Constitution and Health Data Rights (or Lack Thereof)

While users have control over their Facebook pages, they have a lot less control over their health information once it is handled by healthcare providers. In theory, individuals own their health information. However, owning one's health information in principle means relatively little in practice because the medical records that contain patients' medical data are owned by whomever created them – the physician, the hospital, the clinic, and so on.[43] Both state statutes and judicial decisions have confirmed that patients have no property rights attached to their medical records.[44]

Patients also do not have a constitutional right to keep their health information to themselves. In a 2011 case, *National Aeronautics & Space Administration* v. *Nelson*, which involved employment background checks, the Supreme Court had an opportunity to determine whether Americans have a right to informational privacy. However, the Court explicitly declined to determine whether the Constitution establishes such a right and decided the case on other grounds.[45]

6.2.2 *Dignitary Harms*

While the potential for privacy breaches has received significant attention in the literature, other possible harms to the dignity or autonomy of patients have raised concerns as well. If patients are not asked to consent to research that involves their EHRs, they will have no opportunities to determine whether they are willing to accept the risks of dignitary harms. As Professor Mark Rothstein has argued, these harms include group stigmatization, inadvertently supporting medical developments that one finds morally objectionable, and

Maja van der Velden and Khaled El Emam, "'Not All My Friends Need to Know': A Qualitative Study of Teenage Patients, Privacy, and Social Media," *Journal of the American Medical Informatics Association* 20, no. 1 (2013): 20; Stefan Stieger et al., "Who Commits Virtual Identity Suicide? Differences in Privacy Concerns, Internet Addiction, and Personality between Facebook Users and Quitters," *Cyberpsychology, Behavior, and Social Networking* 16, no. 9 (2013): 632.

[43] Marc A. Rodwin, "The Case for Public Ownership of Patient Data," *Journal of the American Medical Association* 302, no. 1 (2009): 87; Mark A. Hall, "Property, Privacy, and the Pursuit of Interconnected Electronic Medical Records," *Iowa Law Review* 95 (2010): 642.

[44] See *Estate of Finkle*, 90 Misc.2d 550, 552 (N.Y. Sur. 1977); *Holtkamp Trucking Co.* v. *Fletcher*, 932 N.E.2d 34, 43–4 (Ill. App. Ct. 2010); *Young* v. *Murphy*, 90 F.3d 1225, 1236 (7th Cir. 1996); FLA. Stat. Ann. § 456.057(1) (West); Miss. Code. Ann. § 41-9-65; S.C. Code Ann. § 44-115-20 (Law. Co-op); Tenn. Code Ann. § 68-11-304(a)(1); Va. Code Ann. § 32.1-127.1:03A (Michie). But see *Person* v. *Farmers Insurance Group of Companies*, 52 Cal. App. 4th 813, 815 (1997) (finding that health records belong to the patient).

[45] *National Aeronautics and Space Administration* v. *Nelson*, 131 S.Ct. 746, 756–7 (2011).

enabling commercial enterprises to garner large profits in which data subjects do not share.[46]

6.2.2.1 Group Stigmatization

Group stigmatization may occur if researchers find that individuals with particular ancestry are more vulnerable to a specific illness than other groups or have better outcomes with treatment that is different from standard therapy.[47] For example, certain abnormalities in the *BRCA1* and *BRCA2* genes are associated with an increased risk of breast and ovarian cancer and are found more commonly in Ashkenazi Jews than in other groups.[48] When genetic testing was developed to identify the *BRCA1* and *BRCA2* mutations, some members of the Jewish community became anxious that Jews would be perceived as having a flawed genetic makeup or as being unusually diseased.[49] Likewise, the Food and Drug Administration's (FDA's) 2005 approval of the drug Bidil for only African Americans generated significant concern about the implications of ethnopharmacology.[50] Would race-based prescriptions lead some to assume that African Americans were biologically different from and measurably inferior to others? Data subjects whose deidentified information is used in research without their consent will not have opportunities to opt out of studies that conceivably might lead to stigmatization of groups with which they identify.

6.2.2.2 Moral Objections

Biomedical research could also lead to outcomes that some data subjects find unacceptable.[51] For example, research may reveal that particular fetal abnormalities can be discovered *in utero*. Testing for the abnormality may ultimately induce parents to abort fetuses that they would have otherwise kept.[52] A patient who opposes abortion may find it abhorrent to have her

---

[46] Mark A. Rothstein, "Is Deidentification Sufficient to Protect Health Privacy in Research?," *American Journal of Bioethics* 10, no. 9 (2010): 5.

[47] *Ibid.*, 6–7; Sharona Hoffman, "'Racially Tailored' Medicine Unraveled," *American University Law Review* 55, no. 2 (2005): 423–6.

[48] Roxana Moslehi, "*BRCA1* and *BRCA2* Mutation Analysis of 208 Ashkenazi Jewish Women with Ovarian Cancer," *American Journal of Human Genetics* 66, no. 4 (2000): 1268–7.

[49] Hoffman, "Racially Tailored" Medicine Unraveled, 423–7.

[50] *Ibid.*, 396–7, 424.

[51] Miller, "Research on Medical Records without Informed Consent," 56.

[52] See Rothstein, "Is Deidentification Sufficient to Protect Health Privacy in Research?," 7; Greely, "Breaking the Stalemate," 760–1 (providing the examples of research concerning "genetic associations with intelligence, violence, or sexual orientation or research into human evolution," all of which might be offensive to some individuals).

medical file play a role in such research, even if it is merely subject to an automated query as part of a large database of deidentified files. Yet, without an informed consent process, she will be given no choice in the matter.

6.2.2.3 No Share in Commercial Profits

Biomedical research, at its most successful, can enable pharmaceutical and device manufacturers to enjoy significant monetary rewards. Manufacturers achieve such commercial success only after the investment of considerable time and money in product development and then only in a minority of instances. The cost of bringing a drug from initial clinical testing to FDA approval has been estimated to be $802 million, and the process takes an average of 90.3 months.[53] Furthermore, according to a study of clinical trial data from 2003–2010, only 10 percent of drugs actually progress from phase I trials to FDA approval.[54] However, when successful medical products such as Lipitor and Viagra are marketed, they can be very lucrative, generating billions of dollars in revenue. These profits are not shared with the research subjects who participated in the relevant clinical trials.[55]

Informed consent forms often include language that explains the possibility that the research sponsor or another party will benefit financially from the research.[56] A 2008 Canadian study found that research participants were particularly concerned about their ability to consent if others might gain financial benefits from use of their data.[57] If patients are not asked to consent, they cannot opt out no matter how strongly they object to this possibility. It should be noted, however, that it is extremely unlikely that lucrative medical products will be developed entirely based on observational studies. Randomized, controlled clinical trials remain the gold standard for drug and device approval. Thus manufacturers seeking to make large profits will still

---

[53] Joseph A. DiMasi et al., "The Price of Innovation: New Estimates of Drug Development Costs," *Journal of Health Economics* 22, no. 2 (2003): 166.

[54] David Thomas, "Release of Bio/Biomedtracker Drug Approval Rates Study," February 15, 2011; available at: www.biotech-now.org/events/2011/02/release-of-biobiomedtracker-drug-approval-rates-study (accessed September 28, 2015).

[55] See Pfizer, Inc., "2010 Pfizer Annual Report to Shareholders: 2010 Financial Report," 25; available at: www.pfizer.com/files/annualreport/2010/financial/financial2010.pdf (accessed September 28, 2015) (indicating that in 2010 Pfizer earned $10.733 billion from Lipitor, $1.928 billion from Viagra, and $1.718 billion from Effexor).

[56] Rothstein, "Is Deidentification Sufficient to Protect Health Privacy in Research?," 7.

[57] Donald J. Willison et al., "Alternatives to Project-Specific Consent for Access to Personal Information for Health Research: Insights from a Public Dialogue," *BMC Medical Ethics* 9, no. 18 (2008): 27.

conduct studies for which they will need to obtain informed consent from participants who will, in turn, have the opportunity to decline enrollment.

6.3 AUTONOMY AND INFORMED CONSENT

Because there is some possibility that record-based research will result in harm to patients, some patient advocates might argue that data subjects should be given an opportunity to refuse to release even deidentified files for EHR studies. This part of the chapter will address the origins of the informed-consent doctrine and the appropriateness of applying it to EHR database studies.

6.3.1 Human Experimentation vs. Record-Based Studies

Informed consent undoubtedly has taken root as a normative component of medical research. But examining the origins of the doctrine reveals that historically the underlying concern was largely protecting subjects from abusive experimental interventions rather than from unwanted observational studies.

A commitment to informed consent in research emerged from the ruins of World War II, during which Nazi doctors conducted brutal experiments on prisoners. The importance of informed consent was initially recognized in the "Nuremberg Code," the first major international document to provide guidelines on research ethics. The "Nuremberg Code" opens by stating that "[t]he voluntary consent of the human subject is absolutely essential."[58] The provision goes on to discuss the need to inform each subject of "the nature, duration, and purpose of the experiment" and "the effects upon his [or her] health or person which may possibly come from his [or her] participation in the experiment." The studies contemplated by the "Nuremberg Code," therefore, involve physical interventions that affect the body, such as the torments that the Nazis perpetrated, rather than the database queries at issue in this chapter.

A second international document that embodies research ethics guidance, the "Declaration of Helsinki," was adopted in 1964 and has been revised multiple times since. Several provisions of the declaration detail informed-consent requirements,[59] though the consent mandate applies only to

---

[58] National Institutes of Health, "Nuremberg Code"; available at: http://ohsr.od.nih.gov/guidelines/nuremberg.html (accessed September 28, 2015).

[59] World Medical Association, "World Medical Association Declaration of Helsinki: Ethical Principles for Medical Research Involving Human Subjects," §§ 24–9; available at: www.wma.net/en/30publications/10policies/b3/17c.pdf.

personally identifiable medical data or biological material.[60] Under the "Declaration of Helsinki," research on deidentified data would not require consent.

In the United States, the National Commission for the Protection of Human Subjects of Biomedical and Behavioral Research issued the *Belmont Report* in 1979.[61] This project was undertaken in the wake of the infamous Tuskegee syphilis trial. The trial took place from 1932 until 1972 and involved 600 African-American men, 399 of whom had syphilis. In the course of the study, researchers withheld penicillin from the subjects after it was proven to be effective in treating syphilis because they wanted to learn about the natural course of disease.[62] The *Belmont Report* identified "respect for persons" as one of three foundational principles for ethical research and established that it demands that investigators obtain informed and voluntary consent from all human subjects. Specifically, the *Belmont Report* states: "Respect for persons requires that subjects, to the degree that they are capable, be given the opportunity to choose what shall or shall not happen to them."[63] This wording and the historical backdrop of the *Belmont Report* suggest that its primary concern is clinical experimentation rather than the collection of data from existing records for observational studies.[64]

6.3.2 *The Trouble with Consent*

While consent requirements promote patient autonomy and may be favored by patients, they also can interfere with the scientific integrity of the research enterprise. Consent requirements can result in selection bias that can actually invalidate research outcomes.[65] In addition, contacting thousands or millions of patients who are included in a database can be a very expensive and

---

[60] *Ibid.*, § 25.

[61] National Commission for the Protection of Human Subjects of Biomedical and Behavioral Research, *The Belmont Report: Ethical Principles and Guidelines for the Protection of Human Subjects of Research* (DHEW Publication No. (OS) 78–0014) (Washington, DC: US Government Printing Office, 1979); available at: www.hhs.gov/ohrp/humansubjects/guidance/belmont.html.

[62] "US Public Health Service Syphilis Study at Tuskegee," Centers for Disease Control and Prevention; available at: www.cdc.gov/tuskegee/timeline.htm.

[63] *Belmont Report*, Part C.1.

[64] The second principle articulated in the *Belmont Report* is beneficence, which encompasses the mandates to do no harm and to maximize potential benefits while minimizing risks in research. The third principle is justice, which requires that the benefits and risks of research be distributed fairly and that selection procedures for human subjects be sound and impartial. *Belmont Report*, Part B.2–3.

[65] Miller, "Research on Medical Records without Informed Consent," 560; IOM Report, 201.

time-consuming undertaking for researchers and might make it impossible for many studies to proceed.[66]

6.3.2.1 Informed Consent Can Lead to Selection Bias

One major difficulty with informed consent is that it can lead to selection bias, which might skew research results. Selection biases result from procedures used to select subjects and from other factors that affect study participation.[67] By one definition, "selection bias" occurs when those who decide to consent to participate in research constitute a subset of individuals who are not representative of the patient population of interest.[68] This could happen if a disproportionate number of people of one ancestry or economic class opt out of a study. It can likewise happen if individuals with certain behavior traits that might be pertinent to a study – such as diet, smoking habits, alcohol or drug consumption, and exercise – disproportionately opt out.

If the process of obtaining patients' informed consent to participate in a research study is subject to this kind of selection bias, then the consenting patients will not comprise a representative sample of the population targeted for study. Consequently, assessments of measures such as disease prevalence or average treatment effect based on the study will tend to yield estimates that differ systematically from the true values of these measures for the target population. That is, the estimates will not generalize from the set of consenters to the target population.

An Institute of Medicine (IOM) report entitled, "Beyond the HIPAA Privacy Rule: Enhancing Privacy, Improving Health through Research," discusses several studies of selection bias.[69] The IOM concluded that the HIPAA Privacy Rule's requirement of patient authorization for use of identifiable health information can indeed generate biased study samples and jeopardizes the validity of outcomes in research involving identifiable data.[70]

6.3.2.2 Obtaining Informed Consent Can Be Costly and Burdensome

In addition to generating selection bias, consent requirements can be very expensive and work-intensive for investigators. Record-based research can include hundreds or thousands of data subjects, and tracking them down to

---

[66] Cate, "Protecting Privacy in Health Research: The Limits of Individual Choice," 1789–93.
[67] Kenneth J. Rothman, Timothy L. Lash, and Sander Greenland, *Modern Epidemiology*, 3rd edn. (Philadelphia: Lippincott Williams & Wilkins, 2008), 136.
[68] Miller, "Research on Medical Records without Informed Consent," 560; IOM Report, 209.
[69] IOM Report, 209–12.
[70] *Ibid.*, 16.

obtain consent, especially if this must be done each time a new study is initiated, could be an overwhelming task. Therefore, consent requirements can constitute a significant obstacle for research projects involving large collections of patient records or even make them impossible to pursue.[71]

Empirical data support the contention that consent requirements are associated with significant costs. A 2007 survey of 1,527 epidemiologists concluded that the HIPAA Privacy Rule's authorization requirements had significantly hindered research.[72] Respondents expressed frustration with the cost and delays associated with regulatory compliance. Other studies reveal similar objections and even suggest that some healthcare providers are opting out of conducting research altogether.[73]

Several studies have attempted to quantify the cost and time demands of consent processes. A study that focused on the Registry of the Canadian Stroke Network, which includes twenty Canadian hospitals, concluded that nurse coordinators spent a median of forty minutes with each patient or surrogate for consent purposes (including the time spent arranging interviews).[74] In addition, of the 2 million Canadian dollars spent on the registry during the first two years, $500,000 was spent on consent activities alone. A British study estimated that the cost of obtaining consent through a combination of e-mail, mail, and telephone calls for review of records of prostate cancer patients was $248 per consented man.[75] In a US study, 2,228 mothers who were likely to deliver preterm infants were approached in person for consent to a study of neonatal care. Consent was found to take between 1,735 and 2,790 hours and to cost between $65,945 and $106,029 based on staff salaries.[76] Yet another study focused on parental consent to 2,496 middle-school-aged children's participation in a survey. Consent, involving three mailings and follow-up telephone calls to nonresponders, was estimated to cost at least $50,000.[77]

[71] For further discussion of different informed consent options, see Hoffman and Podgurski, "Balancing Privacy, Autonomy, and Scientific Needs in Electronic Health Records Research," 119–22.

[72] Roberta B. Ness, "Influence of the HIPAA Privacy Rule on Health Research," *Journal of the American Medical Association* 298, no. 18 (2007): 2167.

[73] IOM Report, 199–209.

[74] Jack Tu et al., "Impracticability of Informed Consent in the Registry of the Canadian Stroke Network," *New England Journal of Medicine* 350, no. 14 (2004): 1418.

[75] Sian Noble, et al., "Feasibility and Cost of Obtaining Informed Consent for Essential Review of Medical Records in Large-Scale Health Services Research," *Journal of Health Services Research & Policy* 14, no. 2 (2009): 79–80. Of the 230 individuals who were sent consent forms, 179 consented.

[76] Wade D. Rich et al., "Antenatal Consent in the SUPPORT Trial: Challenges, Costs, and Representative Enrollment," *Pediatrics* 126, no. 1 (2010): e217–18.

[77] Finn-Aage Esbensen et al., "Differential Attrition Rates and Active Parental Consent," *Evaluation Review* 23, no. 3 (1999): 320, 322, 329.

6.3.3 *The Importance of the Common Good*

The traditional concepts of informed consent centered on the individual rights of research subjects because the research contemplated was generally physically or psychologically invasive. With the advent of large EHR databases and the proliferation of research studies that involve only record review, it is appropriate to turn to the value of the common good as a counterweight to concern about individual risk. When human beings are not subject to any physical or psychological testing in research and only their records are scrutinized, the value of the common good should prevail over individual interests. Society's interests in achieving medical advances should outweigh the individual risks of privacy breaches and non-privacy-related dignitary injuries as long as all reasonable efforts are made to prevent such harms.

All patients benefit from medical care improvements that have been made possible by past research studies. It is thus arguably irresponsible or inequitable for some patients to prohibit researchers from accessing their data and decline to make their own contribution to the research endeavor.[78] Refusal to participate in research can be characterized as "free riding" because there is no practical way to prevent those who do not contribute their records to research from enjoying the benefits of improved treatment resulting from biomedical studies.[79]

Subordinating individual freedom to the common good because individuals profit from societal initiatives is consistent with the philosopher Jean-Jacques Rousseau's theory of social consent. Rousseau spoke of the "social contract" by which individuals willingly gave up freedom and autonomy in order to enjoy the advantages of a body politic.[80] Individuals who are residents of a political state necessarily accept its benefits, and by doing so, citizens tacitly consent to the laws that enable governmental authority to function.[81] The concept of social consent may be applied to the medical arena as well. Because essentially all individuals will at some time in their lives receive medical care, they may be deemed to tacitly consent to having their EHRs available for research that makes treatment possible.

---

[78] Miller, "Research on Medical Records without Informed Consent," 564.

[79] *Ibid.*, 564; Sarah Chan and John Harris, "Free Riders and Pious Sons – Why Science Research Remains Obligatory," *Bioethics* 23, no. 3 (2009): 162–4; G. Owen Schaefer et al., "The Obligation to Participate in Biomedical Research," *Journal of the American Medical Association* 302, no. 1 (2009): 68.

[80] Jean-Jacques Rousseau, *On the Social Contract*, trans. by Maurice Cranston (New York: Penguin, 1987), 23–5.

[81] *Ibid.*, 25–6; Edward A. Harris, "Note: From Social Contract to Hypothetical Agreement: Consent and the Obligation to Obey the Law," *Columbia Law Review* 92 (1992): 676.

A few bioethicists have gone as far as to argue that individuals have a moral duty to participate in biomedical research, that extends even to clinical studies.[82] However, one need not take a position regarding whether participation in research rises to the level of a moral duty to argue that it is ethically sound to prohibit patients from withholding their information from EHR databases.

6.4 NEXT STEPS

Even with greater focus on the principle of promoting the public good, concerns about the privacy vulnerabilities of EHR-based research and the risk of harm to data subjects cannot be taken lightly. The opportunity to consent, however, does not protect data subjects from harm if they choose to participate in research studies.[83] Consent merely allows individuals to assume the risks knowingly or to opt out completely.

As noted earlier, the federal research regulations and the HIPAA Privacy Rule do not prohibit record-based research in the absence of consent. Neither covers deidentified EHRs; limited data sets can be employed without patient authorization; and even research using clearly identifiable information can proceed without informed consent procedures if authorized by an IRB or privacy board. Proposed changes to the Common Rule would further relax consent requirements for EHR-based research.[84]

As Dr. Erik Parens eloquently states, if "we are going to leave informed consent behind, then it should be because we have good reasons. It shouldn't be because we've drifted away on a tide of excitement about our ability to access an astonishing amount of data at a plummeting financial cost."[85] There are good reasons to prioritize liberal use of data over stringent consent requirements, but this approach is ethically justified only if a number of important

---

[82] John Harris, "Scientific Research Is a Moral Duty," *Journal of Medical Ethics* 31 (2005): 247; Rosamond Rhodes, "Rethinking Research Ethics," *American Journal of Bioethics* 5, no. 1 (2005): 15; Rosamond Rhodes, "In Defense of the Duty to Participate in Biomedical Research," *American Journal of Bioethics* 8, no. 10 (2008): 38; Schaefer et al., "The Obligation to Participate in Biomedical Research," 67. But see Stuart Rennie, "Viewing Research Participation as a Moral Obligation: In Whose Interests?," *Hastings Center Report* 41, no. 2 (2011): 46.

[83] Douglas Peddicord et al., "A Proposal to Protect Privacy of Health Information while Accelerating Comparative Effectiveness Research," *Health Affairs* 29, no. 11 (2010): 2087.

[84] See notes 10–12 and accompanying text.

[85] Erik Parens, "Drifting Away from Informed Consent in the Era of Personalized Medicine," *Hastings Center Report* 45, no. 4 (2015): 16, 19. Dr. Parens is a Senior Research Scholar at the Hastings Center.

safeguards are implemented. What follows are recommendations to address privacy and autonomy concerns relating to EHR-based research.

6.4.1 *Privacy and Security*

Data subjects can be protected from privacy harms in two ways. First, researchers and administrators must safeguard data security. Second, researchers should employ identity-concealment techniques whenever possible.

6.4.1.1 Database Security and Deidentification

Chapter 3 discussed the HIPAA Security Rule and data security measures. Healthcare providers should be scrupulous about data security in both the clinical and the research contexts. They must protect patients' medical records in both the treatment and the research contexts.

In addition, researchers should be meticulous about deidentifying data that will be transported to research databases. As noted earlier, the HIPAA regulations provide detailed guidance about deidentification. The HIPAA standard does not fully eliminate the risk of reidentification, but it can reduce it to a fraction of a percent.

Researchers might object to HIPAA-compliant deidentification on the grounds that it strips away too much data that are useful or necessary for their research projects. A lack of details such as dates or localities may indeed have an impact on research quality in some instances. Consequently, researchers may employ "limited data sets" without patient consent if they sign data use agreements containing specified restrictions and privacy protections. Limited data sets are largely deidentified, but they do contain dates and geographic locales, though not patients' exact addresses.[86]

6.4.1.2 Secure Statistical Analysis of Distributed Databases

An alternative to the creation of large research databases is secure statistical analysis of distributed databases.[87] This method involves querying databases that participate in federated systems using special algorithms intended to prevent disclosure of sensitive information.[88] In a federated system, such as

---

[86] 45 CFR §§ 164.514(e)(1)–(4) (2015).

[87] Alan F. Karr et al., "Secure Regression on Distributed Databases," *Journal of Computational and Graphical Statistics* 14, no. 2 (2005): 263–4.

[88] *Ibid.*; Wilson D. Pace et al., "An Electronic Practice-Based Network for Observational Comparative Effectiveness Research," *Annals of Internal Medicine* 151, no. 5 (2009): 338–9; Oren E. Livne, N. Dustin Schultz, and Scott P. Narus, "Federated Querying Architecture for Clinical and Translational Health IT," *Journal of Medical Systems* 35, no. 5 (2011): 1211–24.

the FDA's Sentinel Initiative and DARTNet, each institution manages and maintains control of its own database, but distributed queries are possible through a standard web service.[89] Researchers submit statistical queries via the Internet using software that interfaces with the federated system's distributed query service. The query service interacts with all relevant databases to initiate operations, communicate intermediate results, and return the final results to researchers. Individual databases in the federation cooperate to compute summary statistics, but they do not share individual records or data that would identify particular organizations.[90]

The query service can provide researchers with a somewhat restricted choice of standard statistical query types, enabling them to compute, for example, estimates of population or subpopulation means, proportions, ratios, and regression coefficients. To illustrate, a researcher might query the federated system for the prevalence of disease X among its patient population. After statistical analysis, the investigator would obtain an estimate of the percentage of the population that suffers from the disease.

Privacy protection is a strength of secure statistical analysis of distributed databases. Records do not have to be deidentified and transported to a central database, so there is no risk of flawed deidentification or breaches during the process of data transmission and database creation. However, as in the case of fully deidentified data, statistical queries will not be an appropriate technique for all research projects.

6.4.2 *Data Review Boards*

For some studies, researchers will need extensive details and will seek to use identifiable medical records. In such cases, their studies will be governed by the Common Rule and/or the HIPAA Privacy Rule. By contrast, research using deidentified records or limited data sets is subject to little oversight. Nevertheless, as discussed throughout this chapter, the risk of reidentification and resulting harm to patients is not nonexistent. Consequently, some form of oversight would be appropriate.

I propose that all records-based studies undergo approval by a data review board with expertise in observational research and information security. This task could be assigned to existing IRBs, but because these bodies are already

[89] Griffin M. Weber et al., "The Shared Health Research Information Network (SHRINE): A Prototype Federated Query Tool for Clinical Data Repositiones," *Journal of the American Medical Informatics Association* 16, no. 5 (2009): 624.

[90] Alan F. Karr, "Secure Statistical Analysis of Distributed Databases, Emphasizing What We Don't Know," *Journal of Privacy and Confidentiality* 1, no. 2 (2009): 197, 199.

overworked and may not have the requisite expertise, separate reviewing entities could be established exclusively for records-based studies.[91]

The degree of scrutiny that review boards apply to studies should depend on the extent to which researchers may be able to identify patient data. Research involving fully identifiable data will require patient authorization.[92] But studies using limited data sets that do not require patient consent should nevertheless undergo a thorough approval process. Limited data sets should be subject to careful scrutiny because they can include birth dates and zip codes, which significantly increase the possibility of reidentification.[93] The review board should pay particular attention to the security measures that will be implemented. It should also verify the credentials of applicants to ensure that they are bona fide researchers who have a genuine research project in mind.

Studies in which researchers will view only data that are deidentified in accordance with the HIPAA safe harbor provision should undergo a streamlined process through which investigators register their projects, and their identities are confirmed. The researchers should also sign data use agreements, promising that they will not attempt to reidentify data, will not convey the records they obtain to individuals who are not members of the research team, and will refrain from using data for purposes outside the scope of the study. In addition, researchers should commit to disposing of any records they have obtained at the end of a designated period by approved means.

Furthermore, data review boards should conduct continuing review of all research studies. Researchers should be required to submit annual reports and to inform the board immediately of any adverse events, such as hacking or inappropriate disclosure of data to third parties. If data are not appropriately

[91] Ezekiel J. Emanuel et al., "Oversight of Human Participants Research: Identifying Problems to Evaluate Reform Proposals," *Annals of Internal Medicine* 141, no. 4 (2004): 284; David A. Hyman, "Institutional Review Boards: Is This the Least Worst We Can Do?," *Northwestern Law Review* 101 (2007): 761; Joseph A. Catania et al., "Survey of US Boards That Review Mental Health-Related Research." *Journal of Empirical Research on Human Research Ethics* 3, no. 4 (2008): 71–9.

[92] But see Institute of Medicine Committee on Health Research and the Privacy of Health Information: The HIPAA Privacy Rule, *Beyond the HIPAA Privacy Rule: Enhancing Privacy, Improving Health through Research*, ed. by Sharyl J. Nass, Laura A. Levit, and Lawrence O. Gostin (Washington, DC: National Academies Press, 2009), 34 (suggesting that researchers who wish to use direct identifiers may seek waivers of informed consent from an ethics oversight board if they implement certain data protection measures).

[93] 45 CFR § 164.514c(1) (2015); Benitez and Malin, "Evaluating Re-identification Risks with respect to the HIPAA Privacy Rule," 169. Currently, the Common Rule does not make clear whether research using limited data sets would require IRB approval and consent, and the HIPAA Privacy Rule requires data use agreements but no patient authorization for such studies.

safeguarded, review boards may not approve future studies by the same investigators, may require corrective action, or may withdraw approval of the study and mandate that it be stopped.[94]

The advent of medical big data resources has generated considerable excitement about their potential benefits. Along with the promise of big data, however, comes justifiable anxiety about patient privacy and autonomy. While deidentification of records can protect patient anonymity, it is not always thoroughly and consistently accomplished, and even at its best, it cannot completely remove the possibility that a small number of patients will be recognized. In order to earn public trust and maintain high ethical standards, policymakers must take further steps to safeguard data security and promote responsible research oversight.

---

[94] See 45 CFR § 46.113 (2015).

7

Medical Big Data Quality and Analysis Concerns

In 2009, the *Journal of Psychiatric Research* published an article that linked abortion to psychiatric disorders.[1] The researchers examined "national data sets with reproductive history and mental health variables" to formulate their findings.[2] The study was widely cited among abortion opponents, and several states enacted legislation requiring that women seeking abortions receive counseling that includes warnings about potential long-term mental health problems.[3] In 2012, however, the study was discredited by scientists who scrutinized its design and found that it was severely flawed. The original researchers compared women with unplanned pregnancies who had abortions with all women rather than with women who chose to continue their unplanned pregnancies and have the babies. The study also considered life-time mental disorders, whereas it should have focused only on disorders that manifested after the pregnancies.[4] Thus what appeared to be solid scientific evidence turned out not to be so.

This chapter is based in part on Sharona Hoffman and Andy Podgurski, "The Use and Misuse of Biomedical Data: Is Bigger Really Better?" *American Journal of Law & Medicine* 39 (2013): 497–538.

[1] Priscilla K. Coleman et al., "Induced Abortion and Anxiety, Mood, and Substance Abuse Disorders: Isolating the Effects of Abortion in the National Comorbidity Survey," *Journal of Psychiatric Research* 43, no. 8 (2009): 770.

[2] *Ibid.*

[3] Sharon Begley, "Journal Disavows Study Touted by US Abortion Foes," *Reuters*, March 7, 2012; available at: www.reuters.com/article/2012/03/07/us-usa-abortion-psychiatry-idUSTRE8261U D20120307 (accessed October 25, 2015); Guttmacher Institute, "Counseling and Waiting Periods for Abortion," *State Policies in Brief* (October 1, 2015); available at: www.guttmacher .org/statecenter/spibs/spib_MWPA.pdf (accessed October 25, 2015).

[4] Ronald C. Kessler and Alan F. Schatzberg, "Commentary on Abortion Studies of Steinberg and Finer (*Social Science & Medicine* 2011; 72:72–82) and Coleman (*Journal of Psychiatric Research* 2009;43:770–6 & *Journal of Psychiatric Research* 2011;45:1133–4)," *Journal of Psychiatric Research* 46, no. 3 (2012): 410–11.

The security of electronic health record (EHR) databases and potential privacy breaches are not the only concerns raised by medical big data use. Anyone considering the outcomes of records-based studies must recognize the shortcomings of contemporary EHR data and the challenges of inferring causal effects correctly.[5] This chapter focuses on what can go wrong in the process of EHR data analysis and what precautions must be taken to avoid critical mistakes.

7.1 DATA QUALITY

Medical databases constitute a potentially invaluable research resource, but researchers, analysts, and other stakeholders must appreciate that existing EHRs often contain errors, are incomplete, or suffer from other inadequacies. While any collection of research data may be contaminated by inaccuracies, medical databases may be particularly flawed. The information in EHRs is initially collected for clinical and billing purposes, and thus it might be ill suited for research. Moreover, the sheer volume of information contained in large medical databases and the complex analytical methods and tools required to conduct large-scale observational studies create myriad opportunities for the introduction of errors and omissions. While improved technology may remedy many database shortcomings in the future, these deficiencies are currently of serious concern. This section examines an assortment of potential data quality defects.

7.1.1 *Data Input Errors*

Chapter 1 discussed a variety of EHR problems that can be detrimental to patient care. These same deficiencies can taint the quality of research data that originate in EHRs. Specifically, researchers must be aware that EHR data might be characterized by mistyped words and numbers, sloppy copying and pasting, inaccurate selection of codes and menu items, codes that are not specific or detailed enough, and software failures. In addition, if researchers draw on information that was entered by patients into personal health records (PHRs), the data's accuracy may be compromised by patients' cognitive impairments, lack of medical expertise, or deficient computer skills.

Data errors can skew the outcomes of research projects. A study that focused on pneumonia cases emphasized that even a small number of errors can have

---

[5] Pamela N. Peterson and Paul D. Varosy, "Observational Comparative Effectiveness Research: Comparative Effectiveness and Caveat Emptor," *Circulation: Cardiovascular Quality and Outcomes* 5 (2012): 151.

"a relatively large effect" on mortality estimates.[6] Other researchers have confirmed that error rates as small as 1 to 5 percent could cause significant inaccuracies in mortality and adverse event estimates.[7] Database operators and analysts also cannot ignore the possibility that in the worst-case scenario, hackers could access medical databases and intentionally introduce errors or alter records.[8]

7.1.2 *Incomplete or Fragmented Data*

Incomplete or fragmented data may also compromise the reliability of EHR database information. At times, EHR data do not include all the information needed for particular research projects.[9] Clinicians generally do not approach the task of EHR documentation with research studies in mind.[10] To illustrate, in one instance, a manual review of EHR data from the New York–Presbyterian Hospital clinical data warehouse revealed that when pneumonia patients died in the emergency department, clinicians "spent little time documenting symptoms so that in the electronic health record, the patient appeared to be healthy other than the death."[11] Thus researchers studying these records may find them to be of limited use because of data gaps.

Data about treatment outcomes are particularly likely to be missing.[12] For example, a patient discharged from an emergency room may not seek further care at all or may later visit a physician who has a different EHR system, making it impossible to track whether the emergency treatment was effective over the long term. The absence of information about treatment outcomes in an EHR is difficult to interpret. It could mean that the prescribed therapy

---

[6] George Hripcsak et al., "Bias Associated with Mining Electronic Health Records," *Journal of Biomedical Discovery and Collaboration* 6 (2011): 52.

[7] Steve Gallivan and Christina Pagel, "Modelling of Errors in Databases," *Health Care Management Science* 11, no. 1 (2008): 39; Christina Pagel and Steve Gallivan, "Exploring Potential Consequences on Mortality Estimates of Errors in Clinical Databases," *IMA Journal of Management Mathematics* 20, no. 4 (2009): 391.

[8] Sander Greenland, "Multiple-Bias Modelling for Analysis of Observational Data," *Journal of the Royal Statistical Society: Series A* 168, no. 2 (2005): 267–8; Craig H. Mallinckrodt et al., "Assessing and Interpreting Treatment Effects in Longitudinal Clinical Trials with Missing Data," *Biological Psychiatry* 53, no. 8 (2003): 755.

[9] Craig Newgard et al., "Electronic versus Manual Data Processing: Evaluating the Use of Electronic Health Records in Out-of-Hospital Clinical Research," *Academic Emergency Medicine* 19, no. 2 (2012): 224; Sebastian Haneuse et al., "Learning about Missing Data Mechanisms in Electronic Health Records-Based Research: a Survey-Based Approach," *Epidemiology* 27, no. 1 (2016): 82.

[10] M. Alan Brookhart et al., "Confounding Control in Healthcare Database Research Challenges and Potential Approaches," *Medical Care* 48 (Suppl. 6) (2010): S115.

[11] Hripcsak et al., "Bias Associated with Mining Electronic Health Records," 50.

[12] Newgard et al., "Electronic versus Manual Data Processing," 225.

cured the patient and she required no follow-up. However, it could also mean that the patient experienced no relief or her condition deteriorated and she sought care elsewhere.

Data fragmentation often exists because different facilities have EHR systems that are not interoperable. Thus seriously ill patients who are treated at multiple medical centers as their disease progresses may have their records divided among several EHR systems, and these are unlikely to be integrated into a single research database.[13] EHR fragmentation may well hinder research because analysts will see only pieces of patients' records. It is also possible that at times fragmentation will cause analysts to believe they are examining the records of different patients when in truth they are looking at pieces of a single individual's record.

7.1.3 Data Discrepancies and Extraction

Discrepancies and variability in quality of data may be attributable to a number of factors. According to one source, record keeping was found to be more meticulous if it was relevant to financial gain, contractual obligations, or external viewers and sloppier if it was used internally only.[14] In addition, the existence of multiple fields in which a particular detail could be documented and inconsistent practices used by different personnel (e.g., documenting the originally scheduled date versus actual date of an appointment) can generate irregularities. Yet another complication is that medical offices use terms, phrases, and abbreviations differently. To illustrate, the abbreviation "MS" can mean "mitral stenosis," "multiple sclerosis," "morphine sulfate," or "magnesium sulfate."[15] If the context is not clear from the EHR, a reader might fail to understand what is meant by "MS" in a particular instance.

Further challenges arise from the existence of free-text narrative in EHRs. EHR systems allow providers to enter both coded information and unstructured, natural-language notes about patients.[16] Important information that is

---

[13] Taxiarchis Botsis et al., "Secondary Use of EHR: Data Quality Issues and Informatics Opportunities," *AMIA Joint Summit on Translational Bioinformatics* 2010 (2010): 4 (stating that the EHR system that was mined for purposes of the study did not contain records of patients who were transferred to dedicated cancer centers because of the severity of their disease or who had initially been treated elsewhere).

[14] Jessica S. Ancker et al., "Root Causes Underlying Challenges to Secondary Use of Data," *AMIA Annual Symposium Proceedings Archive* 2011 (2011): 61.

[15] Christopher G. Chute, "Medical Concept Representation," in *Medical Informatics: Knowledge Management and Data Mining in Biomedicine*, ed. by Hsinchun Chen et al. (New York: Springer, 2005), 170, table 6–1.

[16] S. Trent Rosenbloom et al., "Data from Clinical Notes: A Perspective on the Tension between Structure and Flexible Documentation," *Journal of the American Medical Informatics Association* 18, no. 2 (2011): 181–2.

not captured in structured data may be contained in notes, and such information is much more difficult to extract accurately from EHRs for secondary use. For example, database mining may fail to reveal a link between worsening asthma and smoking if the progression of asthma is coded but smoking history is described only in free-text clinical notes.[17] Similarly, family history and information about adverse reactions to drugs may be presented in narrative form rather than coded.[18] Experts may employ natural-language processing tools to extract data from free-text narrative, but these techniques are still developing and are often imperfect.[19]

If diagnoses, measurements, or medical histories contained in EHRs are not standardized or are inaccessible because they are not found in structured form, database contents may be inadequate for secondary uses.[20] Similarly, if medical vocabulary is not harmonized, researchers may misunderstand or be unable to make sense of database records.

7.1.4 *Software Glitches*

Errors may arise when the data are analyzed because of defects in the software used to conduct the analysis. This is particularly likely if the software is complex and if it was developed by scientists or their assistants without the help of skilled software developers.[21] Inexperienced programmers are likely both to create incorrect software and to test it inadequately.[22] However, even commercially developed medical research software may produce erroneous results.[23] Ideally, scientists

---

[17] Naren Ramakrishnan et al., "Mining Electronic Health Records," *Computer* 43, no. 10 (2010): 79.

[18] Isaac S. Kohane, "Using Electronic Health Records to Drive Discovery in Disease Genomics," *Nature Reviews Genetics* 12 (2011): 420.

[19] Ramakrishnan et al., "Mining Electronic Health Records," 79; Kitty S. Chan, J. B. Fowles, and J. P. Weiner, "Electronic Health Records and the Reliability and Validity of Quality Measures: A Review of the Literature," *Medical Care Research and Review* 67, no. 5 (2010): 503, 518 (suggesting that natural-language-processing programs "function more effectively for variables that are narrowly and consistently defined").

[20] Andrea L. Benin et al., "How Good Are the Data? Feasible Approach to Validation of Metrics of Quality Derived from an Outpatient Electronic Health Record," *American Journal of Medical Quality* 26, no. 6 (2011): 441.

[21] Rebecca Sanders and Diane Kelly, "Dealing with Risk in Scientific Software Development," *IEEE Software* 25, no. 4 (2008): 27; Diane F. Kelly, "A Software Chasm: Software Engineering and Scientific Computing," *IEEE Software* 24 (2007): 118; Les Hatton, "The Chimera of Software Quality," *Computer* 40 (2007): 104.

[22] Kelly, "A Software Chasm,"118.

[23] Sanders and Kelly, "Dealing with Risk in Scientific Software Development," 25; Nicole K. Henderson-MacLennan et al., "Pathway Analysis Software: Annotation Errors and Solutions," *Molecular Genetics and Metabolism* 101, no. 2–3 (2010): 137–8.

should work in close cooperation with software experts to develop and thoroughly validate software used in medical research.

7.2 DATA ANALYSIS CHALLENGES

Even if the data themselves are unblemished and no software defects exist, analysts can face many obstacles to drawing correct conclusions. This section analyzes problems of bias affecting observational studies, in particular, selection bias, confounding bias, and measurement bias. An understanding of these issues is crucial for anyone seeking to conduct or interpret the results of medical database studies.

The challenges of bias and causal inference are not unique to studies that use EHR data. They were prevalent in the era of paper records as well. However, as electronic medical big data enables observational research to proliferate exponentially, all potential researchers, policymakers, and the public at large should become educated about data analysis.

7.2.1 Selection Bias

By way of review, if data subjects have the opportunity to opt out of inclusion in a database or if certain individuals' records are otherwise excluded, "selection bias" may arise.[24] Thus the subset of individuals who are included in a study may not be representative of the patient population of interest, perhaps because people of a particular sex, ancestry, or socioeconomic group opted out disproportionately.[25] Selection bias can distort assessments of measures such as disease prevalence and exposure risk because study estimates will differ systematically from the true values of these measures for the target population. That is, the estimates will not be generalizable from the research subjects to the larger population about which analysts wish to draw conclusions.[26]

7.2.2 Confounding Bias

"Confounding bias" can be a significant problem in causal effect studies. These studies typically seek to measure the average beneficial effect on patients of a particular treatment or the average harmful effect on individuals

---

[24] *See* Chapter 6; David L. Faigman et al., *Modern Scientific Evidence: The Law and Science of Expert Testimony* (Eagan, MN: Thomson West, 2011), § 4:16.

[25] Sharyl J. Nass et al., *Beyond the HIPAA Privacy Rule: Enhancing Privacy, Improving Health through Research* (Washington, DC: National Academies Press, 2009), 209.

[26] Herbert I. Weisberg, *Bias and Causation: Models and Judgment for Valid Comparisons* (Hoboken, NJ: Wiley, 2010), 93–4.

of a particular exposure. Confounding occurs because of the presence of a common cause of the treatment/exposure variable and the outcome variable.[27]

The following hypothetical illustrates confounding in an observational study. Suppose that a physician's treatment choices are influenced by the severity or duration of a patient's disease, which also influences the outcome of treatment.[28] Thus patients at a later stage of a progressive disease may receive one treatment (treatment A) and those who are at an earlier stage may receive a different therapy (treatment B). At the same time, sicker patients, as a general matter, will have worse treatment outcomes than healthier individuals. Unless the disease-stage factor, which is called a "confounding variable" or "confounder," is adjusted for appropriately during statistical data analysis, it may induce a spurious association between the treatment variable and the outcome variable, which distorts estimation of the true causal effects of treatment. In other words, researchers may reach incorrect conclusions regarding the efficacy of the two treatments because of the confounding variable: the degree of sickness suffered by patients receiving the different therapies. Treatment A may appear to be less effective than treatment B not because it is in fact an inferior therapy but because the patients receiving treatment A are in a late stage of the disease and would not do well no matter what treatment they received.

Socioeconomic factors and patient lifestyle choices may also be confounders. Those who lack financial resources or adequate health coverage may select less expensive treatments not because they are the best choices for them but because they are the only affordable options. Low income may also separately lead to poor health, for example, because of poor nutrition or stress induced by financial difficulties. In the case of preventive care, a treatment's perceived benefits may be amplified because health-oriented individuals interested in the intervention also pursue exercise, low-fat diets, and other health-promoting behaviors. These patients' impressive outcomes thus would not be associated solely with the preventive measure.[29]

---

[27] M. Maria Glymour and Sander Greenland, "Causal Diagrams" in Kenneth J. Rothman, Sander Greenland, and Timothy L. Lash, *Modern Epidemiology*, 3rd edn. (Baltimore: Lippincott Williams & Wilkins, 2008), 192–93;

[28] Bruce M. Psaty and David S. Siscovick, "Minimizing Bias Due to Confounding by Indication in Comparative Effectiveness Research," *Journal of American Medical Association* 304, no. 8 (2010): 897.

[29] Brookhart et al., "Confounding Control in Healthcare Database Research Challenges and Potential Approaches," S115.

To reduce or eliminate confounding bias in an observational study, those conducting it must strive to ascertain, accurately measure, and adjust for all potential confounding variables.[30] In many studies, however, it is by no means clear which variables are potential confounders. Medical care often depends on a complex web of variables relating to the healthcare system, clinicians, and patients themselves, and the factors at work in each case may not be obvious.[31]

Randomized clinical experiments, when they are well-designed and well-implemented, prevent confounding because randomly assigning treatments to patients (possibly including a placebo) ensures there are no associations between the treatment variable and potential confounding variables. Thus, in our hypothetical situation, regardless of their level of disease severity, patients would have the same probability of receiving treatment A and treatment B. In an observational study, treatment assignment is not under the investigators' control because the treatment has already been given and recorded in patients' medical files. Researchers therefore must attempt to obtain the values of confounding variables and adjust for them during analysis of the study data.[32]

7.2.3 *Measurement Bias*

"Measurement biases" arise from errors in measurement and data collection, and observational study results can be compromised if the medical records that are analyzed contain such errors. Measurement errors occur for a variety of reasons. Measurement instruments might not be calibrated properly or might lack sufficient sensitivity to detect differences in relevant variables.[33] Storage time or conditions for biological samples might be different and affect results when analysis is done. To the extent that patients' own accounts and memories are solicited and recorded, the subjects' ability to recall details may be influenced by the questioner's competence, patience, and apparent sympathy or by the degree to which the patient perceives the topic to be important and relevant to his life.[34]

[30] Sander Greenland, Kenneth J. Rothman, and Timothy L. Lash, "Measures of Effect and Measures of Association," in Rothman, Greenland, and Lash, *Modern Epidemiology*, 58.

[31] Brookhart et al., "Confounding Control in Healthcare Database Research Challenges and Potential Approaches," S114.

[32] Jaclyn L. F. Bosco et al., "A Most Stubborn Bias: No Adjustment Method Fully Resolves Confounding by Indication in Observational Studies," *Journal of Clinical Epidemiology* 63, no. 1 (2010): 64–5.

[33] Gael P. Hammer et al., "Avoiding Bias in Observational Studies," *Deutsches Ärzteblatt International* 106, no. 41 (2009): 665.

[34] *Ibid.*

In addition, patients may have impaired memories or may lie in response to questions if they are embarrassed about the truth.

Of particular concern is the fact that the treatment or outcome itself can affect measurement errors. For example, measurement error might occur in a study of the effect of treatment A on dementia if use of A were determined only by interviewing study participants because dementia affects subjects' ability to recall whether and how they were treated. Moreover, some treatments cause or exacerbate dementia, which, in turn, will render patients unable to provide accurate reports of their treatments and outcomes.[35]

7.3 IMPROVING DATA QUALITY AND ANALYSIS

A number of strategies can be employed to improve medical big data quality and analysis. In this section I discuss advances in technology, data audits, suggested legal interventions, and causal inference techniques.

7.3.1 *Technology Improvements*

As EHR system technology matures, its capacity to capture accurate and comprehensive data sets should continue to improve. Health information technology (IT) experts are increasingly likely to recognize that these systems serve not only as clinical and billing tools but also as data sources for secondary-use purposes. To that end, product designers and vendors should implement a variety of measures to enhance the quality and usefulness of EHR data.

7.3.1.1 Semantic Interoperability

Incompatibility of different EHR systems poses significant challenges for researchers.[36] Reconciling the format and meaning of data that come from different systems constitutes very resource-intensive and burdensome work for analysts.[37] The records of individual patients who see doctors at more than one facility can become fragmented, and it may be nearly impossible to put the pieces together into a cohesive whole if the separate EHR systems are not interoperable. The problem of data fragmentation could be cured through

[35] Miguel A. Hernán and Stephen R. Cole, "Causal Diagrams and Measurement Bias," *American Journal of Epidemiology* 170, no. 8 (2009): 959, 960.

[36] Dipak Karla et al., "Argos Policy Brief on Semantic Interoperability," *Studies in Health Technology and Informatics* 170 (2011): 5.

[37] Carole Goble and Robert Stevens, "State of the Nation in Data Integration for Bioinformatics," *Journal of Biomedical Informatics* 41, no. 5 (2008): 687.

"semantic interoperability," which would enable "information systems to exchange information on the basis of shared, preestablished and negotiated meanings of terms and expressions."[38] Health information exchange capabilities are essential to the research endeavor.[39]

Many barriers hinder the achievement of semantic interoperability. Among them are the extremely large number of stakeholders in the United States; lack of coordination, standardization, trained personnel, and appropriate technology; and government pressure to transition from paper records to EHR systems as quickly as possible.[40] In addition, semantic interoperability is likely unappealing to EHR vendors. If vendors standardize their products, they will make it easier for customers who have one vendor's product to switch to a competitor's EHR system. Customers could learn to use new systems more easily and be able to transfer existing records to new EHR systems with less difficulty.[41] Various organizations, such as the Health Information and Management Systems Society (HIMSS) and the EHR/HIE Interoperability Workgroup, have worked to develop standards to promote interoperability and the exchange of health information, but progress has been slow.[42]

All stakeholders must continue to work together to develop mechanisms to standardize representations of EHR information in order to eliminate data ambiguities and facilitate integration of records from EHR systems produced

[38] Kim H. Veltman, "Syntactic and Semantic Interoperability: New Approaches to Knowledge and the Semantic Web," *New Review of Information Networking* 7 (2001): 167. See also Robert H. Dolin and Liora Alschuler, "Approaching Semantic Interoperability in Health Level Seven," *Journal of the American Medical Informatics Association* 18, no. 1 (2011): 99–100.

[39] Botsis et al., "Secondary Use of EHR," 4; Jane Herwehe et al., "Implementation of an Innovative, Integrated Electronic Medical Record (EMR) and Public Health Information Exchange for HIV/AIDS," *Journal of the American Medical Informatics Association* 19, no. 3 (2012): 448.

[40] Werner Ceusters and Barry Smith, *Semantic Interoperability in Healthcare State of the Art in the US* (Buffalo, NY: Werner Ceusters & Barry Smith New York State Center of Excellence in Bioinformatics and Life Sciences Ontology Research Group, 2010), 4; available at: http://ontology.buffalo.edu/medo/Semantic_Interoperability.pdf (accessed September 29, 2015).

[41] M. Alexander Otto, "Despite Small Steps, EHR Interoperability Remains Elusive," *Internal Medicine News*, January 31, 2011; available at: www.internalmedicinenews.com/?id=495&tx_tt news[tt_news]=21289&cHash=71b93edeb0e05133233a91699964af3f (accessed September 29, 2015).

[42] Mike Miliard, "EHR/HIE Interoperability Workgroup Agrees on Connectivity Specs," *Healthcare IT News*, November 9, 2011; available at: www.healthcareitnews.com/news/ehrhie -interoperability-workgroup-agrees-connectivity-specs (accessed September 29, 2015); HIMSS Innovation Center, "ConCert by HIMSS History and FAQs"; available at: www .himssinnovationcenter.org/concert/overview (accessed August 19, 2016). The EHR/HIE Workgroup involved 19 states and 47 vendors.

by different vendors.[43] The federal government could incentivize the development of semantic interoperability by incorporating increasingly stringent interoperability requirements into the "meaningful use" regulations.[44]

7.3.1.2 Other Improvements

Even with interoperability, many EHRs would be incomplete and contain inaccuracies. These deficiencies could be mitigated in part through increased use of electronic means for collecting patient data, such as remote patient monitoring.[45] A number of devices, including glucometers, implantable cardioverter-defibrillators, and blood pressure monitors, can register clinical measurements at home and report them to patients' healthcare providers.[46]

Several additional improvements would be useful as well. Enhanced user interface design could make it easier for clinicians to navigate EHR systems and accurately record data.[47] When sufficiently advanced, voice-recognition software could also reduce the risk of input errors and allow users to operate systems more quickly so that they would have time to supply more detailed documentation.[48] As discussed earlier, improved and widely available natural-language-processing tools would also enable analysts to extract more comprehensive data from EHRs.

As healthcare facilities become increasingly interested in research endeavors that use electronic databases, they may demand that EHR vendors build systems that encourage or require clinicians to capture research-relevant data. Similarly, healthcare systems may train their employees to be diligent about collecting data that are needed for secondary use. Healthcare providers have

---

[43] See Sharona Hoffman and Andy Podgurski, "Finding a Cure: The Case for Regulation and Oversight of Electronic Health Record Systems," *Harvard Journal of Law & Technology* 22, no. 1 (2008): 152–3.

[44] See 45 CFR §§ 170.205 & 170.207 (2015) for current health information exchange standards.

[45] Kevin D. Blanchet, "Remote Patient Monitoring," *Telemedicine & e-Health* 14, no. 2 (2008): 128–30; Center for Technology and Aging, *Technologies for Remote Patient Monitoring in Older Adults* (Oakland, CA: Center for Technology and Aging, 2009), 4; available at: www .techandaging.org/RPMpositionpaperDraft.pdf (accessed September 29, 2015).

[46] Center for Technology and Aging, *Technologies for Remote Patient Monitoring in Older Adults*, 4.

[47] See Michael E. Wiklund, "Making Medical Device Interfaces More User-Friendly," in *Designing Usability into Medical Products*, ed. by Michael E. Wiklund and Stephen B. Wilcox (Boca Raton, FL: CRC Press, 2005), 151–60; Adrian Williams, "Design for Better Data: How Software and Users Interact Onscreen Matters to Data Quality," *Journal of AHIMA* 77 (2006): 56.

[48] See *ibid.*; Ken Terry, "Voice Recognition Moves Up a Notch: When the Computer Can Type While You Talk, You Save Money and Time," *Medical Economics*, 81, no. 4 (2004): TCP11.

much to gain from observational research using medical databases. New discoveries can lead to better patient care, cost savings, and financial profits from the adoption of more effective treatments. Those who wish to enjoy these benefits should be motivated to do their utmost to produce data that are accurate, complete, and easily usable for research purposes.

7.3.2 *Data Quality Assessment*

Technology alone cannot remedy weaknesses in medical databases and observational study outcomes. Persistent human vigilance will also be critical to the integrity of the research endeavor.

Routine EHR data audits will benefit not only clinicians, who must ensure EHR accuracy for treatment purposes, but also researchers, who must assess data quality.[49] Researchers could randomly select a sample of records, review them, and then verify their accuracy. This could be done through patient and physician interviews or through comparison of EHRs to original documentation such as laboratory reports.[50] This process would enable analysts to estimate error rates for particular databases or federated systems in order to characterize uncertainty about research results.[51]

7.3.3 *Legal Interventions*

The law can serve as an additional, potent tool to improve the quality of data that are put to secondary use. In particular, the federal government can employ three sets of regulations: the meaningful use regulations, the Health Insurance Portability and Accountability Act (HIPAA) Security Rule, and the Common Rule.

---

[49] US Government Accountability Office, *Hospital Quality Data: CMS Needs More Rigorous Methods to Ensure Reliability of Publicly Released Data* (GAO-06-54) (Washington, DC: US Government Printong Office, 2006), 5; available at: www.gao.gov/products/GAO-06-54; Leon G. Fine et al., "How to Evaluate and Improve the Quality and Credibility of an Outcomes Database: Validation and Feedback Study on the UK Cardiac Surgery Experience," *British Medical Journal* 326, no. 7379 (2003): 25–6.

[50] Michael G. Kahn, "A Pragmatic Framework for Single-Site and Multisite Data Quality Assessment in Electronic Health Record-Based Clinical Research," *Medical Care* 50 (2012): S22.

[51] See Douglas Curran-Everett and Dale J. Benos, "Guidelines for Reporting Statistics in Journals Published by the American Physiological Society," *Advances in Physiology Education* 287 (2004): H448.

7.3.3.1 The Meaningful Use Regulations and the HIPAA Security Rule

Stage 3 meaningful use regulations are under development and will be completed by 2017.[52] These or other Centers for Medicare and Medicaid Services (CMS) regulations should focus to a greater extent on interoperability and data harmonization so that documentation can be exchanged among healthcare providers with different EHR systems and be understood by all.[53] Researchers should be able to study complete patient EHRs rather than fragmented EHR pieces and know precisely what terms or acronyms such as "MS" mean regardless of where a particular EHR originated. Just as drivers can look at most car dashboards and have little difficulty reading all the instruments and displays, clinicians who have been trained on one EHR system should be able to navigate and operate other EHR systems.

Furthermore, CMS would be wise to consider incorporating requirements for periodic data audits into future meaningful use regulations. Providers could be instructed to conduct audits to verify that they do not have an unacceptably high error rate and to assess mechanisms to improve data accuracy and completeness.

As noted in Chapter 4, the HIPAA Privacy Rule empowers patients to review their EHRs and to request corrections if they detect errors.[54] Such corrections could both prevent medical errors and enhance the accuracy of EHRs for secondary-use purposes.

The HIPAA Security Rule's "General Requirements" section states that covered entities bear responsibility for ensuring "the confidentiality, integrity, and availability" of electronic health information that they create, receive, maintain, or transmit.[55] The term "integrity" should be interpreted broadly to include data quality. The Department of Health and Human Services' Office of Civil Rights (OCR) should focus on the issue of data quality during audits,

---

[52] Robert Tagalicod and Jacob Reider, "Progress on Adoption of Electronic Health Records," Centers for Medicare and Medicaid Services; available at: www.cms.gov/eHealth/ListServ_S tage3Implementation.html.

[53] Anthony Brino, "Senators Press for EHR Interoperability," *Healthcare IT News*, January 6, 2014; available at: www.huffingtonpost.com/2014/04/26/big-data-discrimination_n_5217990.html (accessed September 29, 2015) (reporting that House and Senate bills call on the Department of Health and Human Services "to adopt a common interoperability standard by 2017, as part of the rules for meaningful use Stage 3"); Daniel R. Verdon, "ONC's DeSalvo Issues Next Health IT Challenge: Build Interoperable EHR Systems," *Medical Economics*, March 4, 2014; available at: http://medicaleconomics.modernmedicine.com/medical-economics/content/tags/health-it/on cs-desalvo-issues-next-health-it-challenge-build-interope?page=full (accessed September 29, 2015) (reporting that Dr. Karen DeSalvo, National Coordinator for Health Information Technology, has declared that interoperability will be a national priority).

[54] 45 CFR §§ 164.524–6 (2015).

[55] 45 CFR § 164.306(a)(1) (2015).

and the agency should require covered entities to demonstrate that they have implemented measures to verify and improve data quality. Furthermore, ensuring patient access to their records and patients' ability to have mistakes corrected in their EHRs should be enforcement priorities for OCR.

7.3.3.2 The Common Rule

The federal research regulations, known as the "Common Rule," can further incentivize physicians to be vigilant about the accuracy and completeness of their EHRs.[56] Many physicians are also researchers, and some of the research projects they conduct are observational studies that involve review of medical records.[57]

Research involving identifiable patient information is currently subject to oversight by institutional review boards (IRBs) pursuant to detailed Common Rule guidance.[58] The regulations specify the criteria for IRB approval of studies that are governed by the regulations.[59] Several provisions address data collection, requiring IRBs to consider how researchers plan to monitor data to ensure the safety of participants and to protect their privacy.[60] An additional approval criterion should be added to the regulations: a requirement that investigators who collect data from EHRs indicate in their research protocols what steps they will take to monitor data quality. A mandate that researchers conduct regular data audits or otherwise double-check information contained in EHRs could enhance the reliability of research findings. In addition, it may induce clinicians who are themselves researchers or are sensitive to the needs of researchers to be more careful about EHR data input.

If proposed modifications to the Common Rule are adopted, EHR-based studies conducted by HIPAA-covered researchers will be governed only by the HIPAA regulations and will not be subject to IRB review.[61] This change would make it all the more important for CMS to focus on data quality in its HIPAA enforcement activities.

---

[56] 45 CFR §§ 46.101–505 (2015).

[57] 45 CFR § 46.102(f) (2015) (explaining that research covered by the Common Rule can be conducted in two ways: (1) intervention or interaction with individuals or (2) study of "identifiable private information").

[58] 45 CFR §§ 46.102(f), 46.107–9 (2015).

[59] 45 CFR § 46.111 (2015).

[60] 45 CFR § 46.111(6) and (7) (2015).

[61] Department of Health and Human Services et al., "Federal Policy for the Protection of Human Subjects," *Federal Register* 80, no. 173 (September 8, 2015): 53978; Kathy L. Hudson and Francis S. Collins, "Bringing the Common Rule into the 21st Century," *New England Journal of Medicine* 373, no. 24 (2015): 2293, 2295–6.

7.3.4 *Causal Inference Techniques*

In the last two decades, researchers have made substantial progress in developing a methodology for making causal inferences from observational data. "Causal diagrams" (also called "causal graphs" and "directed acyclic graphs" [DAGs]) are an important component of this methodology and have become a popular tool in the fields of statistics, biostatistics, epidemiology, and computer science.[62] The use of sound causal inference techniques is essential for analysis of large amounts of complex data from medical databases.

A causal diagram consists of points or vertices, each representing a variable.[63] There is an arrow or "edge" connecting a variable A to a variable B if A is known or assumed to cause B (i.e., $A \rightarrow B$). The variables typically include a treatment or exposure variable (e.g., indicating which medication a patient received), an outcome variable (e.g., representing a patient's disease status), and a number of covariates representing clinical, demographic, and possibly genetic factors. For each study subject, researchers obtain values for all variables, if possible, from the subject's medical record or other sources. A very simple causal diagram, reflecting the relationships between a treatment variable T, outcome variable O, and a confounder C, is shown in Figure 7.1. A causal diagram represents investigators' assumptions about causal relationships between variables in a particular study or about the absence of such relationships. It is intended to be "a map of ... cause and effect relations," allowing researchers to understand relationships among relevant variables so that they can construct valid statistical models, avoid confounding, and correctly interpret study results.[64] In the process of creating causal diagrams, analysts attempt to specify the causal relationships and

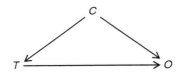

FIGURE 7.1. Simple causal diagram.

[62] Tyler J. VanderWeele and Nancy C. Staudt, "Causal Diagrams for Empirical Legal Research: Methodology for Identifying Causation, Avoiding Bias, and Interpreting Results," *Law, Probability and Risk* 10, no. 4 (2011): 329–30; Judea Pearl, *Causality: Models, Reasoning and Inference*, 2nd edn. (Cambridge University Press, 2009), 65–8.

[63] Jeffrey Swanson and Jennifer Ibrahim, *Picturing Public Health Law Research: Using Causal Diagrams to Model and Test Theory* (Princeton, NJ: Robert Wood Johnson Foundation, 2011), 6; available at: http://publichealthlawresearch.org/sites/default/files/downloads/resource/SwansonIbrahim-CausalDiagrams-March2012.pdf (accessed September 29, 2015); VanderWeele and Staudt, "Causal Diagrams for Empirical Legal Research," 333.

[64] VanderWeele and Staudt, "Causal Diagrams for Empirical Legal Research," 329.

dependencies among all relevant factors involved in a particular problem, leaving the ultimate question of the relationship between the exposure of interest and the outcome to be discovered through research.[65]

Causal diagrams thus can assist analysts in determining the measures to be used in a study and in understanding potential sources of bias.[66] They provide a clear, visual means to depict assumptions about the relationships of variables and highlight complexities that researchers might overlook in the absence of the graphs.[67]

Nevertheless, causal diagrams support valid causal inferences only if they include all relevant variables and reflect the true causal relationships among them. Analysts must make subjective decisions in selecting which variables and arrows to include, and their own erroneous assumptions, biases, or carelessness can contaminate the final product.[68] Thus the causal diagram in Figure 7.1 would be incorrect if there were in truth a selection variable S and a path $T \rightarrow S \leftarrow O$ that was unknown to the researchers.

In the future, expert panels may be able to develop widely accepted causal diagrams for disease-related causal influences about which there is general agreement. Individual researchers would be free to customize them by adding or removing links to reflect their own causal hypotheses, but such diagrams could provide significant guidance to analysts.

Causal diagrams might even be useful as litigation tools. In complex tort cases involving questions of causation, lawyers could ask experts to develop plausible causal diagrams that depict the parties' understanding of how plaintiffs' injuries occurred. Experts on opposing sides are unlikely to agree about the details of causal diagrams and could use causal-inference methodology to attack their opponents' assumptions and assertions. Fact-finders would then determine which diagram is most accurate before deciding which party will prevail.

Medical big data will fulfill its promise only if the data are of high quality and analysis is expertly conducted. Consequently, data quality must be improved not only for purposes of direct patient care but also for purposes of secondary uses such as research, health policy, public health, and more. Technology, health regulations, data audits, and causal inference techniques can all be harnessed to optimize the outcomes of big data analysis.

---

[65] Brookhart et al., "Confounding Control in Healthcare Database Research Challenges and Potential Approaches," S116.

[66] Swanson and Ibrahim, *Picturing Public Health Law Research*, 1.

[67] VanderWeele and Staudt, "Causal Diagrams for Empirical Legal Research," 335.

[68] Brookhart et al., "Confounding Control in Healthcare Database Research Challenges and Potential Approaches," S116.

8

The Special Case of Open Data

I recently logged onto a website called the "Personal Genome Project" and looked at the "Participant Profiles" section. To my surprise, several profiles disclosed the name of the patient along with his or her date of birth, sex, weight, height, blood type, race, health conditions, medications, allergies, procedures, and more.[1] Thus absolutely anyone with a computer would be able to view all these details. Other profiles excluded the name of the participant but provided all the other details, which could potentially allow a clever and motivated viewer to identify the patient.

Earlier chapters discussed medical big data use by professional researchers. This chapter focuses on the phenomenon of "open data." Patient-related medical data can now be easily found on the Internet. With its help, ordinary citizens interested in scientific research are taking matters into their own hands. This is the era of citizen science and do-it-yourself biology.[2] "Citizen science" is "the practice of public participation and collaboration in scientific research" through data collection, monitoring, and analysis for purposes of scientific discovery, usually without compensation.[3] "Do-it-yourself biology" is an international movement "spreading the use of biotechnology

This chapter is based on Sharona Hoffman, "Citizen Science: The Law and Ethics of Public Access to Medical Big Data," *Berkeley Technology Law Journal* 30 (2016): 1741.

[1] "Participant Profiles," Personal Genome Project; available at: https://my.pgp-hms.org/users (accessed September 10, 2015).

[2] Heidi Ledford, "Garage Biotech: Life Hackers," *Science* 467 (2010): 650–2; Amy Dockser Marcus, "Citizen Scientists," *Wall Street Journal*, December 3, 2011; available at: www.wsj.com/articles/SB10001424052970204621904577014330551132036 (accessed September 10, 2015).

[3] "Citizen Science," National Geographic Education; available at: http://education.nationalgeographic.com/education/encyclopedia/citizen-science/?ar_a=1 (accessed September 10, 2015).

beyond traditional academics and industrial institutions and into the lay public."[4]

Increasingly, government and private-sector sources are supplying data collections to the public, and this supply stream will expand considerably in the future. I will call publicly available resources "public-use data" or "open data" in this chapter. Open data are a global phenomenon and are furnished by entities such as the World Health Organization, the UK government, the Canadian Institute for Health Information, Japan's National Institute of Genetics, and many more.[5] The pages that follow will describe representative open data sources, analyze their benefits and risks, and formulate recommendations for responsible handling of open data.

8.1 PUBLICLY AVAILABLE BIG DATA SOURCES

Many large databases offer public access to patient-related health information. These databases have been established by federal and state governments as well as by private-sector enterprises. No comprehensive catalogue of these sources exists. This section focuses on a sample of US databases that feature public-use medical data.

8.1.1 *Federal and State Databases*

On May 9, 2013, President Barack Obama issued an executive order entitled "Making Open and Machine Readable the New Default for Government Information."[6] The order directed that, to the extent permitted by law, the government must release its data to the public in forms that make them easy to find, access, and use.[7] Federal agencies have been working to comply with this order, and many state agencies have adopted similar open data policies.

---

[4] Daniel Grushkin, Todd Kuiken, and Piers Millet, *Synthetic Biology Project: Seven Myths and Realities about Do-It-Yourself Biology* (Washington, DC: Wilson Center, 2013), 4; available at: www.synbioproject.org/process/assets/files/6673/_draft/7_myths_final.pdf (accessed January 7, 2016).

[5] WHO Regional Office for Europe Databases; available at: www.euro.who.int/en/data-and -evidence/databases (accessed January 7, 2016); DATA.GOV.UK; available at: https://data .gov.uk/data/search (accessed January 7, 2016); Canadian Institute for Health Information; available at: www.cihi.ca/en/data-and-standards (accessed January 7, 2016); DNA Data Bank of Japan; available at: www.ddbj.nig.ac.jp/intro-e.html (accessed January 7, 2016).

[6] Exec. Order No. 13,642, *Fed. Reg.* 78: 28111 (May 14, 2013).

[7] The order states, in relevant part:

> To promote continued job growth, Government efficiency, and the social good that can be gained from opening Government data to the public, the default state of new and modernized Government information resources shall be open and machine readable. Government information shall be managed as an asset throughout its life cycle to promote

8.1.1.1 HealthData.gov

HealthData.gov, launched in 2011, is a Department of Health and Human Services website that makes over 1,000 data sets available to researchers, entrepreneurs, and the public free of charge.[8] It thus predates the executive order by two years and establishes a home for the federal government's open data. The data sets are provided by government agencies such as the Centers for Disease Control and Prevention (CDC), the Centers for Medicare and Medicaid Services (CMS), the National Institutes of Health (NIH), the Administration for Children and Families (ACF), and several states.

All users can search for information by keywords, agency type, and subject area.[9] As just one example, users can access a table entitled, "Vaccination Coverage among Children 19–35 Months of Age for Selected Diseases, by Race, Hispanic Origin, Poverty Level, and Location of Residence in Metropolitan Statistical Area."[10] HealthData.gov is the umbrella resource, and through it, users can access a number of separate federal agency databases. Two examples are discussed next.

CDC WONDER. CDC Wonder enables researchers and the public at large to access a wide variety of public health information.[11] This includes data sets about deaths, births, cancer incidence, HIV and AIDS, tuberculosis, vaccinations, census data, and more. The website features statistical research data, reference material, reports, and guidelines related to public health. Users conduct queries by selecting items from drop-down menus and completing fill-in-the-blank forms. Prior to receiving data, users must read a short "data use restrictions" screen and click "I agree," thereby promising to comply with instructions concerning data use and disclosure that are designed to protect the privacy of data subjects.[12]

---

interoperability and openness, and, wherever possible and legally permissible, to ensure that data are released to the public in ways that make the data easy to find, accessible, and usable.

[8] Kathleen Sebelius, "One Thousand Data Sets and Counting," HealthData.gov, February 26, 2014; available at: http://healthdata.gov/.

[9] HealthData.gov; available at: http://healthdata.gov/ (accessed September 11, 2015). The subject areas listed are administrative, biomedical research, children's health, epidemiology, health-care cost, healthcare providers, Medicaid, Medicare, population statistics, quality measurement, safety, treatments, and other.

[10] "Vaccination Coverage among Children 19–35 Months of Age for Selected Diseases, by Race, Hispanic Origin, Poverty Level, and Location of Residence in Metropolitan Statistical Area," Centers for Disease Control and Prevention; available at: www.cdc.gov/nchs/data/hus/2010/081 .pdf (accessed September 10, 2015).

[11] "What Is CDC Wonder?," Centers for Disease Control and Prevention; available at: http:// wonder.cdc.gov/wonder/help/main.html#What_is_WONDER (accessed September 10, 2015).

[12] See, e.g., "About Natality, 2007–2012," CDC Wonder; available at: http://wonder.cdc.gov/nat ality-current.html (accessed September 10, 2015).

CHRONIC CONDITION DATA WAREHOUSE. CMS has established the Chronic Condition Data Warehouse (CCW), from which users can purchase data about Medicare and Medicaid beneficiaries and claims.[13] Researchers can apply for access to identifiable or partially identifiable data, and CCW administrators scrutinize all requests. CCW also offers public-use files that contain aggregated summary-level health information for which no data use agreement or privacy board review is necessary. For example, the "Medicaid State Drug Utilization File" contains information about outpatient drugs for which state Medicaid agencies have paid.[14]

8.1.1.2 State Government Health Data Websites

Like the federal government, many states offer publicly available health data on government websites. Examples are Health Data New York, the New Jersey State Assessment Health Data, the North Carolina State Center for Health Statistics, FloridaHealthFinder.gov, and the Minnesota Center for Health Statistics. All these websites provide a wealth of information free of charge to the public and offer a variety of interactive tools and query options.[15]

8.1.1.3 Healthcare Cost and Utilization Project

The Healthcare Cost and Utilization Project (HCUP) is sponsored by the Agency for Healthcare Research and Quality.[16] It allows users who undergo training and sign data use agreements to purchase a variety of data sets.[17]

[13] "Chronic Condition Data Warehouse," Centers for Medicare and Medicaid Services; available at: www.ccwdata.org/web/guest/home (accessed September 10, 2015).

[14] "Public-Use Files (PUF)/Non-Identifiable Data Requests," Research Data Assistance Center; available at: www.resdac.org/cms-data/request/public-use-files (accessed September 10, 2015); "Medicaid State Drug Utilization File," Research Data Assistance Center; available at: http://resdac.advantagelabs.com/cms-data/files/medicaid-state-drug-utilization (accessed September 10, 2015).

[15] "Health Data New York," New York State Department of Health; available at: https://health.data.ny.gov/ (accessed September 10, 2015); "Welcome to NJSHAD: New Jersey's Public Health Data Resource," New Jersey State Department of Health; available at: www26.state.nj.us/doh-shad/home/Welcome.html (accessed September 10, 2015); "Statistics and Reports," North Carolina State Center for Health Statistics; available at: www.schs.state.nc.us/data/minority.cfm (accessed September 10, 2015); "State Health Data Directory," Agency for Healthcare Administration; available at: www.floridahealthfinder.gov/StateHealthDataDirectory/ (accessed September 10, 2015); "Selected Public Health Data Websites," Minnesota Center for Health Statistics; available at: www.health.state.mn.us/divs/chs/countytables/resources.htm (accessed September 11, 2015).

[16] "Overview of HCUP," Healthcare Cost and Utilization Project; available at: www.hcup-us.ahrq.gov/overview.jsp (accessed September 11, 2015).

[17] "HCUP Central Distributor," Healthcare Cost and Utilization Project; available at: www.hcup-us.ahrq.gov/tech_assist/centdist.jsp (accessed September 11, 2015).

HCUP databases offer "a core set of clinical and nonclinical information found in a typical [hospital] discharge abstract including all listed diagnoses and procedures, discharge status, patient demographics, and charges for all patients, regardless of payer (e.g., Medicare, Medicaid, private insurance, uninsured)."[18] Patient demographics may include sex, age, and, for some states, race but no attributes that more directly identify patients.

8.1.1.4 GenBank

GenBank is the NIH's genetic sequence database, which includes all DNA sequences that are publicly available.[19] The data are free, and GenBank places no restriction on their use. According to scientists at the National Center for Biotechnology Information, GenBank contains "over 900 complete genomes, including the draft human genome, and some 95,000 species."[20]

8.1.1.5 All-Payer Claims Databases

A large number of states have launched all-payer claims databases that collect information about private and public insurance related to medical, dental, and pharmacy services.[21] Typically, the collected data include information regarding patient demographics, insurance contracts, healthcare providers, payments made by insurers and patients, dates on which medical services were received, and codes for diagnoses, procedures, and drugs. Consumers, employers, and other stakeholders can access data in order to learn about healthcare costs, compare prices, and make more informed decisions about insurance plans and healthcare providers.[22] The scope of all-payer claims

---

[18] "Databases and Related Tools from HCUP: Fact Sheet," Agency for Healthcare Research and Quality; available at: http://archive.ahrq.gov/research/findings/factsheets/tools/hcupdata/datah cup.html (accessed September 11, 2015).

[19] "GenBank Overview," GenBank; available at: www.ncbi.nlm.nih.gov/genbank/ (accessed September 11, 2015).

[20] Jo McEntyre and David J. Lipman, "GenBank – A Model Community Resource?," *Nature Debates*; available at: www.nature.com/nature/debates/e-access/Articles/lipman.html (accessed September 11, 2015).

[21] Jo Porter et al., *The Basics of All-Payer Claims Databases: A Primer for States* (Princeton, NJ: Robert Wood Johnson Foundation, January 2014), 1; available at: www.nahdo .org/sites/nahdo.org/files/publications/The%20Basics%20of%20All-Payer%20Claims%20Data bases.pdf (accessed September 11, 2015).

[22] *Ibid.*, 3; "Colorado All-Payer Claims Database"; available at: www.cohealthdata.org/ (accessed September 11, 2015); "Massachusetts All-Payer Claims Database," Center for Health Information and Analysis; available at: www.chiamass.gov/ma-apcd (accessed September 11, 2015) (requiring applications for Massachusetts data).

databases, however, may be limited by a 2016 decision in which the Supreme Court ruled that states may not require all insurers to submit their healthcare claims to the databases.[23]

CMS has released Medicare provider utilization and payment data that are available free of charge.[24] The website offers information pertaining to the 100 most commonly performed inpatient services, thirty frequently provided outpatient services, and more. Thus, for instance, users may obtain hospital-specific charges for particular services and compare prices.[25]

8.1.2 *Private-Sector Databases*

8.1.2.1 Dryad Digital Repository

Dryad is an international repository containing data files that are associated with peer-reviewed scientific articles and other "reputable sources (such as dissertations)."[26] It is a nonprofit organization that is supported by fees from its members and data submitters. Researchers submit data underlying their publications directly to Dryad, and any member of the public can access the collection at no cost. The website provides a search tool that allows users to enter keywords or other search criteria and takes them to data associated with particular publications.[27]

---

[23] *Gobeille* v. *Liberty Mutual Insurance Co.*, 136 S.Ct. 936 (2016) (basing the decision on the Employee Retirement Income Security Act of 1974 (ERISA) preemption principles and finding that self-insured employers and their third-party administrators must be exempt from Vermont's reporting requirement).

[24] "Medicare Provider Utilization and Payment Data," Centers for Medicare and Medicaid Services; available at: www.cms.gov/Research-Statistics-Data-and-Systems/Statistics-Trends -and-Reports/Medicare-Provider-Charge-Data/ (accessed September 11, 2015).

[25] "Medicare Provider Utilization and Payment Data: Inpatient," Centers for Medicare and Medicaid Services; available at: www.cms.gov/Research-Statistics-Data-and-Systems/Statistics -Trends-and-Reports/Medicare-Provider-Charge-Data/Inpatient.html. But see Patrick T. O'Gara, "Caution Advised: Medicare's Physician-Payment Data Release," *New England Journal of Medicine* 371, no. 2 (2014): 101 (discussing the limitations of payment data released by CMS); Dawn Fallik, "For Big Data, Big Questions Remain," *Health Affairs* 33 (2014): 1111 (stating that "Medicare's release of practitioner payments highlights the strengths and weaknesses of digging into big data").

[26] "The Organization: Overview," Dryad; available at: http://datadryad.org/pages/organization (accessed September 11, 2015); "Frequently Asked Questions," Dryad; available at: http://data dryad.org/pages/faq (accessed September 11, 2015).

[27] "The Repository: Key Features," Dryad; available at: http://datadryad.org/pages/repository (accessed September 11, 2015).

8.1.2.2 PatientsLikeMe

PatientsLikeMe is a for-profit website that enables patients who sign up for membership to share their health data and disease experiences.[28] Users can report and obtain information about treatments and connect with others who have the same condition. PatientsLikeMe acknowledges that it sells deidentified information submitted by users to its "partners," which it describes as "companies that can use that data to improve or understand products or the disease market."[29] Members may choose different privacy settings and may determine whether nonmembers will be able to view any of their data.[30] PatientsLikeMe releases reports of aggregated data concerning symptoms and treatments to the public.[31] In addition, members may opt into a public registry that will make their profiles and shared data available to anyone with access to the Internet.[32] PatientsLikeMe makes public-use information available on its website at no cost and does not require applications or data use agreements.[33]

8.1.2.3 The Personal Genome Project

The Personal Genome Project was launched in 2005 by George Church at Harvard University and is now an international enterprise involving thousands of patients.[34] It aims to promote research and offers genomic, environmental, and human trait information from volunteer participants to any interested party. Users can easily access a wealth of information directly from the website, including genome data, genome reports, trait and survey data, participant

---

[28] "Live Better, Together!," PatientsLikeMe; available at:, www.patientslikeme.com (accessed September 11, 2015).

[29] "Does PatientsLikeMe Sell My Data?," PatientsLikeMe; available at: https://support .patientslikeme.com/hc/en-us/articles/201245770-Does-PatientsLikeMe-sell-my-information (accessed September 11, 2015).

[30] "Privacy Policy," effective March 5, 2012, PatientsLikeMe; available at: www.patientslikeme .com/about/privacy (accessed September 11, 2015).

[31] See, e.g., "Treatments," PatientsLikeMe; available at: www.patientslikeme.com/treatments (accessed September 11, 2015).

[32] See, e.g., "Welcome to the PatientsLikeMe Public ALS Registry," PatientsLikeMe; available at: www.patientslikeme.com/registry (accessed September 11, 2015); "What Information Is Visible on Public Profiles?," PatientsLikeMe; available at: https://support.patientslikeme.com/hc/en-us/arti cles/201245830-What-information-is-visible-on-public-profiles- (accessed September 11, 2015).

[33] See, e.g., "Conditions at PatientsLikeMe," PatientsLikeMe; available at: www.patientslikeme .com/conditions (accessed September 11, 2015).

[34] "About the PGP," Personal Genome Project: Harvard; available at: www.personalgenomes.org /harvard/about-pgp (accessed September 11, 2015).

profiles, and microbiome data.[35] The Personal Genome Project states explicitly that its participants must be "willing to waive expectations of privacy" in order to make "a valuable and lasting contribution to science."[36]

8.2 THE BENEFITS OF PUBLIC ACCESS TO HEALTH INFORMATION

Public-use data offer the potential for many valuable benefits. These include new scientific discoveries, research cost savings, the development of tools to help patients navigate the healthcare system, greater government transparency, public education about science and medicine, improvements in healthcare quality, and positive healthcare policy changes.

8.2.1 *Scientific Discovery*

One of the great hopes of health data sharing is that it will promote scientific discovery and medical advances. Citizen scientists may be extremely motivated and dedicated researchers, perhaps especially if they are focusing on diseases that afflict them or their loved ones. Citizen scientists who would not otherwise have access to health data and lack the means to collect original data for studies may nevertheless have the skills, talent, and creativity to make significant contributions given the appropriate data tools.[37]

Citizen scientists have proven themselves to be capable inventors whose contributions aid many people. For example, three Dutch do-it-yourself biologists created Amplino, an inexpensive diagnostic system that can be used in developing countries to detect malaria with a single drop of blood in less than forty minutes.[38] Likewise, Katherine Aull, a graduate of the Massachusetts Institute of Technology whose father suffered from hemochromatosis, a condition that causes the body to absorb excessive amounts of iron and can permanently damage vital organs, developed a homemade genetic

[35] "Data and Samples," Personal Genome Project: Harvard; available at: www.personalgenomes .org/harvard/data (accessed September 11, 2015). Microbiome data focus on "the types of bacteria in and on a participant's body." *Ibid.*

[36] "About PGP Harvard," Personal Genome Project: Harvard; available at: www .personalgenomes.org/harvard/about%E2%80%90pgp (accessed September 11, 2015).

[37] Huseyin Naci and John P. A. Ioannidis, "Evaluation of Wellness Determinants and Interventions by Citizen Scientists," *Journal of the American Medical Association* 314, no. 2 (2015): 121–2.

[38] Thomas Landrain et al., "Do-It-Yourself Biology: Challenges and Promises for an Open Science and Technology Movement," *Systems and Synthetic Biology* 7, no. 3 (2013): 121; Linda Nordling, "DIY Biotech: How to Build Yourself a Low-Cost Malaria Detector," *The Guardian*, April 25, 2014; available at: www.theguardian.com/global-development-professionals-network/2014/apr/25/diy -detector-malaria-eradication-amplino (accessed September 11, 2015).

test to determine whether she was vulnerable to this inherited disease. She built a laboratory in her closet and used equipment purchased from e-Bay or found in her kitchen.[39]

New troves of publicly available data promise to facilitate and accelerate the work of professional researchers and citizen scientists. Public data sources have already led to important discoveries. For example, Project Tycho is a University of Pittsburgh initiative designed to promote the availability and use of public health data by facilitating its analysis and redistribution.[40] Tycho researchers were able to digitize disease surveillance data from the years 1888 to 2011 published in the CDC's *Morbidity and Mortality Weekly Report* and to estimate that since 1924, 103 million incidents of childhood diseases were prevented by immunizations.[41] This finding will be a useful tool for public health authorities who at times meet resistance to vaccination efforts.

8.2.2 *Research Cost Reductions*

Open data resources will be of particular value in an era of diminished research funding.[42] NIH appropriations peaked at $36.4 billion in fiscal year 2010 thanks to funding from the American Recovery and Reinvestment Act. However, they declined to $29.3 billion by fiscal year 2013 and recovered only to $32.31 billion in fiscal year 2016. In 2014, applicants for NIH grants had a 17 percent chance of being funded.[43]

Professional researchers and citizen scientists will be able to use open data to conduct low-cost records-based research. Researchers may find that existing

---

[39] Ana Delgado, "DIYbio: Making Things and Making Futures," *Futures* 48 (2013): 70; "NPR Staff: Biopunks Tinker with the Building Blocks of Life," *NPR Books*, May 19, 2011; available at: www.npr.org/2011/05/22/136464041/biopunks-tinker-with-the-building-blocks-of-life (accessed September 14, 2015).

[40] "About Project Tycho™ Data," University of Pittsburgh; available at: www.tycho.pitt.edu/about.php (accessed September 14, 2015).

[41] Willem G. van Panhuis et al., "Contagious Diseases in the United States from 1888 to the Present," *New England Journal of Medicine* 369, no. 22 (2013): 2152, 2156.

[42] Lauren Ingeno, "Crowdfunding Academic Research," *Inside Higher Ed.*, June 10, 2013; available at: www.insidehighered.com/news/2013/06/10/academic-researchers-using-crowdfunding -platforms#sthash.ziC5DeXs.dpbs (accessed September 14, 2015).

[43] Judith A. Johnson, "Brief History of NIH Funding: Fact Sheet," December 23, 2013; available at: www.fas.org/sgp/crs/misc/R43341.pdf; Jeannie Baumann, "Neuroscientist Says NIH Funding Squeeze Causing 'Crisis in Biomedical Enterprise,'" *Bloomberg BNA Medical Research Law & Policy Report* 13 (2014): 407; Mike Lauer, "NIH Budget Highlights for 2016"; available at: https://nexus.od.nih.gov/all/2016/01/27/nih-budget-highlights-for-2016/ (accessed August 19, 2016); Sally Rockey, "What Are the Chances of Getting Funded"; available at: https://nexus.od.nih.gov/all/2015/06/29/what-are-the-chances-of-getting-funded/ (accessed August 19, 2016)

data collections contain all the raw data they need and be spared the work and cost of recruiting human subjects to gather original data.[44]

While many researchers will focus on well-known and widespread health problems, open data may also stimulate study of subjects for which little to no public funding is available. For example, because of vigorous lobbying by the National Rifle Association, the CDC was prohibited from analyzing the impact of firearms on public health for many years.[45] Likewise, there is often very limited interest in or funding for research relating to rare diseases.[46] Citizen scientists, however, may be highly motivated, for personal rather than profit-seeking reasons, to research those diseases.

Furthermore, relatively inexpensive big data projects can be funded by an emerging trend called "crowdfunding."[47] Crowdfunding is an Internet-based method of fundraising by which one can solicit money from numerous donors, who usually contribute small amounts.[48] Typically, crowdfunding for scientific projects raises less than $10,000, but enterprising fund-raisers have frequently surpassed that sum.[49] Public-use data may enable a growing

---

[44] Centers for Disease Control and Prevention, *CDC/ATSDR Policy on Releasing and Sharing Data*, by Coleen Boyle (NCDPHD CIO) et al. (CDC-GA-2005-14), 6; available at: www.cdc .gov/maso/policy/releasingdata.pdf (accessed September 14, 2015).

[45] Michael Luo, "NRA Stymies Firearms Research, Scientists Say," *New York Times*, January 25, 2011; available at: www.nytimes.com/2011/01/26/us/26guns.html (accessed September 14, 2015). The moratorium was lifted by an executive order signed by President Obama in January 2013, entitled "Engaging in Public Health Research on the Causes and Prevention of Gun Violence." *Fed. Reg.* 78: 4295. (accessed September 14, 2015)

[46] "Research Grant Policy," National Organization for Rare Disorders; available at: http://rarediseases .org/wp-content/uploads/2015/05/NORD-Research-Grant-Policy.pdf (accessed September 14, 2015).

[47] Vural Özdemir et al., "Crowd-Funded Micro-Grants for Genomics and 'Big Data': An Actionable Idea Connecting Small (Artisan) Science, Infrastructure Science, and Citizen Philanthropy," *OMICS: A Journal of Integrative Biology* 17, no. 4 (2013): 162.

[48] Stuart R. Cohn, "New Crowdfunding Registration Exemption: Good Idea, Bad Execution," *Florida Law Review* 64, no. 5 (2012): 1434.

[49] Rachel E. Wheat et al., "Raising Money for Scientific Research through Crowdfunding," *Trends in Ecology & Evolution* 28, no. 2 (2013): 72; Ethan O. Perlstein, "Anatomy of the Crowd4Discover Crowdfunding Campaign," *SpringerPlus* 2 (2013): 561 (reporting that the authors raised $25,460 from 390 donors in fifteen countries for a pharmacological research project); Joe Palca, "Scientists Pass the Hat for Research Funding," *NPR Special Series: Joe's Big Idea*, February 14, 2013; available at: www.npr.org/2013/02/14/171975368/scientist-gets -research-donations-from-crowdfunding (accessed September 15, 2015) (reporting that UBiome and American Gut together raised over $600,000 for projects designed to discover how microbiomes [tiny organisms that reside in the human body] influence health when donors were promised an analysis of the bacteria in their own digestive tracts). The Internet offers a large number of platforms for crowdfunding, including the aptly named Kickstarter, Experiment, and Indiegogo, among others. Kickstarter: www.kickstarter.com/; Experiment: https://experiment.com/; Indiegogo: www.indiegogo.com/. Crowdfunding has become so pop-ular that it is being used not only by enterprising individuals and companies but also by several

number of projects to have very limited costs that researchers can cover in creative ways rather than through the traditional channels of government-allocated grant awards.

8.2.3 *Tools to Help Patients Navigate the Healthcare System*

Open health data can promote not only research but also services that are helpful for patients. Several enterprises are developing tools to help patients obtain suitable and affordable medical care. Aidin is a small startup that uses CMS data on health facilities and nursing homes to provide hospitals and patients with information about options for care after discharge from the hospital.[50] Aidin offers its clients listings of available providers, quality-of-care ratings, and reviews. It also helps hospitals to track patient experiences and outcomes so that they can determine which providers are the best fit for patients with specific health conditions.

Similarly, iTriage is a free mobile app and website that allows patients to look up their symptoms and learn about possible causes and treatments.[51] In addition, it assists patients in locating and selecting appropriate care options by providing information such as hospital wait times and physician ratings. iTriage uses publicly available data from the Department of Health and Human Services (HHS), the Food and Drug Administration (FDA), and other sources.[52]

Other examples are the state all-payer claims databases, Medicare's provider utilization and payment data, and Medicare's Hospital Compare.[53] These

---

universities, such as the University of Virginia and Tulane University, which are seeking to compensate for the dearth of funding from traditional sources. Morgan Estabrook, "New Crowdfunding Site Allows Public to Advance U.Va. Research Projects through Targeted Donations," *UVA Today*, May 15, 2013; available at: http://news.virginia.edu/content/new-crowdfunding-site-allows-public-advance-uva-research-projects-through-targeted-donations (accessed September 15, 2015); Keith Brannon, "Tulane University Launches Crowdfunding Partnership for Medical Research," *Tulane University New Wave*, December 10, 2013; available at: http://tulane.edu/news/releases/pr_12102013.cfm (accessed September 15, 2015).

[50] Sebelius, "One Thousand Data Sets and Counting" and "Our Story," Aidin; available at: www.myaidin.com/ourstory.html (accessed September 15, 2015).

[51] "Your Healthcare. Simplified," iTriage; available at: https://about.itriagehealth.com/PDF/iTriage_Consumer_Overview-LR4.pdf (accessed September 15, 2015).

[52] "About Our Medical Content," iTriage; available at: https://about.itriagehealth.com/company-info/medical-content/ (accessed September 15, 2015); Sebelius, "One Thousand Data Sets and Counting."

[53] See "Hospital Compare," Medicare.gov; available at: www.medicare.gov/hospitalcompare/search.html?AspxAutoDetectCookieSupport=1 (accessed September 15, 2015).

enable patients to become more educated about healthcare costs and quality and to compare prices for various inpatient and outpatient services.

8.2.4 *Government Transparency and Public Education*

Proponents of government transparency will be pleased by the proliferation of open data. Databases such as HealthData.gov, Genbank, and others allow viewers to gain significant insight into the information that the government has collected about individuals and the healthcare industry. In some cases, such insight may generate public debate and critique of government investigative policies that could lead to positive policy changes.[54]

In addition, public-use data can function as an important educational tool. Patients can research their own conditions, find doctors with special expertise, be better prepared for their medical appointments, and assess different treatment options that they are given.[55] Furthermore, the general public can learn about the healthcare system, healthcare costs, disease trends, genetics, research and public health initiatives, and much more. Ordinary citizens and students at all levels will be able to access raw data themselves and engage in research exercises, either within the framework of academic programs or on their own. For example, New York University School of Medicine is leveraging open data resources to enhance its curriculum. It is creating patient snapshots from New York hospital discharge data and developing sophisticated training tools based on these real cases.[56] Active learning and engagement with health data might also inspire greater public enthusiasm about medical research and more vocal support for government funding of this vital activity.

8.2.5 *Improvements in Healthcare Quality and Public Health Policy*

Open data can fuel improvements in healthcare quality and health policies. A report from New York State provided a number of compelling illustrations. In 2011, in preparation for Hurricane Irene, nursing home administrators used publicly available weekly bed census reports to identify facilities to which they

---

[54] Centers for Disease Control and Prevention, *CDC/ATSDR Policy on Releasing and Sharing Data*, 4.

[55] Internet searches, however, should not replace consultation with medical experts and often have pitfalls. Patients should not panic based on their independent research and become convinced that they suffer from a dreaded disease or have a poor prognosis before a physician examines them. Patients also should not go to the doctor with a closed mind, unwilling to accept the expert's own assessment and treatment recommendations.

[56] Erika G. Martin et al., "Liberating Data to Transform Healthcare: New York's Open Data Experience," *Journal of the American Medical Association* 311, no. 24 (2014): 2481.

could evacuate residents. In addition, annual reports of cardiac surgery mortality rates, linked to the hospitals and surgeons who provided care, induced low-scoring facilities to undertake quality-improvement initiatives and several physicians who had performed poorly to leave practice. A different study, published in 2015 in *Health Affairs*, concluded that Medicare's Hospital Compare "slowed the rate of price increases in a majority of states that had not previously been exposed to comparable information through their own public reporting systems."[57]

Once data are released, they are available not only to the general public but also to the media. Media stories about health-related inequities can be particularly potent tools to effect policy changes. After officials released New York childhood obesity statistics, organized by school district, and news outlets highlighted the disparities in 2013, some school administrators decided to improve school policies despite cost concerns. A 2014 report in *Crain's New York Business* that publicized hospital cost disparities (e.g., hip replacements that cost $103,725 at New York University Hospitals Center but only $15,436 at Bellevue Hospital Center) may likewise catalyze pricing and reimbursement changes.[58]

8.3 RISKS OF PUBLIC ACCESS TO HEALTH DATA

Although the benefits of opening health data resources to the public are considerable, the risks of doing so are not inconsequential. The federal research regulations do not cover studies that are not funded or conducted by federal government agencies or that use publicly available data, and therefore, such studies are not subject to any formal oversight.[59] Furthermore, the Health Insurance Portability and Accountability Act (HIPAA) Privacy Rule and state privacy laws most likely will not govern open databases. This section analyzes several potential risks associated with open access to patient-related health information: (1) privacy threats, (2) discrimination and special

---

[57] Avi Dor et al., "Medicare's Hospital Compare Quality Reports Appear to Have Slowed Price Increases for Two Major Procedures," *Health Affairs* 34 (2015): 75 (focusing on coronary artery bypass grafts and percutaneous coronary interventions).

[58] Martin et al., "Liberating Data to Transform Healthcare: New York's Open Data Experience," 2481.

[59] 45 CFR §§ 46.101(a) & (b)(4) (2015). Under proposed changes to the Common Rule, the regulations would extend to all privately funded clinical trials that are conducted at institutions funded for human subjects research. Kathy L. Hudson and Francis S. Collins, "Bringing the Common Rule into the 21st Century," *New England Journal of Medicine* 373, no. 24 (2015): 2293–4.

targeting by employers, financial institutions, and marketers, among others, and (3) propagation of incorrect and harmful research conclusions.

8.3.1 *Privacy Threats*

Privacy concerns are the first risk that may come to mind with respect to public use of patient-related medical big data. As emphasized throughout this book, they cannot be minimized.

8.3.1.1 HIPAA and State Privacy Laws

Chapter 6 discussed the HIPAA Privacy Rule[60] at length and the state privacy laws.[61] By way of review, the laws and regulations do not cover all data holders who make medical information publicly available. The HIPAA Privacy Rule covers only healthcare providers, insurers, healthcare clearinghouses, and their business associates.[62] Government entities, website operators, and private data-collection initiatives are thus left outside of its jurisdiction. Consequently, HIPAA does not regulate many of the websites discussed in this chapter, such as those operated by state governments, the CDC, Dryad, or PatientsLikeMe. In addition, public-use data are generally presented in deidentified form and thus are exempt from the disclosure restrictions established in these laws and regulations.

8.3.1.2 The Privacy Act

One other law may apply to government-held data. The Privacy Act of 1974 is a federal law that governs the collection, storage, use, and disclosure of information by the federal government.[63] The law provides that the federal government may not disclose records without the data subject's permission unless specific exceptions apply. However, the Privacy Act defines the term "record" as an item that contains a person's "name, or the identifying number, symbol, or other identifying particular assigned to the individual."[64]

---

[60] 45 CFR §§ 160.101–534 (2015).
[61] Americans Health Lawyers Association, *State Healthcare Privacy Law Survey* (2013); "Public Health Departments and State Patient Confidentiality Laws Map," LawAtlas; available at: http://lawatlas.org/preview?dataset=public-health-departments-and-state-patient-confidentiality-laws (accessed September 15, 2015).
[62] 45 CFR §§ 160.102–60.103 (2015); 42 USC § 17934 (2010).
[63] 5 USC § 552a (2010).
[64] 5 USC § 552a(a)(4).

Consequently, the Privacy Act exempts the government's dissemination of deidentified information on HealthData.gov or other websites.

8.3.1.3 Reidentification Concerns

Recall that the rigorous HIPAA safe harbor deidentification requirements, discussed in Chapter 6, apply only to healthcare providers, healthcare clearinghouses, insurers, and their business associates. Consequently, entities not covered by the regulations may be more lax about deidentification practices and thus cause data subjects to incur a higher risk of reidentification.

Data holders' deidentification practices do, in fact, vary. A 2013 survey found that thirty-three states released patient hospital discharge data to the public, but only seven deidentify them in a manner that would conform to the HIPAA Privacy Rule's safe harbor standard.[65] Many states released the month or quarter of hospital admission and/or discharge and five-digit zip codes. Data sets with these details are more vulnerable to reidentification than those that are deidentified in accordance with HIPAA guidance. This is so because the more personal details a publicly available health record contains, the more likely it is to be matched to other open data sets that include names, such as voter registration lists, purchasing records, and news reports.[66] Thus the more overlapping information fields there are between the medical records and other datasets, such as zip codes, ages, and details of illness, the more likely it is that an adversary will be able to link names to the purportedly "anonymized" health information.

Experienced data miners, aided by contemporary technology, often have no difficulty achieving reidentification. Interested buyers can purchase lists of patients with depression, erectile dysfunction, diabetes, Alzheimer's disease, and Parkinson's disease.[67] In a 2010 article, two computer scientists, Arvind Narayanan and Vitaly Shmatikov, went so far as to say that "advances in the art and science of re-identification,

---

[65] Sean Hooley and Latanya Sweeney, "Survey of Publicly Available State Health Databases," Data Privacy Lab White Paper 1075-1, June 2013, 4; available at: http://dataprivacylab.org/proj ects/50states/1075-1.pdf (accessed September 15, 2015). See Chapter 6 for a discussion of the safe harbor standard.

[66] Arvind Narayanan and Vitaly Shmatikov, "Privacy and Security: Myths and Fallacies of 'Personally Identifiable Information'," *Communications of the ACM* 53 (2010): 26; "Re-Identification," Electronic Privacy Information Center; available at: http://epic.org/privacy/re identification (accessed September 15, 2015).

[67] Shannon Pettypiece and Jordan Robertson, "For Sale: Your Name and Medical Condition," *Bloomberg Business*, September 18, 2014; available at: www.bloomberg.com/bw/articles/2014 -09-18/for-sale-your-name-and-medical-condition (accessed September 15, 2015).

increasing economic incentives for potential attackers, and ready availability of personal information about millions of people (for example, in online social networks) are rapidly rendering [deidentification] ... obsolete."[68]

8.3.2 *Discrimination and Special Targeting*

Medical big data can serve as a treasure trove of information for many parties who will use it to further their own economic best interests.[69] The release of patient data for public use and advances in reidentification capabilities raise significant concern regarding potential discrimination or targeting by parties with a stake in individuals' health and economic welfare.[70]

8.3.2.1 Employers

Employers go to great lengths to select employees carefully in order to maximize business productivity and profitability. Sick or disabled employees can be very expensive for employers because of absenteeism, performance shortcomings, high insurance costs, loss of customers who are uncomfortable interacting with the individual, erosion of workforce morale if other workers feel overburdened while the employer accommodates the ill or impaired employee, and other problems.[71] Employers may have good economic reasons to strive for the healthiest possible workforce, but they are constrained by federal and state laws that prohibit discrimination based on a variety of protected classifications, including disability and genetic information.[72]

[68] Narayanan and Shmatikov, "Myths and Fallacies of 'Personally Identifiable Information,'" 26. See also "Re-Identification," Electronic Privacy Information Center.

[69] Kate Crawford and Jason Schultz, "Big Data and Due Process: Toward a Framework to Redress Predictive Privacy Harms," *Boston College Law Review* 55, no. 93 (2014): 96–9; Danielle Keats Citron and Frank Pasquale, "The Scored Society: Due Process for Automated Predictions," *Washington Law Review* 89 (2014): 3 (stating that in today's world "[p]redictive algorithms mine personal information to make guesses about individuals' likely actions and risks" and "[p]rivate and public entities rely on predictive algorithmic assessments to make important decisions about individuals").

[70] Executive Office of the President, *Big Data: Seizing Opportunities, Preserving Values* (Washington, DC: White House, May 2014), 51; available at: www.whitehouse.gov/sites/defa ult/files/docs/big_data_privacy_report_may_1_2014.pdf (accessed September 15, 2015).

[71] See Bruce Japsen, "US Workforce Illness Costs $576B Annually from Sick Days to Workers' Compensation," *Forbes*, September 12, 2012; available at: www.forbes.com/sites/brucejapsen/ 2012/09/12/u-s-workforce-illness-costs-576b-annually-from-sick-days-to-workers-compensation/ (accessed September 15, 2015); Jessica L. Roberts, "Healthism and the Law of Employment Discrimination," *Iowa Law Review* 99 (2014): 580–9.

[72] See Sharona Hoffman, "The Importance of Immutability in Employment Discrimination Law," *William & Mary Law Review* 52 (2011): 1489–94 (discussing the forms of discrimination prohibited by antidiscrimination legislation).

The statutes seek to prevent employers from depriving qualified individuals of job opportunities for discriminatory reasons such as bias or negative stereotyping.

Nevertheless, the advent of publicly available data may enable employers to discriminate against individuals who are perceived to be at high risk of poor health in ways that are subtle and difficult to detect. Some employers are already embracing advanced technologies such as smart badges that enable them to monitor employee conduct and analyze workplace interactions as never before.[73] They may well pursue opportunities to use identifiable, reidentifiable, and even nonidentifiable medical data to develop new screening tools and hiring policies.

USING IDENTIFIABLE OR REIDENTIFIABLE DATA. Individuals who agree to share identifiable or easily reidentifiable medical data with the public on websites such as PatientsLikeMe or the Personal Genome Project should understand that it will be accessible to anyone and everyone. This includes not only fellow patients or others with benign interests but also employers who may take adverse action based on health concerns.

Many employers reportedly access public profiles that applicants post on social media sites as part of their investigation of candidates' credentials.[74] They also ask applicants for permission to obtain their credit reports.[75] It is therefore not far-fetched to assume that they will search publicly available health profiles as well.

It is also possible that employers will hire data miners to reidentify medical information when doing so is not excessively difficult. Employers or their agents may be able to reidentify health records that feature certain items such as postal codes, birth dates, and gender with the aid of demographic information and names contained in voter registration lists, credit reports, or job applications. In addition, data miners may be able to obtain individuals' detailed purchasing histories or web-browsing histories from database

---

[73] Steve Lohr, "Unblinking Eyes Track Employees: Workplace Surveillance Sees Good and Bad," *New York Times*, June 21, 2014; available at: www.nytimes.com/2014/06/22/technology/workplace-surveillance-sees-good-and-bad.html?emc=eta1 (accessed September 15, 2015).

[74] Greg Fish and Timothy B. Lee, "Employer Get Outta My Facebook," *Bloomberg Businessweek*; available at: www.businessweek.com/debateroom/archives/2010/12/employers_get_outta_my_facebook.html (accessed September 15, 2015); Phyllis Korkki, "Is Your Online Identity Spoiling Your Chances?," *New York Times*, October 9, 2010; available at: www.nytimes.com/2010/10/10/jobs/10search.html (accessed September 15, 2015).

[75] Gary Rivlin, "The Long Shadow of Bad Credit in a Job Search," *New York Times*, May 11, 2013; available at: www.nytimes.com/2013/05/12/business/employers-pull-applicants-credit-reports.html?pagewanted=all (accessed September 15, 2015).

marketers such as Acxiom,[76] and by some estimates, approximately 4,000 data brokers already exist.[77] If these lists suggest that particular workers have certain health conditions, data miners may be able to link "anonymized" health records to names on the lists and thereby identify patients and obtain all their medical details.

The Americans with Disabilities Act prohibits employers from engaging in disability-based discrimination.[78] The law allows employers to conduct medical inquiries and examinations within certain limits to determine fitness for duty,[79] but workers who feel that employers denied them job opportunities because of information they discovered may sue the employers.[80] Unlike medical examinations, publicly shared medical data would enable employers to view workers' health information without the individuals' knowledge and, consequently, with little concern about being accused of disability discrimination in case of adverse employment decisions.

DEIDENTIFIED INFORMATION AS A BASIS FOR MULTIFACTOR DISCRIMINATION AND DISCRIMINATION BY PROXY. Employers may use publicly available medical data for purposes of screening workers even without attempting to reidentify records. Some websites feature information concerning disease trends that might induce employers to try to exclude certain classes of employees. For instance, CDC Wonder allows users to search for cancer incidence by age, sex, race, ethnicity, and region.[81] As a hypothetical example, the results of a search might lead an employer to conclude that Hispanic women over age fifty are more prone to several cancers than other individuals and, consequently, to decline to hire Hispanic women over age fifty.[82]

---

[76] See Alice E. Marwick, "How Your Data Are Being Deeply Mined," *New York Review of Books*, January 9, 2014; available at: www.nybooks.com/articles/archives/2014/jan/09/how-your-data-are-being-deeply-mined/ (accessed September 15, 2015) (discussing the development of "database marketing," an industry that collects, aggregates, and brokers personal data from sources such as "home valuation and vehicle ownership, information about online behavior tracked through cookies, browser advertising, and the like, data from customer surveys, and "offline" buying behavior"); Acxiom; available at: www.acxiom.com/ (accessed January 7, 2016).

[77] Frank Pasquale, "The Dark Market for Personal Data," *New York Times*, October 16, 2014; available at: www.nytimes.com/2014/10/17/opinion/the-dark-market-for-personal-data.html?_r=0 (accessed September 15, 2015).

[78] 42 USC § 12112(a) (2010).

[79] 42 USC § 12112(d) (2010).

[80] 42 USC § 12117(a) (2010).

[81] "United States Cancer Statistics, 1999–2010 Incidence Archive Request," CDC Wonder; available at: http://wonder.cdc.gov/cancer-v2010.HTML (accessed September 15, 2015).

[82] See Jourdan Day, "Closing the Loophole – Why Intersectional Claims Are Needed to Address Discrimination against Older Women," *Ohio State Law Journal* 75, no. 2 (2014): 448.

The civil rights laws prohibit discrimination by race, color, sex, and age, among other categories,[83] but discrimination based on a combination of two or more factors would be very difficult to detect and prove. If accused of discrimination, the employer may be able to show that it has Hispanic, female, and older employees in its workforce. A plaintiff would need to be clever enough to discern that the employer is excluding only a subgroup that falls at the intersection of several protected categories and then somehow decipher the employer's motivation for doing so.

"Anonymized" data can provide other opportunities for discrimination as well.[84] Employers who are highly motivated to develop means to screen out workers at high risk of health problems may undertake their own citizen science projects or hire experts to do so. Employers or their agents may mine medical data using sophisticated algorithms in order to detect associations between individual characteristics or behaviors and poor physical or mental health.[85] Then they could try to determine from job applications, interviews, and reference or background checks whether applicants have those attributes or behaviors.

Already some employers are known to reject candidates who are obese or smoke because of anticipated health problems.[86] In the future, they might disqualify applicants for many more forms of conduct or characteristics. Applicants could routinely be questioned during interviews about their eating, exercise, travel, and other habits. Employers may then base employment decisions on proxies for disease or predictions of later illness based on big data research without violating state and federal antidiscrimination laws. As Professor Jessica Roberts explains, existing statutes prohibit discrimination based on attributes (e.g., race or disability) rather than on behavior (e.g., consumption of fatty foods or a sedentary lifestyle).[87] Furthermore, the laws focus only on *current* disabilities and do not govern any assumptions employers might make about individuals' future ailments, unless such assumptions are based on genetic information, which is off-limits to employers.[88]

---

[83] See Title VII of the Civil Rights Act of 1964, 42 USC § 2000e-2(a) (2010); the Age Discrimination in Employment Act, 29 USC §§ 623(a), 631(a) (2010).

[84] Michael Schrage, "Big Data's Dangerous New Era of Discrimination," *Harvard Business Review*, January 29, 2014; available at: https://hbr.org/2014/01/big-datas-dangerous-new-era-of -discrimination (accessed September 15, 2015).

[85] See Executive Office of the President, *Big Data*, 45–7.

[86] Roberts, "Healthism and the Law of Employment Discrimination," 577–9.

[87] *Ibid.*, 604–7.

[88] See Hoffman, "The Importance of Immutability in Employment Discrimination Law," 1489–94. The Genetic Information Nondiscrimination Act prohibits employers from

8.3.2.2 Financial Institutions and Marketers

Like employers, financial institutions collect information about individuals. Banks routinely maintain databases with data about customers who previously overdrew their accounts or bounced checks.[89] Nothing will prevent them from adding health information to their databases in order to hone their ability to screen out applicants with a high risk of defaulting on loans if such data are attainable at low cost. As suggested earlier, financial institutions may use identifiable and easily reidentifiable information and may mine databases to discern associations between health risks and various attributes or behaviors.

The Americans with Disabilities Act prohibits disability-based discrimination by places of public accommodation, that is, establishments that provide services to the public, including banks and other financial institutions.[90] However, customers are unlikely to suspect or discover that banks viewed their health information while assessing their loan applications, and thus such acts of discrimination will most probably go unchallenged.

Marketers and advertisers too have an interest in individuals' health data. The more they know about potential customers, the more they can tailor their materials to appeal to those individuals.[91] For example, individuals who are known to have diabetes might receive advertisements about sugar-free products, which some may perceive as a troubling invasion of privacy. Consumers may be particularly resentful when the health condition at issue is sensitive, as noted in a 2012 *Forbes* magazine article entitled "How Target Figured Out a Teen Girl Was Pregnant before Her Father Did."[92]

Marketers may also engage in discriminatory practices, offering promotions and discounts to some customers but not others or advertising selectively so

discriminating based on genetic information, and therefore, employers should refrain from mining data collections for genetic information even if it is abundantly available. Genetic Information Non-Discrimination Act, Pub. L. No. 110–233, 122 Stat. 881 §§ 201(4) & 202(a) (2008); 42 USC §§ 2000ff(4) & 2000ff-1a(a) (Supp. 2010).

[89] Jessica Silver-Greenberg and Michael Corkery, "Bank Account Screening Tool Is Scrutinized as Excessive," *New York Times*, June 15, 2014; available at: http://dealbook.nytimes.com/2014/06/15/bank-account-screening-tool-is-scrutinized-as-excessive/?_php=true&_type=blogs&emc=eta1&_r=0 (accessed September 15, 2015).

[90] 42 USC § 12181(7)(F) & 12182(a) (2010).

[91] Lori Andrews, "Facebook Is Using You," *New York Times*, February 4, 2012; available at: www.nytimes.com/2012/02/05/opinion/sunday/facebook-is-using-you.html?pagewanted=all&_r=0 (accessed September 15, 2015).

[92] Kashmir Hill, "How Target Figured Out a Teen Girl Was Pregnant before Her Father Did," *Forbes*, February 16, 2012; available at: www.forbes.com/sites/kashmirhill/2012/02/16/how-target-figured-out-a-teen-girl-was-pregnant-before-her-father-did/ (accessed September 15, 2015) (discussing Target's practice of data mining its customers' purchasing records in order "to figure out what you like, what you need, and which coupons are most likely to make you happy").

that they reach only certain consumers. They may mine health records for clues regarding individuals' purchasing potential and aggressively pursue the most likely or wealthiest customers. A 2014 presidential report provided the following account:

> [S]ome ... retailers were found to be using an algorithm that generated different discounts for the same product to people based on where they believed the customer was located. While it may be that the price differences were driven by the lack of competition in certain neighborhoods, in practice, people in higher-income areas received higher discounts than people in lower-income areas.[93]

While this practice already exists, access to open medical data may enable industry to refine marketing campaigns even further, to the dismay of some customers. Moreover, selective advertising or promotional offers and discounts are unlikely to be found to violate antidiscrimination laws.[94] Marketers will generally be able to argue convincingly that their decisions were based on economic factors rather than on race, disability, or other protected categories.[95]

8.3.3 *Propagation of Incorrect and Harmful Research Conclusions*

Citizen science, that is, research conducted by individuals who are not professional researchers, can lead to valuable and illuminating discoveries. At the same time, however, amateurs may reach incorrect conclusions.[96] Furthermore, anyone can widely publicize information on the Internet, whether it is correct or erroneous. Advice as to how to gain broad exposure is abundantly available on the Internet and can be found in web pages such as "12 Ways to Promote Your Blog" and "How to Promote Your Article Online."[97]

---

[93] Executive Office of the President, *Big Data: Seizing Opportunities, Preserving Values*, 46–7.

[94] Schrage, "Big Data's Dangerous New Era of Discrimination" (stating that it is unclear "where value-added personalization and segmentation end and harmful discrimination begins").

[95] Crawford and Schultz, "Big Data and Due Process: Toward a Framework to Redress Predictive Privacy Harms," 101 (stating that "housing providers could design an algorithm to predict the relevant PII [personally identifiable information] of potential buyers or renters and advertise the properties only to those who fit these profiles" and do so without violating fair housing laws).

[96] Institute of Medicine, *Discussion Framework for Clinical Trial Data Sharing: Guiding Principles, Elements, and Activities* (Washington, DC: National Academies Press, 2014), 4; available at: https://globalhealthtrials.tghn.org/site_media/media/medialibrary/2014/01/IOM _data_sharing_Report.pdf (stating that "shared clinical trial data might be analyzed in a manner that leads to biased effect estimates or invalid conclusions").

[97] Sally Kane, "12 Ways to Promote Your Blog: Blog Promotion Tips for Lawyers and Legal Professionals," About.com; available at: http://legalcareers.about.com/od/practicetips/tp/10 -Ways-To-Promote-Your-Blog.htm (accessed September 15, 2015); Daniel Vahab and Lisa Chau, "How to Promote Your Article Online," *Social Media Monthly*, November 30,

In some cases, the media, celebrities, and politicians highlight the work of ordinary citizens, and they may well do so with respect to scientific discoveries that they find intriguing or that support their own agendas. In other cases, individuals can gain attention through word of mouth and social media, as happens when a YouTube video or blog post "goes viral."[98]

While professional researchers most often seek publication in peer-reviewed journals that carefully scrutinize submissions, nothing will stop citizen scientists from posting their study results on blogs, personal web pages, and other electronic publications, making them instantaneously available to a worldwide audience.[99] Many reports published on websites look highly professional and may seem credible to general readers, who are not always sophisticated about distinguishing between reliable and questionable sources of information.[100]

Incorrect findings are unlikely to be a rarity. Open data analysis may often be tainted by poor data quality as well as selection, confounding, and measurement biases, all discussed in Chapter 7.

In addition, researchers must be particularly sensitive to the difference between *association* and *causation*.[101] They may identify associations between certain behaviors, exposures, or treatments and particular outcomes but

2012; available a: http://thesocialmediamonthly.com/how-to-promote-your-article-online/ (accessed September 15, 2015).

[98] See Seth Mnookin, "One of a Kind: What Do You Do if Your Child Has a Condition That is New to Science?," *New Yorker*, July 21, 2014; available at: www.newyorker.com/reporting/2014/07/21/140721fa_fact_mnookin?currentPage=all&mobify=0 (accessed September 15, 2015) (describing how a father posted a blog entry about his disabled son's extremely rare genetic abnormality in order to identify other patients with the condition, and the blog went viral, yielding contact with several other families).

[99] R. J. Cline and K. M. Haynes, "Consumer Health Information Seeking on the Internet: The State of the Art," *Health Education Research* 16, no. 6 (2001): 679.

[100] See, e.g., Geraldine Peterson et al., "How Do Consumers Search for and Appraise Information on Medicines on the Internet? A Qualitative Study Using Focus Groups," *Journal of Medical Internet Research* 5, no. 4 (2003): e33 (concluding "that there was a range of search and appraisal skills among [study] participants, with many reporting a limited awareness of how they found and evaluated Internet-based information on medicines."); Cline and Haynes, "Consumer Health Information Seeking on the Internet: the State of the Art," 680 (cautioning that many consumers have weak information-evaluation skills); Miriam J. Metzger, "Making Sense of Credibility on the Web: Models for Evaluating Online Information and Recommendations for Future Research," *Journal of the American Society for Information Science and Technology* 58, no. 13 (2007): 2079 (noting that "studies have found that users are seldom diligent in checking the accuracy of the information they obtain online").

[101] Austin Bradford Hill, "The Environment and Disease: Association or Causation," *Proceedings of the Royal Society of Medicine* 58 (1965): 295–300; Arvid Sjolander, "The Language of Potential Outcomes," in *Causality: Statistical Perspectives and Applications*, ed. by Carlo Berzuini, Philip Dawid, and Luisa Bernardinell (Hoboken, NJ: Wiley, 2012), 6, 9.

wrongly assume that there is a causal relationship between the two.[102] To illustrate, suppose that a citizen scientist concludes that people who eat acai berries live longer than those who do not eat this fruit. Does this mean that acai berry consumption prolongs life? Probably not. The explanation for this finding may well be that individuals who purchase this exotic fruit are generally well off and have the means to make careful food choices, to exercise, to limit their stress, and to obtain top-notch medical care. Thus it may in fact be true that eating acai berries is *associated* with a longer life on average; but it does not follow that acai berries have some property that actually *causes* people to live longer.

8.3.3.1 Potential Harms

While many mistaken research conclusions will be benign, some could be harmful. Patients reading incorrect information about their diseases may become unnecessarily anxious or, in the opposite case, overly sanguine about their symptoms and fail to seek needed medical care.

Furthermore, individuals with personal agendas may undertake scientific studies with malevolent intent. They may use findings to inflame passion and prejudice against particular minority groups. Some may attempt to further political agendas by "proving" that their opponents' policies have adverse effects on human health or the healthcare system. Others with selfish economic interests may aim to hurt competitors by claiming that their products cause particular ailments.[103]

Even peer-reviewed journals have published articles whose conclusions are false. A notorious example is the 1998 study published in the prestigious journal *Lancet*, that suggested a link between autism and the measles, mumps, rubella (MMR) vaccination.[104] While the study was later retracted,[105] the belief that vaccinations can lead to autism gained a considerable foothold and still needs to be explicitly repudiated on the CDC website.[106]

---

[102] Stephen Choi et al., "The Power of Proxy Advisors: Myth or Reality?," *Emory Law Journal* 59 (2010): 879–85.

[103] Michelle Mello et al., "Preparing for Responsible Sharing of Clinical Trial Data," *New England Journal of Medicine* 369, no. 17 (2013): 1653 (cautioning that public access to clinical trial data "could lead unskilled analysts, market competitors, or others with strong private agendas to publicize poorly conducted analyses").

[104] Andrew J. Wakefield et al., "Ileal-Lymphoid-Nodular Hyperplasia, Non-Specific Colitis, and Pervasive Developmental Disorder in Children," *Lancet* 351 (1998): 641.

[105] Simon H. Murch et al., "Retraction of an Interpretation," *Lancet* 363 (2004): 750.

[106] "Measles, Mumps, and Rubella (MMR) Vaccine," Centers for Disease Control and Prevention; available at: www.cdc.gov/vaccinesafety/Vaccines/MMR/MMR.html (accessed September 15, 2015).

Researchers who are media or web savvy and do not submit their findings to peer-reviewed journals for review by experts may be all the more likely to propagate incorrect and potentially harmful views. Manuscripts that are not submitted to journals will not be scrutinized by experts before their authors post them on the Internet, and no filtering mechanism exists to indicate to readers whether the material is valid or trustworthy. The Internet provides publishing opportunities without any need for intermediaries and oversight. Therefore, potentially, millions of readers could view and believe even nonsensical conclusions, especially when authors assert that they based their research on data that the government furnished.

Many myths have in fact gained considerable traction despite the existence of abundant evidence to negate them. Two examples are climate change denial and the outcry that the Patient Protection and Affordable Care Act (aka "Obamacare") would authorize "death panels" to decide which patients should live and which should die.[107] In both cases, the arguments gained popularity because high-profile public figures embraced them to further their own political and economic agendas, which may occur in many other instances as well.

8.4 RECOMMENDATIONS

The growing trend of opening patient-related data held by the government and private entities to the public raises hopes for considerable benefits at the same time that it provokes significant concerns. Should legislators and regulators respond in any way to this emerging phenomenon? The law must balance the interests of a variety of stakeholders: patients, professional researchers, citizen scientists, the government, industry, and the public at large. An excessively heavy-handed approach to regulation might discourage citizen scientists from pursuing projects and making important contributions and may deter data custodians from releasing records. However, a regulatory approach that is too timid may result in privacy breaches, discrimination, and other societal harms. This section formulates recommendations for regulatory and policy modifications to address open data concerns.

---

[107] Aaron M. McCright and Riley E. Dunlap, "Cool Dudes: The Denial of Climate Change among Conservative White Males in the United States," *Global Environmental Change* 21, no. 4 (2011): 1163; Brian Beutler, "Republicans' 'Death Panel' Smear Was Appallingly Effective," *New Republic*, June 23, 2014; available at: www.newrepublic.com/article/118313/gop-obamacare-death-panel -smear-putting-peoples-lives-risk (accessed September 15, 2015).

8.4.1 HIPAA Privacy Rule Amendments

The emergence of open data makes it all the more important to revise the HIPAA Privacy and Security Rules so that they cover all entities that handle identifiable health information for business purposes. This recommendation has already been detailed in Chapter 3. The proposed change should not inhibit the release of data to the public. Rather, it would provide all data holders with clear instructions regarding security safeguards and create uniform, national standards for data disclosure and deidentification.

The HIPAA Privacy Rule should also be amended to include a general prohibition of any attempt to reidentify information that would apply to any user of deidentified data.[108] This restriction is already an element of HIPAA data use agreements, which require the recipients of limited data sets to promise that they will not "identify the information or contact the individuals."[109] The proposed change would extend this regulatory proscription to anyone using deidentified information, including employers, financial institutions, and all other parties. The provision could specify exceptions, such as permitting reidentification that is necessary in order to respond to medical or public health emergencies. Violators should be subject to HIPAA's enforcement provisions, which incorporate civil and criminal penalties.[110]

8.4.2 Other Privacy Protections

8.4.2.1 Data Review Boards

All data custodians who will release electronic health record (EHR) data to the public should establish data review boards. The boards should scrutinize all data sets that are proposed for release to the public, no matter how thoroughly they will be deidentified. At institutions with data review boards that review proposed observational studies, as described in Chapter 6, the same board could fulfill this review function as well.

This approach is embraced by the CDC in its "Policy on Releasing and Sharing Data."[111] The boards, composed of data-mining and privacy experts, would review any data that are to be released to ascertain that they are as

---

[108] If the HIPAA Privacy Rule's scope of coverage is expanded as suggested earlier, the prohibition would apply to all covered entities and individuals. If not, the HIPAA statute itself should be amended to include a reidentification prohibition that applies broadly to all deidentified health data users.

[109] 45 CFR § 164.514(e)(4)(ii)(C)(5) (2015).

[110] 45 CFR §§ 160.300–552 (2015).

[111] Centers for Disease Control and Prevention, *CDC/ATSDR Policy on Releasing and Sharing Data*, 9.

effectively deidentified as possible. In addition, the data-release review board should oversee all privacy and data-quality safeguards that data holders implement. Finally, if the released information will be identifiable or easily reidentifiable data, the board should also oversee data subject consent procedures, as described in the next section.

8.4.2.2 Data Use Agreements, Privacy Training, Registries, and Consent Procedures

Data custodians who release medical information to the public should implement several privacy-protection measures beyond board review, and the extent of these procedures should depend on the type of data at issue. Users who access any database of medical information, including aggregate, summary-level data, should be alerted to the fact that the information is sensitive and raises privacy concerns. For example, the CDC Wonder website asks viewers who are seeking mortality information from its database to agree to a short list of data use restrictions by clicking an "I agree" icon.[112]

For patient-level data that are not aggregated, more elaborate procedures are needed. The Healthcare cost and Utilization Project's "National (Nationwide) Inpatient Sample" (NIS) furnishes a useful model. The NIS contains information concerning millions of hospital stays.[113] It provides detailed information about patients and hospitals but is careful to remove identifiers and most likely meets the HIPAA safe harbor standard. Nevertheless, NIS requires purchasers of the data to take a 15-minute online training course that addresses privacy concerns.[114] It also requires purchasers to sign a detailed data use agreement that specifies a variety of use restrictions designed to protect individual and institutional data subjects from privacy violations and other abuses, such as attempts to gain commercial or

---

[112] "About Underlying Cause of Death, 1999–2013," CDC Wonder; available at: http://wonder.cdc .gov/ucd-icd10.html (accessed September 15, 2015). Users agree that they will

- Use these data for health statistical reporting and analysis only.
- For sub-national geography, not present or publish death counts of nine or fewer or death rates based on counts of nine or fewer (in figures, graphs, maps, tables, etc.).
- Make no attempt to learn the identity of any person or establishment included in these data.
- Make no disclosure or other use of the identity of any person or establishment discovered inadvertently and advise the NCHS Confidentiality Officer of any such discovery.

[113] "Overview of the National (Nationwide) Inpatient Sample (NIS)," Healthcare Cost and Utilization Project, May 2015; available at: www.hcup-us.ahrq.gov/nisoverview.jsp#purchase (accessed September 15, 2015).

[114] "HCUP Data Use Agreement Training," Healthcare Cost and Utilization Project, May 2015; available at: www.hcup-us.ahrq.gov/tech_assist/dua.jsp (accessed September 15, 2015).

competitive advantage through analysis of released NIS data.[115] A useful supplement to the NIS's requirements would be an online test in which examinees would have to demonstrate that they read and understood the training materials and contents of the data use agreement.

Admittedly, training courses and data use agreements will not prevent all privacy violations because they can easily be ignored. However, these measures will alert the public to the importance of privacy and responsible data handling and may well avert innocent breaches by citizen scientists who wish to do no harm.

Equally important is the fact that the data use agreement requirement will create a record of those accessing data. Data custodians should maintain functional registries of users. Signatories can be required to provide their names, affiliations, and contact information. Those who are found to violate data use agreements by reidentifying data or engaging in other misconduct could be precluded from downloading information in the future and be subjected to other penalties.[116]

In some cases, privacy requirements should apply not only to data users but also to data subjects. Specifically, individuals choosing to allow public access to identifiable or easily reidentifiable data, such as data sets that include birth date, sex, and zip code, should undergo a comprehensive informed consent process. Such data subjects should understand that their personal health information could be viewable not only by researchers who have good intentions but also by employers, marketers, financial institutions, and others who may not have their best interests in mind. To this end, the Harvard Personal Genome Project requires participants to read and sign a lengthy consent document. They also must pass an examination and thereby demonstrate their understanding of the material contained in the consent form.[117] Testing data subjects' comprehension of the privacy risks they are accepting would be an important component of any informed consent process pertaining to publicly sharing individually identifiable data.

[115] "Data Use Agreement for the Nationwide Databases from the Healthcare Cost and Utilization Project Agency for Healthcare Research and Quality," Healthcare Cost and Utilization Project, May 20, 2015; available at: www.hcup-us.ahrq.gov/team/NationwideDUA.pdf (accessed September 15, 2015).

[116] "About Underlying Cause of Death, 1999–2013," CDC Wonder (describing sanctions for violations and stating that "[r]esearchers who violate the terms of the data use restrictions will lose access to WONDER and their sponsors and institutions will be notified").

[117] "Participation Documents," Personal Genome Project: Harvard; available at: www .personalgenomes.org/harvard/sign-up#documents (accessed September 15, 2015).

8.4.3 *Addressing Data Mining through the Americans with Disabilities Act*

The ADA defines "disability" very broadly[118] and prohibits employers, financial institutions, and others from discriminating against individuals because of their disabilities or because they are believed to have physical or mental impairments, even if the belief is unfounded. The ADA's "regarded as" provision explicitly states that an individual is protected by the statute if "he or she has been subjected to an action prohibited under this chapter because of an actual or perceived physical or mental impairment whether or not the impairment limits or is perceived to limit a major life activity."[119]

Despite its liberal definition of the term "disability," the ADA does not reach individuals who are deemed vulnerable to future disabilities. The statute does not ban discrimination against those who are neither currently impaired nor perceived as impaired but are deemed to be at risk of being unhealthy in the future because of their eating habits, exposure to toxins, or a myriad of other concerns.[120]

If discrimination against high-health-risk individuals is enabled by open data and becomes increasingly common, legislators would be wise to respond to it. An easy fix would be to add language to the "regarded as" provision indicating that individuals are also regarded as disabled if they have been subjected to an adverse action because they are perceived as likely to develop physical or mental impairments in the future.

Legislators should also consider requiring disclosure of any data-mining practices on which businesses might base decisions regarding employees or consumers. A tweak of the ADA's medical inquiry and examination provision could adds a requirement that employers disclose in writing to applicants and employees any medical data-mining activities that they intend to use for purposes of making employment decisions.[121] This information would then be available to plaintiffs' attorneys and government enforcement agencies such as the Equal Employment Opportunity Commission (EEOC), which could investigate whether

---

[118] *See* 42 USC § 12102 (2010).

[119] 42 USC § 12102(3)(A) (2010).

[120] Note, however, that the Genetic Information Nondiscrimination Act prohibits employers from discriminating based on genetic information. Thus employers may not make adverse employment decisions based on genetic vulnerabilities to future diseases. Genetic Information Non-Discrimination Act, Pub. L. No. 110–233, 122 Stat. 881 §§ 201(4) & 202(a) (2008); 42 USC §§ 2000ff(4) & 2000ff-1(a) (Supp. 2010).

[121] 42 USC § 12112(d) (2010).

these activities resulted in unlawful discrimination.[122] Likewise, the ADA's public accommodation title could feature the same provision to cover financial institutions and other businesses.[123] Disclosure statements could appear on employment or loan application forms as long as they were in sufficiently large and readable print or on separate sheets given to applicants.

8.4.4 *Citizen-Scientist Chaperoning*

Several mechanisms should be developed to assist citizen scientists in conducting, validating, and publishing their research. Chaperoning citizen scientists by means of research support and filtering tools could reduce the potential for widespread dissemination of erroneous and harmful research conclusions.

First, government agencies, academic institutions, and other research experts should develop educational resources and best-practices guidelines to assist citizen scientists in conducting research. These documents or videos could be posted on database websites, and users could be required or encouraged to review them, along with the privacy training materials, before signing data use agreements.

Second, citizen scientists should have opportunities to have their work vetted, validated, and published on platforms that are recognized as reliable. Without such mechanisms, readers will have no way to discern whether citizen scientists' findings are trustworthy.

One option is to follow the Wikipedia paradigm. Wikipedia allows any member of the public to post articles and anyone to edit those entries, but it provides some degree of oversight and quality control.[124] Authors can request reviews of their entries from peers, and Wikipedia administrators have authority to delete and undelete pages, protect pages from editing, and take other actions.[125] In extreme cases, administrators, of whom there are over 1,400, can temporarily or permanently bar authors from contributing to Wikipedia because of intentional and persistent misconduct. In addition, Wikipedia has an extensive dispute-resolution system for disagreements about the

---

[122] The Equal Employment Opportunity Commission is the federal agency tasked with enforcing the federal anti-discrimination laws.

[123] 42 USC § 12182 (2010).

[124] "Wikipedia: Policies and Guidelines," Wikipedia; available at: http://en.wikipedia.org/wiki/Wikipedia:Policies_and_guidelines (accessed September 15, 2015).

[125] "Wikipedia: Editor Review," Wikipedia; available at: http://en.wikipedia.org/wiki/Wikipedia:Editor_review (accessed January 2, 2016); "Wikipedia: Administrators," Wikipedia; available at: http://en.wikipedia.org/wiki/Wikipedia:Administrators (accessed January 2, 2016).

contents of Wikipedia pages.[126] Readers who find passages that are biased or erroneous are encouraged to improve them and discuss the problem with the original author. Parties may also ask for a "Third Opinion" or for a moderated discussion through the "Dispute Resolution Noticeboard," or they can initiate open requests for comments from the community at large or requests for mediation with help from the "Mediation Committee."

A similar venue could be established for the publication of citizen scientists' reports and findings that are not submitted to traditional journals. Opportunities for responsible editing by other professional and amateur scientists, dispute-resolution mechanisms, and other forms of oversight would significantly enhance the reliability of posted materials. The venue's policy should also require authors to disclose any computer programs that they used so that their research can be replicated and verified.[127]

The future may herald different models to chaperone citizen scientists. Whether these follow the Wikipedia paradigm or another path, they would assist not only researchers in improving and publicizing their work but also the reading public in filtering out research findings that have no reliable basis.

In his May 2013 executive order, President Obama asserted that "making information resources easy to find, accessible, and usable can fuel entrepreneurship, innovation, and scientific discovery that improves Americans' lives."[128] Unfortunately, without well-considered responses to the legal and ethical implications of open data, the new trend may generate more harm than good. However, with careful data stewardship, society may well enjoy the new policy's promised bounty.

---

[126] "Wikipedia: Dispute Resolution," Wikipedia; available at: http://en.wikipedia.org/wiki/Wikip edia:Dispute_resolution (accessed January 2, 2016).

[127] Ari B. Friedman, "Preparing for Responsible Sharing of Clinical Trial Data (letter to the editor)," *New England Journal of Medicine* 370, no. 5 (2014): 484.

[128] Exec. Order No. 13,642.

Conclusion

Electronic health record (EHR) systems hold great promise for improved patient care, but thus far they have not yet fulfilled their potential. The United States is not alone in facing EHR system implementation hurdles. In 2002, England's National Health Service launched an ambitious "National Programme for IT" designed to create a national EHR system for the United Kingdom. In 2011, the British government announced that the program was being dismantled because of delays and budget problems.[1] Nevertheless, in 2013, the UK Health Secretary announced a new "paperless NHS" project whose target completion date is 2018.[2] Likewise, in 2011 the Dutch Parliament rejected legislation to establish a national federated EHR system because of privacy concerns, but in 2013 the national information exchange became fully operational after these concerns were addressed.[3] Indeed, the vast majority of medical practices in the United Kingdom, the Netherlands, the United States, and other developed countries use EHR systems, however imperfect.[4]

[1]   Department of Health, "Dismantling the NHS National Programme for IT," September 22, 2011; available at: www.gov.uk/government/news/dismantling-the-nhs-national-pro gramme-for-it; Aziz Sheikh et al., "Adoption of Electronic Health Records in UK Hospitals," *Lancet* 384, no. 9937 (2014): 8.

[2]   eHealth Stakeholder Group, "Patient Access to Electronic Health Records: eHealth Stakeholder Group," led by Illaria Passarani, European Commission, June 12, 2013; available at: http://ec.europa.eu/digital-agenda/en/news/commission-publishes-four-reports-ehealth -stakeholder-group (accessed January 7, 2016).

[3]   *Ibid.*, 10.

[4]   Owen A. Johnson et al., "Electronic Health Records in the UK and USA," *Lancet* 384, no. 9947 (2014): 954; Christine P. Stone, "A Glimpse at EHR Implementation around the World: The Lessons the US Can Learn," *Health Institute for E-Health Policy* (2014); available at: www .e-healthpolicy.org/docs/A_Glimpse_at_EHR_Implementation_Around_the_World1_ChrisS tone.pdf; Robin Osborn et al., "Primary Care Physicians in Ten Countries Report Challenges Caring for Patients with Complex Health Needs," *Health Affairs* 34, no. 12 (2015): 2104–12; available at: http://content.healthaffairs.org/content/34/12/2104.full?keytype=ref&siteid=healt haff&ijkey=Wvt51Tp9QSL/g#T4.

Because contemporary EHR systems suffer from many shortcomings, the medical big data that they produce is also often flawed. Data-quality problems can compromise the value of databases for scientific research, quality assessment, public health, and other purposes.

Robert Wachter, author of *The Digital Doctor: Hope, Hype, and Harm at the Dawn of Medicine's Computer Age*, imagines a future of optimally effective EHR systems. He describes them as follows:

> Computerized decision support for clinicians will … be taken to a new level. While physicians will still be ultimately responsible for making a final diagnosis, the EHR will suggest possible diagnoses for the physician to consider, along with tests and treatments based on guidelines and literature that are a click or a voice command away. Color-coded digital dashboards will show at a glance whether all appropriate treatments have been given …
>
> Big-data analytics will be constantly at work, mining the patient's database to assess the risk of deterioration (infection, falls, bedsores, and the like) before such risks become clinically obvious. These risk assessments will seamlessly link to the dashboards, suggesting changes in monitoring, staffing, or treatments when a patient's risk profile changes. Alerts (both those in the EHR and those from in-room monitoring devices) will be far more intelligent and far less frequent. Like the Boeing cockpit alerts, they will be graded, and the alert for "you're about to give a 39-fold overdose" will look nothing like the alert that fires for "these two medications sometimes have a significant interaction you should be aware of …
>
> [Many details in the medical record] will be automatically entered through voice recordings, by sensors (vital signs, for example), and by patients themselves. The combination of intelligent algorithms and automatic data entry will allow each healthcare professional to practice far closer to the top of her license. As less time is wasted on documenting the care, doctors and nurses will have more direct contact with patients and families, restoring much of the joy in practice that has been eroding, like a coral reef, with each new wave of nonclinical demands.[5]

Thanks to the Health Information Technology for Economic and Clinical Health (HITECH) Act and the meaningful use incentive program that commenced in 2011, we have made significant progress in the arena of digitization, and we continue to strive to realize all of its potential benefits. But much work remains to be done.

---

[5] Robert Wachter, *The Digital Doctor: Hope, Hype, and Harm at the Dawn of Medicine's Computer Age* (New York: McGraw Hill Education, 2015), 260–1.

As the preceding passage from *The Digital Doctor* suggests, special attention must be paid to the nature of the physician–patient relationship in the computerized era. Will physicians have time to continue to nurture relationships with patients or will too many of their work hours be consumed by EHR-related tasks? Will they remain caregivers in the true sense of the word or will their role be reduced essentially to that of data entry and review of data output? Will the human aspect of the medical encounter survive digitization or will patients increasingly become faceless computer entries?[6]

EHR systems, quality of care, and medical big data can all improve through a combination of technological, policy, and regulatory interventions. To that end, this book offers a wide array of recommendations, which are summarized next.

TECHNOLOGICAL ADVANCES

- Automation through voice-recognition software and automatic transmission of data from medical devices such as thermometers and heart monitors
- Improved decision support through alerts that are better customized for particular medical practices and appear in a variety of colors and formats so that they are differentiated by level of significance
- Alerts that warn clinicians if implausible or clearly erroneous data are entered into the computer
- Continued vigilance concerning data security and diligent efforts to develop security measures that effectively address emerging security threats
- Standardization and harmonization of EHR terminology so that terms have the same meanings in all EHRs
- Improved natural-language-processing tools to extract data from EHRs for secondary use
- EHR system default settings that encourage or require clinicians to capture data that are vitally important for secondary use even if they are less important for clinical care

---

[6]   See Lisa Rosenbaum, "Transitional Chaos or Enduring Harm? The EHR and the Disruption of Medicine," *New England Journal of Medicine* 373, no. 17 (2015): 1585.

POLICIES FOR HEALTHCARE PROVIDERS, RESEARCHERS, AND MEDICAL DATA HOLDERS

- Required periodic data audits to assess EHRs' accuracy and error rates
- Measures to address high error rates, including workforce training and consultations with EHR vendors to determine whether any user-interface changes might reduce the likelihood of input mistakes
- Professionally trained scribes to perform data entry tasks
- Thoughtful policies regarding secure messaging to ensure that patients understand the limitations of electronic communication and use it in appropriate circumstances
- Thoughtful policies regarding release of data to patients through personal health records
- Guidance regarding the handling of excessive or incorrect EHR alerts and how decisions to override alerts should be documented in the record
- Guidance regarding when and how the copy and paste function should be used
- Educational materials that encourage patients to review their own EHRs and flag errors
- Meticulous deidentification of all data sets that will be released to researchers or to the public
- Use of expert data review boards to scrutinize record-based studies that do not require institutional review board (IRB) approval and to review medical data sets that will be released to the public to ensure that there is minimal risk of reidentification or other harms to data subjects
- Training for clinicians regarding the importance of collecting data needed for secondary use even if it is not obviously relevant to clinical care
- Training for researchers regarding best practices for conducting observational research and up-to-date causal inference techniques
- Required data use agreements and privacy training for individuals accessing public databases that contain patient records regardless of the degree to which the records are deidentified
- Thorough consent procedures for individuals who agree to release their own identifiable medical information on public websites
- Creation of venues in which citizen scientists can publish their work with some degree of oversight so that published findings can gain both credibility and visibility

LEGAL INTERVENTIONS

- Expansion of the Health Insurance Portability and Accountability Act (HIPAA) Privacy and Security Rules' definition of "covered entity" to include any person or entity that "for commercial, financial, or professional gain, monetary fees, or dues, or on a cooperative, nonprofit, or pro bono basis, engages, in whole or in part, and with real or constructive knowledge, in the practice of assembling, collecting, analyzing, using, evaluating, storing, or transmitting protected health information"
- Expansion of the HIPAA definition of "health information" to include "any information, recorded in any form or medium, that relates to the past, present, or future physical or mental health or condition of an individual, the provision of healthcare to an individual, or the past, present, or future payment for the provision of healthcare to an individual"
- Addition of a private cause of action to the HIPAA Privacy and Security Rules
- A new HIPAA Privacy Rule provision that prohibits reidentification of deidentified data
- Department of Health and Human Services scrutiny of data quality as part of its HIPAA Privacy and Security Rule enforcement
- A Common Rule requirement that investigators indicate in research protocols what measures they will implement to monitor data quality (e.g., data audits)
- Required disclosure of metadata when EHRs are produced in discovery during litigation
- Much more extensive clinical testing of EHR systems prior to their approval in order to ascertain their usability and safety
- Continuing review of EHR systems after they are launched in the marketplace to ensure that they function as expected
- Required reporting of EHR system adverse events
- Regulatory mandates that promote EHR system interoperability at the regional and national levels
- Expansion of the Americans with Disabilities Act's (ADA's) definition of "disability" to include individuals who are predicted to develop physical or mental impairments in the future
- New ADA provisions that require disclosure of any data-mining practices on which businesses might base decisions regarding employees or consumers

The federal government's "Meaningful Use Incentive Program" began in 2011 and is scheduled to end in 2021.[7] Thereafter, the government will no longer finance and directly promote implementation of EHR systems. But the law will continue to play a vital role in the health information technology arena. Because EHR systems manage many aspects of clinical care and are thus safety-critical for patients, the government must engage in robust oversight activities, regulating EHR systems' approval and continuous monitoring. Because computerized records are susceptible to privacy breaches, privacy and security regulations will never be superfluous. Likewise, regulations are needed to incentivize the development of functions such as interoperability that are not necessarily financially profitable for vendors but are of great benefit to society. Finally, statutory antidiscrimination mandates must protect vulnerable individuals and address emerging forms of discrimination that new technology enables.

Regulators must partner with medical and health information technology experts to ensure that regulations fit the needs of clinicians, industry, and the public at large. Excessively aggressive or otherwise unreasonable regulation can discourage innovation and hinder patient care. At the same time, the law must not lag behind technology and fail to address evolving threats to data security, data quality, or other aspects of public welfare.

EHR systems and medical big data were introduced with much fanfare and aspirations for dramatic improvements in treatment outcomes and public health. As of this writing, many remain skeptical about the degree to which these benefits will be realized. Nevertheless, with dedicated efforts and genuine collaboration among the legal, medical, health policy, and health information technology communities, our enormous investment in medical digitization can lead to its hoped-for benefits and beyond.

---

[7] Centers for Medicare and Medicaid Services, "Medicare and Medicaid EHR Incentive Program Basics"; available at: www.cms.gov/Regulations-and-Guidance/Legislation/EHRInc entivePrograms/Basics.html (accessed August 25, 2015).

Index

Acxiom, 112, 185
ADA. *See* Americans with Disabilities Act
Administration for Children and Families, 170
Agency for Healthcare Research and Quality, 126, 171
Aidin, 178
Akron General Hospital, 1
all-payer claims databases, 172, 178
Allscripts Healthcare Solutions, 89
American College of Physicians, 30
American Health Information Management Association, 26
  statement regarding copy/paste functionality, 26
American Medical Association (AMA), 50, 51
  framework for improving EHR system usability, 99–100
  guidance, physicians' use of e-mail, 102–3
American National Standards Institute, 47
Americans with Disabilities Act (ADA), 185, 187, 195–6, 202
  definition of disability, 195, 202
  "regarded as" provision, 195
  See also discrimination
Amplino, 175
anonymized health information. *See* deidentified information
Anthem Blue Cross and Blue Shield, 35
Association of Korean Medicine, 59
audit trails, 96, 98, 107. *See also* discovery and litigation; metadata
Aull, Katherine, 175

Benitez, Kathleen, 136–7
big data. *See* medical big data
Bipartisan Policy Center, 37

Birkmeyer, John, 33
Blue Cross and Blue Shield of Tennessee, 67
Brandeis, Louis, 56
breaches, 34–5, 53, 56–61, 81, 93–5, 149
  breaches affecting 500 or more individuals, 35, 53, 68
  breach notification. *See* HIPAA: breach notification rule
  consequent harms, 59–60, 66–7
  cost of breaches, 66–7
  insurance for, 60–1
  prevention of, 70–2
Broccolo, Bernadette, 72
Burlington Northern and Santa Fe Railway Company, 123–4
Bush, George W., 1

Cable Communications Policy Act, 76
Canadian Institute for Health Information, 169
Cancer Biomedical Informatics Grid, 127
Cassidy, Bill, 54
Centers for Disease Control and Prevention (CDC), 121, 170, 177, 190, 192
  CDC Wonder, 185, 193
  Morbidity and Mortality Weekly Report, 176
  Vaccine Safety Datalink (VSD), 121–2
Centers for Medicare & Medicaid Services (CMS), 22, 38, 42, 45–7, 53–4, 119–20, 173
  Chronic Condition Data Warehouse (CCW), 125, 171
  Hospital Compare, 22, 120, 178, 180
  provider utilization and payment data, 173, 178
  See also Medicare and Medicaid EHR Incentive program
Cerner, 14